CHAOSOPHY

SOFT SUBVERSIONS

FÉLIX GUATTARI

D1319670

EDITED BY SYLVÈRE LOTRINGER

TRANSLATED BY DAVID L. SWEET AND CHET WIENER

Semiotext(e)

Special thanks to Emmanuelle Guattari, Jarred Becker,
Sande Cohen, Jeanine Herman, Andrea Loselle,
Benjamin Meyers, Gianna Quach, Danielle Sivadon,
Bernard Schütze, and Charles Wolfe

Semiotext[e] Offices:

522 Philosophy Hall	POB 568
Columbia University	Williamsburgh Station
New York, New York	Brooklyn, New York
10027 USA	11211-0568 USA

Phone & Fax: 718-963-2603

Printed in the United States of America

CONTENTS

1

MOLECULAR REVOLUTIONS

There are a number of things I would like to share and discuss with you now, but I get the feeling that I could talk about absolutely anything—my private life, how I vote—except desire or revolution. They would seem truly obscene here at Columbia University.*

It has reached the point where I wonder if one wouldn't really have to be a member of the CIA in order to undertake such a thing.[1] There is something like a CIA virus here that seems to have contaminated many people and that keeps reoccuring at different times, and I can't help asking myself whether I haven't caught the bug.

If one could get beyond these walls or through this muffling that constitutes a sort of wall of sound within the university, I think one might begin to recognize that the world crisis is accelerating at a considerable pace. Am I simply caught up in an accelerating schizo-process? For some years now we have been experiencing a process comparable to that of 1929—a full range of regional conflicts, of local political confrontations, of economic crises. There are no extreme, salient characters of a Hitler or Mussolini magnitude on the political scene right now, yet extermination camps do exist. The entire country of Bangladesh is such a camp; thousands, tens of thou-

---

* Guattari is addressing here the Schizo-Culture Conference organized by *Semiotext(e)* in November, 1975 at Columbia University.

sands of people are dying there, or on the verge of it, because they are locked in a particular economic situation, which results from a specific governmental policy, and no alternatives exist except being exterminated. I do believe that a whole series of factors are leading to an absolute crisis at all levels of social organization throughout the world. This situation should call for revolutionary solutions, but nothing, no one, no organization is prepared to deal with it and its imperatives. The obscene thesis I wish to defend before you now is this: all these organizations—Bolshevik, Marxist-Leninist, Communist, Spontaneist (in one form or another), Social Democratic—are missing an essential aspect of this revolutionary struggle and its development.

There are two ways of rejecting the revolution. The first is to refuse to see it where it exists; the second is to see it where it manifestly will not occur. These are, in a nutshell, the reformist and the dogmatic pathways. Indeed, a revolution of great amplitude is developing today, but at the molecular or microscopic level.

I believe that this molecular revolution can only develop in a parallel way with the general, political crisis. Some people say that the social turmoil in the United States during the 1960s, or in France in '68, was a spontaneist event—transitory, marginal—and that such a utopian revolution leads nowhere. But in my opinion, important things began happening only *after* that revolution, which perhaps was the last revolution in the old style. Molecular revolution develops in relatively unknown areas. Gilles Deleuze was just telling us[2] there isn't much to try to understand. We see students rebelling, playing at the barricades. We see teenagers changing life in the high schools. We see prisoners setting half the French prisons on fire. We see the President of the French Republic shaking hands with the prisoners. Women's revolts are moving in all sorts of directions, at many levels: against inherited politics, on the problem of abortion, on the question of prostitution. We see the struggles of immigrants or ethnic minorities, the struggle of homosexuals, of drug-users, of mental patients. We even find previously unimaginable social categories being mobilized in France, for example some judges....

When we put this all together on the table, side by side, we may ask: what does all this have in common? Can we use all this to start a revolution? Does this have anything to do, for example, with what is going on right now in Portugal, where officers of the colonial army are playing the Cohn-Bendits?[3] We can certainly dismiss these phenomena as marginal, try to recoop them as excess force, which is precisely the attitude most of the groupuscules have; or—and this is my hypothesis—we can assume that the molecular revolution of which I spoke is located and developing here in an irreversible manner and that each time these movements fail because the old forms and structures of organization take power, holding the rhizomatic element of desire in a system of arborescent power. Therefore, the main question for me is a radical change of attitude with regard to political problems. On the one hand, there are the "serious" things one sees in the papers, on television— the questions of power in the parties, the unions, the groupuscules; on the other hand, there are the little things, the things of private life: the militant's wife who stays at home to look after the children; the petty bureaucrat making deals in the corridors of Congress—these are at the root of most political schisms and assume a programmatic aspect, but are invariably linked to the phenomena of bureaucratic investment and the special caste that runs these organizations.

I believe that revolutionary movements, whatever they may be, do not change their orientation because of ideology. Ideology does not weigh very heavily compared to the libidinal trafficking that effectively goes on among all these organizations. It all comes to the same thing: either political objectives are the echo of all kinds of struggles, and are associated with an analysis of the phenomena of desire and of the social unconscious within the present organizations, or else the bureaucratic impasses and recuperations will necessarily recur, the desire of the masses and of interest groups go through representatives, and result from a representation.

We all have experienced these kinds of militant initiatives. We should be able to understand why things work that way, why desire is being delegated to representatives and bureaucrats of all kinds, why revolutionary desire is turned into organizational microfascism.

Certainly there must be a more powerful investment that comes to replace revolutionary desire. My explanation, provisionally, arises from the fact that capitalist power is not only exercised in the economic domain and through the subjugation of class, nor is it exercised only through police, foremen, teachers, and professors, but also on another front which I would call the *semiotic subjugation* of all individuals. Children begin learning about capitalism in the cradle, before they have access to speech. They learn to perceive capitalist objects and relations on television, through the family, in the nursery. If they somehow manage to escape semiotic subjugation, then specialized institutions are there to take care of them: psychology, psychoanalysis, to name but two.

Capitalism cannot successfully put together its work force unless it proceeds through a series of semiotic subjugations. The difficult thing—and one that raises a basic theoretical problem—is how to conceive the articulation and unification of struggles on all these fronts: the front of traditional political and social struggle; the liberation of oppressed ethnic groups and regions; linguistic struggles; struggles for a better neighborhood, for a more communal way of life; struggles to change family life or whatever takes the place of it; struggles to change modes of subjugation that recur in couples, whether heterosexual or homosexual. I put all these struggles under the term "microfascist," although I don't particularly like it. I use it simply because it startles and annoys people. There is a microfascism of one's own body, of one's organs, the kind of bulimia that leads to anorexia, a perceptual bulimia that blinds one to the value of things, except for their exchange value, their use value, to the expense of the values of desire.

This raises an important theoretical question, a question that, for me, Deleuze, and several others, has changed somewhat lately. We thought the most formidable enemy was psychoanalysis because it reduced all forms of desire to a particular formation, the family. But there is another danger, of which psychoanalysis is but one point of application: it is the reduction of all modes of semiotization. What I call *semiotization* is what happens with perception, with movement in space, with singing, dancing, mimicry, caressing, contact, everything that concerns the body. All these modes of semiotization are being reduced to the dominant language, the language of power which coordinates its syntactic regulation with speech production in its totality. What one learns at school or in the university is not essentially a content or data, but a behavioral model adapted to certain social castes.

What you require of your students before all else when you make them take an exam is a certain style of semiotic moulding, a certain initiation to the given castes. This initiation is all the more brutal in the context of manual formation, with the training of workers. Exams, the movement from position to position in factory work, always depend on whether one is Black, Puerto Rican, or raised in a well-to-do neighborhood, whether one has the right accent, is a man or woman. There are signs of recognition, signs of power that operate during instructional formation, and they are veritable rites of initiation. I have taken the example of the university, I could easily have taken examples from many other formations of power.

Dominant power extends the semiotic subjugation of individuals unless the struggle is pursued on every front, particularly those of power formations. Most people don't even notice this semiotic subjugation; it's as though they do not want to believe it exists, yet this is what political organizations with all their bureaucrats are about; this is what contributes to create, engender, and maintain all forms of recuperation.

There is something that interests me very much in the United States. It has been happening for a number of years, notably with the Beat generation, and is probably due to the very acuteness of the problems concerning the semiotics of the body, of perception. This is much less true in Europe where one is tied down to a certain intellectualist conception of relations and of the unconscious. The various rationalizations or justifications that are given here for reintroducing a semiotics of the body interest me less. Some involve Zen Buddhism, or various forms of technology, like the Tai Chi that was being done just now on the stage…. It seems to me that something is being sought there in some sort of blind way. Blindness takes multiple forms. In France, for example, we have networks of gurus in psychoanalytic societies; we even have a personality like Reverend Moon heading an important psychoanalytic organization. But psychoanalysis only involves a particular set of people. In the United States, apparently, the virus of psychoanalysis has been more or less averted, but I sometimes wonder if its hierarchical systems aren't reproduced in the systems of gurus, the systems for representing desire.

The problem is this: one cannot strive toward a political objective without identifying as well all the microfascisms, all the modes of semiotic subjugation of power that reproduce themselves through that struggle, and no myth of a return to spontaneity or to nature will change anything. However naively one assumes to be innocent in this regard, whether in relation to our children, our partner, or our students (for professors), I believe this innocence is equivalent to guilt and engenders guilt. The question is neither of innocence or guilt but of finding the microfascism one harbors in oneself, particularly when one does not see it. The last thing I would want to bring up here, of course, is that it can receive an individual solution. It can only be dealt with a new type of *arrangement of enunciation.* One example of these arrangements of enunciation—an impossible, truly awful arrangement from the vantage point of the arrangements of desire—is that of this room itself, with some individual raised above everyone else, with a prepared discussion which would make it impossible for anyone really to start a discussion. Yesterday I proposed changing the whole format, the whole type of work we are doing here, and to my great surprise, I realized that everyone wanted the conference to remain as it was. Some people even asked for their money back, although no one here was being paid to speak.[4]

At various times there were attempts to produce this kind of dialogue. The only people who came forward to try and start a dialogue—completely phony, but full of real desire—were those who falsely accused us of being CIA agents.

As one invests in the libidinal economy of the micropolitics of desire, of microfascism, so must one precisely identify the alliances and possibilities that exist concretely at the level of political struggles and which are completely different in nature. I once told Jean-Jacques Lebel, regarding his workshop on Portugal, that the judgment one makes concerning the attitude of the Portuguese Communist Party is necessarily different from Spinola's and his own, and yet the mechanisms of bureaucratization and the ignorance about the desire of the masses are comparable in both cases.

Another example. In France we have some groups, gangs of people who wear swastikas on their backs and who walk around covered with all sorts of fascist insignia. Yet one should not confuse their microfascism with the fascism of political groups like Occident, etc. To the extent that one fights microfascism at the molecular level, one can also prevent it from happening at the level of large political groups. If one believes that each one of us is immunized against microfascist contamination, against semiotic contamination by capitalism, then we can surely expect to see unbridled forms of macrofascism well up.

Translated by David L. Sweet

1. Attracted by world-wide media coverage, agent provocateurs, presumably from Larouche's Labor Committee, tried a few times to disrupt the Conference by publicly accusing R. D. Laing and Michel Foucault of being paid by the CIA. See *Foucault Live*. New York: Semiotext(e) "Double Agents" series, 1995. [Ed.]

2. Gilles Deleuze spoke in French in the afternoon about trees and rhizomes while drawing graphs on the blackboard, an idea later developed in "Rhizomes." See *On the Line*. New York: Semiotext(e), 1983. [Ed.]

3. Daniel Cohn-Bendit, called "Danny the Red," was the most outspoken leader of the May '68 uprising. [Ed.]

4. The previous day Guattari had suggested replacing the formal lecture format with short summaries followed by discussions, and the audience split in two over this proposal in the middle of Joel Kovel's paper. Half of the audience remained in the main hall, the rest moved with Guattari to a smaller room where Foucault had his paper on "Infant Sexuality" read in English. It is at that point that a provocateur accused Foucault of being a CIA agent. It should be noted the Conference was not sponsored by Columbia University and that registration fees for the Conference were entirely used to pay for the lecture rooms at Teacher's College. [Ed.]

2

DESIRE IS POWER, POWER IS DESIRE
Answers to the Schizo-Culture Conference

After a systematic attack (at least I think so) on psycho-analysis, Gilles Deleuze and I began asking ourselves about the linguistic and semiotic conceptions underlying formations of power in psychoanalysis, in the university, and in general.

A sort of generalized suppression of what I call the *semiotic components of expression* takes place in a certain type of writing, such that even when people speak, they speak as if they were writing. At the same time, the rules of their speech not only depend on a certain syntax, but on a certain *law of writing*.

Unlike primitive societies, our society doesn't think much of speech—only writing, writing that is signed, attested. Subjugation in capitalist societies is basically a semiotic subjugation linked to writing. Those who escape writing give up any hope of survival. They end up in specialized institutions. Whether at work or in any other area of life, one must always make sure that the semiotic modes one uses relate to a phenomenon of the law of writing. If I make a gesture, it must relate to a text that says: "Is it appropriate to make this gesture at this point?" If my gesture is incoherent, there will be, as in a computer, some written or digitalized device that will say: "This person may be mad, or drugged, perhaps we should call the police, or maybe he is a poet: that individual belongs to a certain society and should be referred to a written text." I think, therefore, that the problem posed in this colloquium—whether

15

to read certain texts or not—is basically a problem of the formation of power that goes beyond the university.

Q: Doesn't this relate to what Antonin Artaud said about the written text?

FG: Absolutely. Artaud understood theater and cinema in their multiplicity of semiotic components. Most of the time a film is based on a written text, a script, and the plastic and aural elements are referred to, and alienated from, the text.

Q: Isn't it more a question here of linearity rather than of writing, strictly speaking?

FG: Certainly, or what could be called digitalization, putting everything into digits.

Q: Is the problem of linearity specific to capitalism, or is there a form of writing specific to capital?

FG: Yes, I believe so. The whole evolution of systems of enunciation tends toward the individuation of enunciation and toward the degeneration of collective arrangements of enunciation. In other words, one moves toward a situation where the entirety of complex systems of expression—as in dance, tattoo, mime, etc.—is abandoned for an individuation that implies the position of a speaker and an auditor, such that the only thing that remains of a communication is the transmission of information quantified in "bits." Yet, in another arrangement, the essence of communication is a communication of *desire.* A child who plays, or a lover who courts someone, does not transmit information, he creates a richly expressive situation in which a whole series of semiotic components are involved.

Capitalism refuses to take these components into consideration; what it wants is: 1. people to express themselves in a way that confirms the division of labor; 2. desire to be only expressed in a way that the system can recoup, or only if it is linearized, quantified in systems of production. A number of people here have remarked that the linearization is the best way of transmitting data for a given purpose, even in genetic systems. For example, consider what happens in a primitive society when a purchase is made. The purchase is often a body linked to interminable discussions; it is more often like a donation, even though it is presented as an exchange. Today, shopping ideally demands that the salesperson behaves like a computer. Even if the salesperson is someone affable, and displays all the iconic components of seduction, she nonetheless seduces according to a precise code. Her skirt must be a certain length, her smile artificial, etc. The best way for capitalism to insure semiotic subjugation is to encode desire in a linear way. Whether in a factory or a bank, capitalism does not want people who bring the totality of what they are, with their desire and their problems. One doesn't ask them to desire, to be in love, or to be depressed; one asks them to do the work. They must suppress what they feel, what they are, their entire perceptive semiotics, all their problems. To work in capitalist society implies isolating the usable quantity of semiotization which has a precise relation to a law of writing.

Q: That's questioning capitalism in an extremely broad sense.

FG: Clearly, one must also include bureaucratic socialism.

Q: To take up the question of linearity again, what consequence follows, according to you, from the critique and rejection of the Oedipal triangle in Lacan? What is the impact of such a critique in terms of revolutionary action; not just as critical exegesis, but as intellectual praxis?

FG: To me, the Lacanian definition of the unconscious seems particularly pertinent if one remembers that it forgets the unconscious of the capitalist-socialist bureaucratic social field. What, in fact, does Lacan say? He says that the unconscious is structured like a language and that a signifier represents the subject for another signifier. One gains access to the unconscious through representation, the symbolic order, the articulation of persons in the symbolic order, through the triangle and castration. In fact, and this is really what it's all about, desire can only exist insofar as it is represented, as it passes through representatives. Otherwise, one falls into the black night of incestuous indifferentiation, of drives, etc. For the whole question lies here; if one follows Lacan closely to the end, what does he ultimately say? You accede to desire by the signifier and by castration, and the desire to which you accede is an impossible desire.

I think that Lacan is completely right in terms of the unconscious of the capitalist social field, for as soon as someone represents our desire, as soon as the mother represents the desire of the child, as soon as the teacher represents the desire of the students, as soon as the orator represents the desire of the audience, or the leader, the desire of the followers, or ourselves in our ambition to be something for someone who represents our desire (I've got to be "macho," or else what will she think of me), then there is no more desire. I think the position of the subject and the object in the unconscious is one that continually implies not a metaphysical, general subject, but a particular subject, a type of particular object in a definite socioeconomic field. Desire as such escapes the subject as well as the object, and in particular the series of so-called partial objects. Partial objects of psychoanalysis only appear in a repressive field. For those who remember Freud's monograph *The Little Hans,* the anal partial object appears when all the other objects have been forbidden, the little girl next door or crossing the street, going for a walk, sleeping with the mother, or masturbating—then, when everything has become impossible, the phobic object appears, the phobic subject appears.

Systems of signification are always linked with formations of power and each time the formations of power intervene in order to provide the significations and the significative behaviors, the goal is always to hierarchize them, to organize and make them compatible with a central formation of power, which is that of the state, of capitalist power mediated by the existence of a national language, the national language being the machine of a system of general law that is differentiated into as many particular languages as will specify the particular positions of each one. The national language is the instrument of translatability which specifies each person's way of speaking. An immigrant does not speak the same way as a teacher, as a woman, as a manager, etc., but in any case each is profiled against a system of general translatability. I do not believe one should separate functions of transmission, of communication, of language, or the functions of the power of law. It is the same type of instrument that institutes a law of syntax, that institutes an economic law, a law of exchange, a law of labor division and alienation, of extortion, of surplus value.

And yet I am so talkative myself that I don't see how one could accuse me of denying language and power. It would be absurd to go to war against power in general. On the contrary, certain types of politics of power, certain types of arrangements of power, certain uses of language, notably national languages, are normalized in the context of an historical situation, which implies the seizure of power by a certain linguistic caste, the destruction of dialects, the rejection of special languages of all kinds—professional as well as infantile or feminine (see Robin Lakoff's study)—I think that is what happens. It would be absurd to oppose desire and power. Desire is power; power is desire. What is at issue is what type of politics is pursued with regard to different linguistic arrangements that exist. Because—and this seems essential to me—capitalist and bureaucratic socialist power infiltrate and intervene in all modes of individual semiotization; today, it proceeds more through semiotic subjugation than through direct subjugation by the police, or by explicit use of physical pressure. Capitalist power injects a microfascism into all the attitudes of the individuals, into their relation to perception, to the body, to children, to sexual partners, etc. If a struggle can be led against the capitalist system, it can only be done, in my opinion, through combining a struggle—with visible, external objectives—against the power of the bourgeoisie, against its institutions and systems of exploitation, with a thorough understanding of all the semiotic infiltrations on which capital is based. Consequently, each time one detects an area of struggle against bureaucracy in the organizations, against reformist politics, etc., one must also see just how much we ourselves are contaminated by, are carriers of, this microfascism.

Everything is done, everything organized in what I will call the *individuation of the enunciation,* so that one is prevented from taking up such work, so that an individual is always coiled up in himself, his family, his sexuality, so that such work of liberation is made impossible. Thus, this process of fusing a revolutionary political struggle with analysis is only conceivable on condition that another instrument be forged. In our terminology (i.e., with Gilles Deleuze), this instrument is called *a collective arrangement of enunciation.* This doesn't mean it's necessarily a group: a collective arrangement of enunciation can bring both people and individuals into play—but also machines, organs. This can be a microscopic endeavor, like that of certain characters we find in novels (I am thinking of Beckett's *Molloy*); it can be transcendental meditation or a group work. But the collective arrangement of enunciation is not a solution by the group. It is simply an attempt to create opportunities of conjunction between different semiotic components in order that they not be systematically broken, linearized, separated.

In the previous talk, the person who was "discoursing" came to me and said: "If I spoke a long time, all at once, it was because I felt inhibited, because I could not speak." We did not function as a collective arrangement of enunciation; I didn't manage to relate my own inhibition about hearing him with his inhibition about speaking. It always comes back to the idea that if you abandon the discourse of reason, you fall into the black night of passions, of murder, and the dissolution of all social life. But I think the discourse of reason is the pathology, the morbid discourse par excellence. Simply look at what happens in the world, because it is the discourse of reason that is in power everywhere.

Q: In your collective arrangement of enunciation, how do you prevent the reimposition of linearity and syntax?

FG: It would also be absurd to want to suppress the information, the redundancies, the suggestions, the images all the powers-that-be want to suppress. The question, then, is not semiotic, or linguistic, or psychoanalytic—it is political. It consists in asking oneself where the emphasis is put on the politics of significative redundancy or on the multiple connections of an entirely different nature.

Q: You have to be more precise. You speak of semiotics, of information, of collective arrangements of enunciation, i.e., of linguistics, and then you displace your argumentation from the linguistic or psychological system to that of politics. I no longer follow you.

FG: Each time it is the same thing. Let's take a concrete example: teaching writing in school. The question is often posed in a different, global method. Society being made as it is, even in a completely liberated school, one can hardly imagine refusing to teach children how to write or to recognize linguistic traffic signs. What matters is whether one uses this semiotic apprenticeship to bring together power and the semiotic subjugation of the individual, or if one does something else. What school does is not to transmit information; but impose a semiotic modeling on the body. And that is political. One must start modeling people in a way that ensures their semiotic receptiveness to the system if one wants them to accept the alienations of the bureaucratic capitalist-socialist system. Otherwise they would not be able to work in factories or offices; they would have to be sent away to asylums, or universities.

Q: Do you completely reject the system of knowledge elaborated by Lacan through linguistics and psychoanalysis?

FG: Completely. I believe Lacan described the unconscious in a capitalist system, in the socialist bureaucratic system. This constitutes the very ideal of psychoanalysis.

Q: But is it valid as a system for describing this system?

FG: Certainly. Psychoanalytic societies (and this is why we pay them dearly) represent an ideal, a certain model that can have great importance for the other domains of power—in the university and elsewhere—because they represent a way of making sure desire is invested in the signifier and only the signifier, in pure listening, even the silent listening of the analyst. It is the ideal of semiotic subjugation pushed to its highest expression.

Q: According to Nietzsche, one assumes or goes beyond one's own weaknesses in adjusting oneself to them, in refining them. Yet Nietzsche is a reactionary. Is it possible for someone who is a radical to propose going further into psychoanalytic discourse and industrial discourse?

FG: First of all, I am no Nietzschean. Second, I do not think of going beyond my weaknesses. Third, I am soaked to my neck in psychoanalysis and in the university, and I do not see what I could bring to this domain. All the more so since I do not believe that anything can be changed by a transmission of information between speaker and listener. This is not, then, even a problem of ideological striving or of striving for truth, as one could have understood it here. It is simply this: either there will be other types of arrangement of enunciation in which the person will be a small element juxtaposed to something else (beginning with me), or there will be nothing—and worse than nothing: the development of fascism in continuous linear fashion is taking place in many countries, and there you have it.

Translated by David L. Sweet

3

LETTER TO THE TRIBUNAL

For nearly ten years now, researchers and practitioners in the social sciences have collaborated on the journal *Recherches*. They have addressed problems of childhood, education, mental illness, delinquency, the effects of contemporary urban development, etc.—always by establishing close contacts with the subjects involved. It must be said that, in France, university research and laboratory research have too often remained aloof from practice in the field. The rapid evolution of social problems and the development of new techniques have only aggravated this gap between theory and practice. For a long while now the liveliest research in pedagogy—far removed from the schools dealing with pedagogy—has been carried out by isolated and unsupported teachers: the Freinet school, F. Oury's institutional pedagogy, etc. The same may be said of psychiatry, of childhood psychological disorders, of educational systems, etc. Thus the groups connected with *Recherches* have sought to work directly with these teachers, social workers, nurses, architects, etc., as well as with children, delinquents, and those having psychological problems.

It was in this spirit that the issue of *Recherches* on homosexuality was produced. In the course of recent years, the position of homosexuals in society has changed a great deal. But here as well we can observe a gap between the reality on the one hand and the psychiatric theory and medical-legal practice on the other. Homosexuality is seen less and less as a shameful illness, a monstrous deviance, or a crime. This evolution of opinion was accentuated after May '68, when social struggles began to take into consideration subjects that had previously been neglected, such as prison life, orphanages, the condition of women, the problem of abortion, the quality of life, and so forth. A completely new kind of homosexual political movement appeared. For a long time there had existed homosexual movements that saw themselves as a marginalized minority and sought to defend their human dignity and assert their civil rights. Some of these movements, for example those in the USA, had even allied themselves to anti-Vietnam War movements, to Black and Puerto Rican liberation movements, to feminist movements, etc.

In France, the story was different: the revolutionary homosexual movement, the FHAR (Front Homosexuel d'Action Révolutionnaire) was based from the start on a political program. There was never a grafting of marginalized homosexual movements onto political movements; instead the problems of homosexuality were posed directly in terms of a political movement. This self-generated Maoist movement, gathered around the magazine *Tout,* arose in May '68. It not only refused to regard homosexuality as an illness or a perversion, but went on to assert that every normal sexual life had some direct link to homosexuality. In much the same way, the Women's Liberation Movement considers female homosexuality not only as a form of struggle against male chauvinism, but also a radical critique of the dominant forms of sexuality.

Thus homosexuality may be regarded not only as a dimension of everyone's existence, but also as cause to think critically about a whole series of social phenomena, including hierarchies and bureaucratization, etc. In short, the question has been re-framed: male and female homosexuals refuse the identity of oppressed minority, and instead undertake a political offensive against the subjugation of the values of capitalist and bureaucratic socialist societies. We must speak not about homosexuality but about the transcendence of sexual categories. We must define what sexuality consists of in a society liberated from capitalist exploitation and freed from the relationships of alienation that capitalism creates at all levels of the social structure. From this point of view, the struggle for homosexual liberation becomes an essential part of struggles for the liberation of society.

These themes, this current of thought, explored in the recent issue of *Recherches,* have caused me—as the editor of the publication—to be charged with "offenses against common decency." In fact, the issue of *Recherches* in question addresses only political concerns. It has absolutely nothing to do with those magazines found in sex shops, which exploit the sexual misery and ingenuousness of the general public regarding such themes. Collectively edited by researchers, university professors, and homosexuals, the issue of the journal attempted to present documentation and elucidate new problems. All the members of the editorial collective consider themselves jointly responsible for the publication, and when advised of the legal proceedings, requested (in vain) to have their names included in the citation. But the true motive for the charges has nothing to do with any "offense against common decency." Instead, a political trial is being set in motion, one that will attack the new homosexual politics. It is an assault implicitly aimed at suppressing any similar sort of political development in other domains as well, including the fields of psychiatry and law. The charge of pornography is only a pretext, readily invoked against this kind of subject matter. The important thing is to "set an example" by repressing. No doubt it will be claimed that the trial does not involve any fundamental question, but only the mode of expression—hence justifying charges being lodged only against the editor. Perhaps the intention is to limit the question to a simple violation of laws about what may be published. No doubt the obscenity of the illustrations, the brutality of the expressions, etc. will be cited.

Recherches, like a number of other contemporary publications, has sought to break with the common practice of radio, TV, and most other means of communication. It does not select information on the basis of the reigning prejudices, nor does it judge decency or indecency, nor transpose into so-called decent language the words of people who are dealing directly with a particular issue. In other words, it does not pretend to speak for others. Speaking of prison conditions, for example, the press might cite a judge, a police officer, and a former prisoner—but the latter would be some sort of exceptional character, perhaps someone who has murdered for passion. It would never occur to anyone to cite an average prisoner. The same goes for mental illness. At the most, the press might quote some creative person with a mental disturbance—but it would never think to ask for testimony about the miserable conditions in psychiatric hospitals.

So we decided to let homosexuals speak for themselves. And what was the result? We are accused of indecency. But what sort of indecency is this, if not of a political order? Indeed what that issue of *Recherches* has to say, and the way in which it said it, was not only milder than what one can find in publications produced for sex shops—and once again, let me repeat that we did not intend to compete with that type of literature—but also milder than what one finds in scientific journals. The originality of our special issue—the thing that shocks, the thing for which we have really been charged—is that perhaps for the first time homosexuals and non-homosexuals speak openly and on their own behalf of the problems they face.

Perhaps our opponents will refuse to debate the fundamental question and instead will keep to the current legislation on these matters. They will tell us that the issue of *Recherches* did not fall under regulations governing material available in sex shops, nor, on the other hand, did it appear in the form usually taken by works of erudition. But these are artificial objections. Shouldn't we be angry precisely because dirty material and scientific material must be so rigidly segregated? And must we repeat that many young people, including minors, find it quite easy to gain access to so-called specialized books? Some of the professors who collaborated on our issue can testify that quite a few minors are well acquainted with the works of Kraft–Ebbing. And these works, supposedly reserved for legal scholars and doctors, speak of sexual perversions with a tone and a crudity quite beyond anything found in *Recherches*.

Thus we are not just saying that this volume should be accessible to any young person; we are saying even more: that it could have been written by any number of young people.

What I want to assert in the course of this trial—though under our present social system it may not constitute a "mitigating circumstance"—is that we had no intention of producing pornography, but only wished to participate in a contemporary movement which is becoming more important everyday, and which is based on letting people speak directly about the problems that concern them.

Translated by Jarred Becker

4

IN ORDER TO END THE MASSACRE
OF THE BODY*

No matter how much it proclaims its pseudo-tolerance, the capitalist system in all its forms (family, school, factories, army, codes, discourse…) continues to subjugate all desires, sexuality, and affects to the dictatorship of its totalitarian organization, founded on exploitation, property, male power, profit, productivity….

Tirelessly it continues its dirty work of castrating, suppressing, torturing, and dividing up our bodies in order to inscribe its laws on our flesh, in order to rivet to our subconscious its mechanisms for reproducing this system of enslavement.

With its throttling, its stasis, its lesions, its neuroses, the capitalist state imposes its norms, establishes its models, imprints its features, assigns its roles, propagates its programs…. Using every available access route into our organisms, it insinuates into the depths of our insides its roots of death. It usurps our organs, disrupts our vital functions, mutilates our pleasures, subjugates all lived experience to the control of its condemning judgments. It makes of each individual a cripple, cut off from his or her body, a stranger to his or her own desires.

To reinforce its social terror, which it forces individuals to experience as their own guilt, the capitalist army of occupation

---

* Published anonymously in the special issue of *Recherches* on "Three Billion Perverts," March 1973.

strives, through an ever more refined system of aggression, provocation and blackmail, to repress, to exclude, and to neutralize all those practices of desire which do not reproduce the established form of domination.

In this way the system perpetuates a centuries–old regime of spoiled pleasures, sacrifice, resignation, institutionalized masochism, and death. It is a castrating regime, which produces a guilty, neurotic, scrabbling, submissive drudge of a human being.

This antiquated world, which stinks everywhere of dead flesh, horrifies us and convinces us of the necessity of carrying the revolutionary struggle against capitalist oppression into that territory where the oppression is most deeply rooted: the living body.

It is the body and all the desires it produces that we wish to liberate from "foreign" domination. It is "on that ground" that we wish to "work" for the liberation of society. There is no boundary between the two elements. I oppress myself inasmuch as that I is the product of a system of oppression that extends to all aspects of living.

The "revolutionary consciousness" is a mystification if it is not situated within a "revolutionary body," that is to say, within a body that produces its own liberation.

Women in revolt against male power—a power that has been forced on their bodies for centuries—homosexuals in revolt against a terroristic "normality," young people in revolt against the pathological authority of adults: these are the people who, collectively, have begun to make the body a means of subversion, and have begun to see subversion as a means for meeting the "immediate" needs of the body.

These are the people who have begun to question the mode of production of desires, the relationship between pleasure and power, the relationship between the body and the individual. These are the people who question the function of such relationships in all spheres of capitalist society, including within militant groups.

These are the people, of both sexes, who have finally broken that perennial barrier between "politics" and reality as it is actually lived—a barrier that has served the interests of both the leaders of bourgeois society and those who have claimed to represent and speak for the masses.

These are the people, of both sexes, who have opened the way for a great uprising of life against the forces of death—even as these latter continue to infiltrate our organisms in order to subjugate, with greater and greater subtlety, our energies, our desires, and our reality to the demands of the established order.

A new cutting edge, a new line of more radical and more definitive attack has been opened up, and because of it there will necessarily be new alignments among revolutionary forces.

We can no longer sit idly by as others steal our mouths, our anuses, our genitals, our nerves, our guts, our arteries, in order to fashion parts and works in an ignoble mechanism of production which links capital, exploitation, and the family.

We can no longer allow others to turn our mucous membranes, our skin, all our sensitive areas into occupied territory—territory controlled and regimented by others, to which we are forbidden access.

We can no longer permit our nervous system to serve as a communications network for the system of capitalist exploitation, for the patriarchal state; nor can we permit our brains to be used as instruments of torture programmed by the powers that surround us.

We can no longer allow others to repress our fucking, control our shit, our saliva, our energies, all in conformity with the prescriptions of the law and its carefully defined little transgressions. We want to see frigid, imprisoned, mortified bodies explode to bits, even if capitalism continues to demand that they be kept in check at the expense of our living bodies.

This desire for a fundamental liberation, if it is to be a truly revolutionary action, requires that we move beyond the limits of our "person," that we overturn the motion of the "individual," that we transcend our sedentary selves, our "normal social identities," in order to travel the boundary-less territory of the body, in order to live in the flux of desires that lies beyond sexuality, beyond the territory and the repertories of normality.

So it is that some of us have felt the vital need to act as a group in liberating ourselves from those forces that have crushed and controlled desire in each one of us.

Everything that we have experienced on the level of personal, intimate life we have tried to approach, explore, and live collectively. We want to break down the concrete wall, erected by the dominant social organization, that separates being from appearance, the spoken from the unspoken, the private from the social.

Together, we have begun to explore all the workings of our attractions, repulsions, our resistances, our orgasms, the universe of our representations, our fetishes, our obsessions, our phobias. The "unconfessable secret" has become for us a matter for reflection, public discussion, and political action—where politics is taken as the social manifestation of the irrepressible aspirations of the "living being."

We have decided to break the intolerable seal of secrecy which the power structure has placed on the reality of sensual, sexual, and affective practices; thus we will break the power structure's ability to produce and reproduce forms of oppression.

As we have explored collectively our individual histories, we have seen to what extent all of our desiring life has been dominated by the fundamental laws of the bourgeois capitalist state and the Judeo-Christian tradition; all of our desires are subjected to capitalism's rules concerning efficiency, surplus value, and reproduction. In comparing our various "experiences," no matter how free they may have appeared, we recognized that we are always and forever obliged to conform to the officially sanctioned sexual stereotypes, which regulate all forms of lived experience and extend their control over marriage beds, houses of prostitution, public bathrooms, dance floors, factories, confessionals, sex shops, prisons, high schools, buses, etc.

Let us discuss this officially sanctioned sexuality, which has been defined as the one and only possible sexuality. We do not wish to manage it, as one manages the conditions of one's imprisonment. Rather, we wish to destroy it, eliminate it, because it is nothing more that a mechanism for castrating and re-castrating; it is a mechanism for reproducing everywhere, in every individual, over and over again, the bases for a system of enslavement. "Sexuality" is a monstrosity, whether in its restrictive forms, or in its so-called "permissive" forms. It is clear that "liberalizing" attitudes and "eroticizing" the social reality through advertising is something organized and controlled by the managers of "advanced" capitalism for the sake of a more efficacious reproduction of the officially sanctioned libido. Far from reducing sexual misery, these transactions only increase frustrations and feelings of "failure," hence permitting the transformation of desire into a compulsive consumer need, while also guaranteeing "the production of demand," which of course is the very motor of capitalist expression. There is no real difference between the "immaculate conception" and the seductive female of advertising, between dutifully-fulfilled marital obligations and the promiscuity of bourgeois women on the go. The same censorship is at work in all cases. The same will to put to death the body-that-desires perpetuates itself. Only a change of strategy has occurred.

What we want, what we desire, is to burst through the screen of sexuality and its representations in order to know the reality of our bodies, of our bodies-that-desire.

We want to free this living body, make it whole again,

33

unblock it, clear it, so that it may experience the liberation of all its energies, desires, intensities, which at present are crushed by a social system that prescribes and conditions.

We want to recover the full use of all our vital functions, complete with their particular potentials for pleasure.

We want to recover such elementary faculties as the pleasure of breathing, which has literally been strangled by the forces that oppress and pollute. We want to recover the pleasure of eating and digesting, which has been disrupted by the rhythms imposed by productivity and by the bad food that is produced and prepared according to criteria of marketability. And let us not forget the pleasure of shitting and the pleasures of the anus, systematically destroyed by the coercive conditioning of the sphincter—a conditioning used by capitalist authority to inscribe even onto the flesh its fundamental principles (relationships of exploitation, neurotic accumulation, the mystique of property and of cleanliness, etc.). Or the pleasure of masturbating happily and without shame, with no anguished feelings about failure and compensation, but simply for the pleasure of masturbating. Or the pleasures of shaking oneself, of humming, of speaking, of walking, of moving, of expressing oneself, of feeling delirious, of singing, of playing with one's body in every possible way. We want to recover the pleasures of producing pleasure and of creating—pleasures which have been ruthlessly quashed by educational systems charged with manufacturing obedient worker-consumers.

We want to open our bodies to the bodies of other people, to other people in general. We want to let vibrations pass among us, let energies circulate, allow desires to merge, so that we can all give free reign to our fantasies, to our ecstasies, so that at last we can live without guilt, so that we can practice without guilt all pleasures, whether individual or shared by two or more people. All of this pleasure we desperately need if we are not to experience our daily reality as a kind of slow agony

34

which capitalist, bureaucratic civilization imposes as a model of existence on its subjects. And we want to excise from our being the malignant tumor of guilt, which is the age-old root of all oppression.

Obviously we are aware of the formidable obstacles that we will have to overcome if our aspirations are not to remain simply the dream of a tiny set of marginalized people. We are quite aware that the liberation of the body and the freeing of sensual, sexual, affective, and ecstatic feelings are indissolubly linked to the liberation of women and the abolition of every kind of sexual categorization. Revolutionizing desire means destroying male power and rejecting all its modes of behavior and its ideas about couples; revolutionizing desire means destroying all forms of oppression and all models of normality.

We want to put an end once and for all to the roles and identities instituted by the Phallus.

We want to put an end once and for all to any rigid assigning of sexual identity. We do not want to think of ourselves anymore as men and women, homosexuals and heterosexuals, possessors and possessed, older and younger, masters and slaves, but rather as human beings who transcend such sexual categorization, who are autonomous, in flux, and multifaceted. We want to see ourselves as beings with varying identities, who can express their desires, their pleasures, their ecstasies, their tenderness without relying on or invoking any system of surplus value, or any system of power at all, but only in the spirit of play.

We have begun with the body, the revolutionary body, as a place where "subversive" energies are produced—and a place where in truth all kinds of cruelties and oppressions have been perpetuated. By connecting "political" practice to the reality of this body and its functioning, by working collectively to find means to liberate this body, we have already begun to create a new social reality in which the maximum of ecstasy is combined with the maximum of consciousness. This is the only way that we will be able to directly combat the hold that the Capitalist State exercises over us. This is the only step that will truly make us STRONG against a system of domination that continues to strengthen its power, that aims to weaken and to undermine each individual in order to force him or her to bow to the system, that seeks, in effect, to reduce us all to the level of dogs.

Translated by Jarred Becker

5

I HAVE EVEN MET HAPPY DRAG QUEENS

The Mirabelles are experimenting with a new type of militant theatre, a theatre separate from an explanatory language, and long tirades of good intentions, for example, on gay liberation. They resort to drag, song, mime, dance, etc., not as different ways of illustrating a theme, to "change the ideas" of the spectators, but in order to trouble them, to stir up uncertain desire-zones that they always more or less refuses to explore. The question is no longer to know whether one will play feminine against masculine or the reverse, but to make bodies, all bodies, break away from the representations and restraints of the "social body," and from stereotyped situations, attitudes and behaviors, of the "breast plate" of which Wilhelm Reich spoke. Sexual alienation, one of capitalism's foundations, implies that the social body is polarized in masculinity, whereas the feminine body is transformed into an object of lust, a piece of merchandise to which one cannot have access except through guilt and by submitting to all the system's mechanisms (marriage, family, work, etc.). Desire, on the other hand, has to manage as best it can. In fact it deserts man's body in order to emigrate to the side of the woman, or more precisely, to the becoming-woman side. What is essential here is not the object in question, but the transformational movement. It's this movement, this passage, that the Mirabelles help us explore: a man who loves his own body, a man who loves a woman's body or another man's is himself always secretly characterized by a "becoming-woman." This is, of course, much different than an identification to the woman, even less to the mother, as psychoanalysts would have us believe. Instead, it is a question of a different becoming, a state in order to become something other than that which the repressive social body has forced us to be. Just as workers, despite the exploitation of their work power, succeed in establishing a certain kind of relationship to the world's reality, women, despite the sexual exploitation which they undergo, succeed in establishing a true relationship to desire. *And they live this relationship primarily on the level of their bodies.* And if at the economic level the bourgeoisie is nothing without the proletariat, men aren't much where bodies are concerned, if they do not achieve such a becoming-woman. From whence comes their dependence on the woman's body or the woman image which haunts their dreams and their own bodies, or which they project onto their homosexual partner's body. From whence comes the counter-dependence to which they try to reduce women or the predatory sexual behaviors which they adopt in regard to them. Economic and sexual exploitation cannot be dissociated. Bureaucracies and the bourgeoisie maintain their power by basing themselves on sexual segregation, age, classes, races, the codification of attitudes and class stratification. Imitation of these same segregations and stratifications by militants (for example, refusal to look closely at the concrete alienation of women and children, at possessive and dominating attitudes, at respect for the bourgeois separation of private life and public activity, etc.) constitutes one of the foundations of the present bureaucratization of the revolutionary worker's movement. Listening for the real desires of the people implies that one is capable of listening to one's own desire and to that of one's most immediate entourage. That doesn't at all mean that we should put class struggles way down on the ladder beneath desire struggles. On the contrary, each juncture between them will bring an unexpected energy to the former.

That is the "front" on which, with much modesty and tenacity, the Mirabelles work. But they especially don't want us to take them seriously; they are struggling for something more important than what is "serious". (Their motto: "Drag and monetary crisis. Drag green bean…") What interests them is to help pull homosexuality out of its ghetto, even if it is a militant ghetto; what interests them is that shows like theirs touch not only homosexual circles, but also the mass of people who just don't feel good about themselves.

Translated by Rachel McComas

6

BECOMING-WOMAN

In the global social field, homosexualities function somewhat as movements, chapels with their own ceremonial,
their initiation rites, their myths of love as Renée Nelli puts
it.[1] Despite the intervention of groupings of a more or less corporatist nature like Arcadia, homosexuality continues to be tied
to the values and interactional systems of the dominant sexuality. Its dependence in regard to the heterosexual norm is
manifested in a politics of the secret, a hiddenness nourished
by repression as well as by a feeling of shame still lively in
"respectable" milieus (particularly among businessmen, writers, show-biz people, etc.) in which psychoanalysis is presently the reigning master. It enforces a second degree norm, no
longer moral, but scientific. Homosexuality is no longer a
moral matter, but a matter of perversion. Psychoanalysis
makes an illness of it, a developmental retardation, a fixation
at the pre-genital stage, etc.

On another, smaller and more avant-garde level is found
militant homosexuality, of the FHAR type. Homosexuality
confronts heterosexual power on its own terrain. Now heterosexuality must account for itself; the problem is displaced,
phallocratic power tends to be put into question; in principle, a
conjunction between the actions of feminists and homosexuals
then becomes possible.

However, we should perhaps distinguish a third level, a
more molecular one in which categories, groupings and "special instances" would not be differentiated in the same way, in

which clear cut oppositions between types would be repudiated, in which, on the contrary, one would look for similarities among homosexuals, transvestites, drug addicts, sado-masochists, prostitutes, among women, men, children, teenagers, among psychotics, artists, revolutionaries, let's say among all forms of sexual minorities once it is understood that in this realm there could only be minorities. For example, it could be said, both at the same time 1) that all forms of sexuality, all forms of sexual activity are fundamentally on this side of the personological oppositions homo-hetero; 2) that nonetheless, they are closer to homosexuality and to what could be called a feminine becoming.

On the level of the social body, libido is caught in two systems of opposition: class and sex. It is expected to be male, phallocratic, it is expected to dichotomize all values—the oppositions strong/weak, rich/poor, useful/useless, clean/dirty, etc.

Conversely, on the level of the sexed body, libido is engaged in a becoming-woman. More precisely, the becoming-woman serves as a point of reference, and eventually as a screen for other types of becoming (example: becoming-child in Schumann, becoming-animal in Kafka, becoming-vegetable in Novalis, becoming-mineral in Beckett).

Becoming-woman can play this intermediary role, this role as mediator vis-à-vis other sexed becomings, because it is not too far removed from the binarism of phallic power. In order to understand the homosexual, we tell ourselves that it is sort of "like a woman." And a number of homosexuals themselves join in this somewhat normalizing game. The pair feminine/passive, masculine/active therefore remains a point of reference made obligatory by power in order to permit it to situate, localize, territorialize, control intensities of desire. Outside of this exclusive bi-pole, no salvation: or else it's the plunge into the non-sensical, to the prison, to the asylum, to psychoanalysis, etc. Deviance, various forms of marginalism are themselves coded to work as safety valves. Women, in short, are the only official trustee of a becoming-sexed body. A man who detaches himself from the phallic types inherent in all power formations will enter such a becoming-woman according to diverse possible modalities. It is only on this condition, moreover, that he will be able to become animal, cosmos, letter, color, music.

Homosexuality, by the very nature of things, cannot be dissociated from a becoming-woman—even non-oedipal, non-personological homosexuality. The same holds true for infantile sexuality, psychotic sexuality, poetic sexuality (for instance: the coincidence, in Allen Ginsberg's work, of a fundamental poetic mutation together with a sexual mutation). In a more general way, every "dissident" organization of libido must therefore be directly linked to a becoming-feminine body, as an escape route from the repressive socius, as a possible access to a "minimum" of sexed becoming, and as the last buoy vis-à-vis the established order. I emphasize this last point because the becoming-feminine body shouldn't be thought of as belonging to the woman category found in the couple, the family, etc. Such a category only exists in a specific social field that defines it. There is no such thing as woman per se, no maternal pole, no eternal feminine…. The man/woman opposition serves as a foundation to the social order, before class and caste conflicts intervene. Conversely, whatever shatters norms, whatever breaks from the established order, is related to homosexuality or a becoming-animal or a becoming-woman, etc. Every semiotization in rupture implies a sexualization in rupture. Thus, to my mind, we shouldn't ask which writers are homosexual, but rather, what it is about a great writer—even if he is in fact heterosexual—that is homosexual.

I think it's important to destroy "big" notions like woman, homosexual…. Things are never that simple. When they're reduced to black-white, male-female categories, there's an ulterior motive, a binary-reductionist operation meant to sub-jugate them. For example, you cannot qualify a love univocal-ly. Love in Proust is never specifically homosexual. It always has a schizoid, paranoid component, a becoming-plant, a becoming-woman, a becoming-music.

Orgasm is another over-blown notion whose ravages are incalculable. Dominant sexual morality requires of the woman a quasi-hysterical identification of her orgasm with the man's, an expression of symmetry, a submission to his phallic power. The woman *owes* her orgasm to the man. In "refusing" him, she assumes the guilt. So many stupid dramas are based on this theme. And the sententious attitude of psychoanalysts and sex-ologists on this point doesn't really help. In fact, it frequently happens that women who, for some reason or other, are frozen with male partners achieve orgasm easily by masturbating or having sex with another woman. But the scandal would be much worse if everything is out in the open. Let's consider a final example, the prostitute movement. Everyone, or just about, at first yelled "Hurrah, prostitutes are right to rebel. But wait, you should separate the good from the bad. Prostitutes, OK, but pimps, people don't want to hear about them." And so, prostitutes were told that they should defend themselves, that they're being exploited, etc. All that is absurd. Before explain-ing anything whatsoever, one should first try to understand what goes on between a whore and her pimp. There's the whore-pimp-money triangle. But there also is a whole micro-politics of desire, extremely complex, which is played out between each pole in this triangle and various characters like the John and the cop. Prostitutes surely have very interesting things to teach us about these questions. And, instead of perse-cuting them, it would be better to subsidize them, as they do in research laboratories. I'm convinced, personally, that in study-ing all this micropolitics of prostitution, one might shed some new light on whole areas of conjugal and familial micro-politics—the money relations between husband and wife, parents and children, and ultimately, the psychoanalyst and his patient. (We should also recall what the anarchists of the turn of the century wrote on the subject.)

Translated by Rachel McComas and Stamos Metzidakis

1. Renée Nelli, *Les Troubadours.* (Paris: Desdée de Brouwer, 1960–66).

7

A LIBERATION OF DESIRE

GEORGE STAMBOLIAN: In 1970 the authorities forbade the sale to minors of Pierre Guyotat's novel, *Eden, Eden, Eden*. More recently they outlawed and seized the special issue of the magazine *Recherches* ("Encyclopedia of homosexualities") to which you had made important contributions. You were even taken to court on the matter. How would you explain these reactions by the French government?

FÉLIX GUATTARI: They were rather old-fashioned reactions. I do not think that the present government would behave the same way because there is, on the surface at least, a certain nonchalance regarding the literary and cinematographic expression of sexuality. But I don't have to tell you that this is an even more subtle, cunning, and repressive policy. During the trial the judges were completely ill at ease with what they were being asked to do.

GS: Wasn't it because this issue of *Recherches* treated homosexuality, and not just sexuality?

FG: I'm not sure, because among the things that most shocked the judges was one of the most original parts of this work—a discussion of masturbation. I think that a work devoted to homosexuality in a more or less traditional manner would have had no difficulty. What shocked perhaps was the expression of sexuality going in all directions. And then there were the illustrations—they were what set it off.

GS: In your opinion, what is the best way to arrive at a true sexual liberation, and what dangers confront this liberation?

FG: The problem, as I see it, is not a sexual liberation but a liberation of desire. Once desire is specified as sexuality, it enters into forms of particularized power, into the stratification of castes, of styles, of sexual classes. The sexual liberation— for example, of homosexuals, or transvestites, or sado-masochists—belongs to a series of other liberation problems among which there is an a priori and evident solidarity, the need to participate in a necessary fight. But I don't consider that to be a liberation as such of desire, since in each of these groups and movements one finds repressive systems.

GS: What do you mean by "desire"?

FG: For Gilles Deleuze and me desire is everything that exists *before* the opposition between subject and object, *before* representation and production. It's everything whereby the world and affects constitute us outside of ourselves, in spite of ourselves. It's everything that overflows from us. That's why we define it as flow. Within this context we were led to forge a new notion in order to specify in what way this kind of desire is not some sort of undifferentiated magma, and thereby dangerous, suspicious, or incestuous. So we speak of machines, of "desiring machines," in order to indicate that there is as yet no question here of "structure," that is, of any subjective position, objective redundancy, or coordinates of reference. Machines arrange and connect flows. They do not recognize distinctions between persons, organs, material flows, and semiotic flows.

GS: Your remarks on sexuality reveal a similar rejection of established distinctions. You have said, for example, that all forms of sexual activity are minority forms and reveal themselves as being irreducible to homo-hetero oppositions. You have also said that these forms are nevertheless closer to homosexuality and to what you call a "becoming-woman." Would you develop this idea, in particular by defining what you mean by "feminine"?

FG: Yes, that was a very ambiguous formulation. What I mean is that the relation to the body, what I call the semiotics of the body, is something specifically repressed by the capitalist-socialist-bureaucratic system. So I would say that each time the body is emphasized in a situation—by dancers, by homosexuals, etc.—something breaks with the dominant semiotics that crush these semiotics of the body. In heterosexual relations as well, when a man becomes body, he becomes feminine. In a way, a successful heterosexual relation becomes homosexual and feminine. This does not at all mean that I am speaking of women as such; that's where the ambiguity lies, because the feminine relation itself can lose the semiotics of the body and become phallocentric. So it is only by provocation that I say feminine, because I would say first that there is only one sexuality, it is homosexual; there is only one sexuality, it is feminine. But I would add finally: there is only one sexuality, it is neither masculine, nor feminine, nor infantile; it is something that is ultimately flow, body. It seems to me that in true love there is always a moment when the man is no longer a man. This does not mean that he becomes a woman. But because of her alienation woman is relatively closer to the situation of desire. And in a sense, perhaps from the point of view of representation, to accede to desire implies for a man first a position of homosexuality as such, and second a feminine becoming. But I would add as well a becoming-animal, or a becoming-

47

plant, a becoming-cosmos, etc. That's why this formulation is very tentative and ambiguous.

GS: Isn't your formulation based in part on the fact that our civilization has associated body and woman?

FG: No, it's because woman has preserved the surfaces of the body, a bodily *jouissance* and pleasure much greater than that of man. He has concentrated his libido on—one can't even say his penis—on domination, on the rupture of ejaculation: "I possessed you" "I had you." Look at all the expressions like these used by men: "I screwed you," "I made her." It's no longer the totality of the body's surface that counts, it's just this sign of power: "I dominated you," "I marked you." This obsession with power is such that man ultimately denies himself all sexuality. On the other hand, in order to exist as body he is obliged to beg his sexual partners to transform him a bit into a woman or a homosexual. I don't know if homosexuals can easily accept what I'm saying, because I don't mean to say that homosexuals are women. That would be a misunderstanding. But I think that in a way there is a kind of interaction between the situation of male homosexuals, of transvestites, and of women. There is a kind of common struggle in their relation to the body.

GS: "Interaction," "transformation," "becoming," "flow"— these words suggest a recognition of our sexual or psychic multiplicity and fluidity which, as I understand it, is an essential aspect of what you call schizo-analysis. What then is the basic difference between schizo-analysis and psychoanalysis which, I believe, you have completely abandoned?

FG: I was Lacan's student. I was analyzed by Lacan, and I practiced psychoanalysis for twelve years; and now I've broken with that practice. Psychoanalysis transforms and deforms the unconscious by forcing it to pass through the grid of its system of inscription and representation. For psychoanalysis the unconscious is always already there, genetically programmed, structured, and finalized on objectives of conformity to social norms. For schizo-analysis it's a question of constructing an unconscious, not only with phrases but with all possible semiotic means, and not only with individuals or relations between individuals, but also with groups, with physiological and perceptual systems, with machines, struggles, and arrangements of every nature. There's no question here of transfer, interpretation, or delegation of power to a specialist.

GS: Do you believe that psychoanalysis has deformed not only the unconscious but the interpretation of life in general and perhaps of literature as well?

FG: Yes, but even beyond what one imagines, in the sense that it's not simply a question of psychoanalysts or even of psychoanalytical ideas as they are propagated in the commercial press or in the universities, but of interpretative and representational attitudes toward desire that one finds in persons who don't know psychoanalysis, but who put themselves in the position of interpreters, of gurus, and who generalize the technique of transfer.

GS: With Gilles Deleuze, you have just finished a schizo-analysis of Kafka's work. Why *this* method to analyze and to comprehend literature?

FG: It's not a question of method or of doctrine. It's simply that I've been living with Kafka for a very long time. I therefore tried, together with Deleuze, to put into our work the part of me that was, in a way, a becoming-Kafka. In a sense the book is a

49

schizo-analysis of our relation to Kafka's work, but also of the period of Vienna in 1920 and of a certain bureaucratic eros which crystallized in that period, and which fascinated Kafka.

GS: In a long note you speak of Kafka's joy, and you suggest that psychoanalysis has found only Kafka's sadness or his tragic aspect.

FG: In his *Diaries* Kafka gives us a glimpse of the diabolic pleasure he found in his writing. He says that it was a kind of demonic world he entered at night to work. I think that everything that produces the violence, richness, and incredible humor of Kafka's work belongs to this world of his.

GS: Aren't you really proposing that creation is something joyful, and that this joy can't be reduced to a psychosis?

FG: Absolutely—or to a lack.

GS: In the same book on Kafka you say that a "minor literature," which is produced by a minority in a major language, always "deterritorializes" that language, connects the individual to politics, and gives everything a collective value. These are for you, in fact, the revolutionary qualities of any literature within the established one. Does homosexuality necessarily produce a literature having these three qualities?

FG: Unfortunately, no. There are certainly homosexual writers who conduct their writing in the form of an Oedipal homosexuality. Even very great writers—I think of Gide. Apart from a few works, Gide always transcribed his homosexuality and in a sense betrayed it.

GS: Despite the fact that he tried to prove the value of homosexuality in works such as *Corydon?*

FG: Yes, but I wonder if he did it in just one part of his work and if the rest of his writing isn't different.

GS: In *Anti-Oedipus* you and Deleuze note that Proust described two types of homosexuality—one that is Oedipal and therefore exclusive, global, and neurotic, and one that is a-Oedipal or inclusive, partial, and localized. In fact, the latter is for you an expression of what you call "transsexuality." So if there are two Gides, aren't there also two Prousts, or at least the possibility of two different readings of his work?

FG: I can't answer for Proust the man, but it seems to me that his work does present the two aspects, and one can justify the two readings because both things in effect exist.

GS: You spoke of the demonic in Kafka. Well, Gide, Proust, and Genet have been accused of being fascinated by the demonic aspect of homosexuality. Would you agree?

FG: To a point. I wonder sometimes, not specifically concerning the three names you mention, if it isn't a matter of persons who were more fascinated by the demonic than by homosexuality. Isn't homosexuality a means of access to the demonic? That is, they are the heirs of Goethe in a certain way, and what Goethe called the demonic was in itself a dimension of mystery.

GS: But the fact remains that in our civilization homosexuality is often associated with the demonic.

FG: Yes, but so is crime. There's a whole genre of crime literature that contains a similar demonic aspect. The demonic or the mysterious is really a residue of desire in the social world. There are so few places for mystery that one looks for it everywhere, in anything that escapes or becomes marginal. For example, there's something demonic in the life of a movie star. That's why it's used by the sensationalist press.

GS: Doesn't that tell us that we are hungry for the demonic; that we are hungry for things that aren't "natural"; that we have exploited movie stars and homosexuals to satisfy our need for the demonic?

FG: I'm not against that because I'm not at all for nature. Therefore artifice, the artificially demonic, is something that rather charms me. Only it is one thing to live it in a relationship of immediate desire, and another thing to transform it into a repressive machine.

GS: Let's go back to the homosexual writers. I'd like to quote here a remark of yours that struck me. It's the last paragraph of your interview published in the August 1975 issue of *La Quinzaine littéraire.* You say: "Everything that breaks something, everything that breaks with the established order, has something to do with homosexuality, or with a becoming-animal, a becoming-woman, etc. Any break in semiotization implies a break in sexuality. It is therefore not necessary, in my opinion, to raise the question of homosexual writers, but rather to look for what is homosexual, in any case, in a great writer, even if he is in other respects heterosexual." Doesn't this idea contain a new way to approach or perhaps to go beyond a question that has so obsessed certain Freudian critics and psychoanalysts—namely, the connection between homosexuality, or all sexuality, and creativity?

FG: Yes, of course. For me, a literary machine starts itself, or can start itself, when writing connects with other machines of desire. I'd like to talk about Virginia Woolf in her relation to a becoming-man which is itself a becoming-woman, because the paradox is complete. I'm thinking about a book I like very much, *Orlando*. You have this character who follows the course of the story as a man, and in the second part of the novel he becomes a woman. Well, Virginia Woolf herself was a woman, but one sees that in order to become a woman writer, she had to follow a certain trajectory of a becoming-woman, and for that she had to begin by being a man. One could certainly find in George Sand things perhaps more remarkable than this. So my question is whether writing as such, the signifier as such, relates to nothing, only to itself, or to power. Writing begins to function in something else, as for example for the Beat Generation in the relation with drugs; for Kerouac in the relation with travel, or with mountains, with yoga. Then something begins to vibrate, begins to function. Rhythms appear, a need, a desire to speak. Where is it possible for a writer to start this literary machine if it isn't precisely outside of writing and of the field of literature? A break in sexuality—therefore homosexuality, a becoming-woman, addict, missionary, who knows? It's a factory, the means of transmitting energy to a writing machine.

Q: Can a break in semiotization precede a break in sexuality?

FG: It's not a break in semiotization, but a semiotic connection. I'll give you a more familiar example. Take what are called mad people from a poor background from the point of view of intellectual formation—peasants who never read anything, who only went to grade school. Well, when they have an attack of dissociation, a psychotic attack, it happens sometimes that they begin to write, to paint, to express extraordinary things, extraordinarily beautiful and poetic! And then when they are "cured," they return to the fields, to the sugar-beets and asparagus, and they stop writing altogether. You have something of a psychotic attack in Rimbaud. When he became normal, he went into commerce; all that stopped. It's always a question of a connection. Something that was a little scholastic writing machine, really without any quality, connects with fabulously perceptive semiotics that start in psychosis, or in drugs, or in war, and that can animate this little writing machine and produce extraordinary things. You have a group of disconnected machines, and at a given moment there is a transmission among them, and everything begins not only to function but to produce an acceleration of operations. So you see, I'm not talking about sexuality. Sexuality is already specified as sex, caste, forms of sexual practice, sexual ritual. But creativity and desire are for me the same thing, the same formula.

GS: I'd still like to ask you the following question. Could you begin the search for what is homosexual in a heterosexual writer with a great writer like, for example, Beckett, whose work offers us a "homosexuality" which seems at times to be the product of extraordinary semiotic connections, and which, in any case, confounds all previous representations and goes beyond them?

FG: I think of those characters who travel by twos and who have no sexual practice because they live completely outside of sexuality, but who nevertheless represent a kind of collective set-up of enunciation, a collective way of perceiving everything that happens. And so many things are happening that it's necessary to select, to narrow down, in order to receive and distill each element, as if one were using a microscope to capture each of the intensities. Indeed, there is perhaps in

Beckett a movement outside of the sexes, but then there is the absolutely fabulous relation to objects, a sexual relation to objects. I'm thinking of the sucking stones in *Molloy.*

GS: Then how does one explain the elements of homosexuality, of sadomasochism, in his work?

FG: But that's theater, because if there's a constant in Beckett's work, it's that even when he writes novels, he creates theater, in the sense of a *mise en scène,* an acting out, of giving something to be seen. So then inevitably, he gathers up representations, but he articulates them to create literature. What's more, Beckett is someone, I think, who was very interested in the insane, in psychopathology, and therefore he picked up a lot of representations. The use he makes of them is essentially literary, of course, but what he uses them for is not a translation, it's a collage, it's like a dance. He plays with these representations, or rather, he makes them play.

GS: You said in your article on the cinema[1] that any representation expresses a certain position with respect to power. But I wonder if Beckett hasn't succeeded in writing a politically "innocent" text.

FG: I no more believe in innocence than I do in nature. One thing should be made clear—if one finds innocence, there's reason to worry, there's reason to look not for guilt, of course—that's the same thing as innocence, it's symmetry— but for what is politically in germination, for a politics in dotted lines. Take Kafka again. Although his text isn't innocent, the supremely innocent character is K., and yet he is neither innocent nor guilty. He's waiting to enter a political scene. That's not fiction; it's not Borges, because he did enter a political scene in Prague, where one of the biggest political dramas was played around Kafka's work. So, innocence is always the anticipation of a political problem.

GS: Everything that's written is therefore linked in one way or another to a political position?

FG: Yes, with two fundamental axes: everything that's written in refusing the connection with the referent, with reality, implies a politics of individuation of the subject and of the object, of a turning of writing on itself, and by that puts itself in the service of all hierarchies, of all centralized systems of power, and of what Gilles Deleuze and I call all "arborescences," the regime of unifiable multiplicities. The second axis, in opposition to arborescence, is that of the "rhizome," the regime of pure multiplicities. It's what even innocent texts, even gratuitous games like those of the Dadaists, even collages, cut-ups, perhaps especially these things, will make it possible one day to reveal the pattern of similar breaks in reality, in the social field, and in the field of economic, cosmic, and other flows.

GS: So sexual liberation is not going to rid us of political connections.

FG: Sexual liberation is a mystification. I believe in, and will fight for, the taking of power by other castes and sexual systems, but I believe that liberation will occur when sexuality becomes desire, and desire is the freedom to be sexual, that is, to be something else at the same time.

GS: How does one escape from this dilemma in which one caste replaces another?

FG: What these liberation movements will reveal by their failures and difficulties is that there really aren't any castes. There's the possibility that society will reform itself through other types of subjective arrangements that are not based on individuals in constellation or on relations of power that communication institutes between speaker and listener. There will be arrangements, I don't know what, based neither on families, nor on communes, nor on groups, where the goals of life, politics, and work will always be conjugated with the analysis of unconscious relations, of relations of micro-power, of micro-fascism. On the day when these movements fix as their goals not only the liberation of homosexuals, women, and children, but also the struggle against themselves in their constant power relations, in their relations of alienation, of repression against their bodies, their thoughts, their ways of speaking, then indeed, we will see another kind of struggle appear, another kind of possibility. The micro-fascist elements in all our relations with others must be found, because when we fight on the molecular level, we'll have a much better chance of preventing a truly fascist, a macro-fascist formation on the molar level.

GS: You and Deleuze often speak of Artaud, who wanted to rid us of masterpieces and perhaps even of written texts. Can one say that the written text already contains a form of microfascism?

FG: No, because a written text can be lengthened. Graffiti in the street can be erased or added to. A written text can be contradictory, can be made into a palimpsest. It can be something extremely alive. What is much less alive is an *oeuvre* and Artaud himself did not write a work or a book. But then, one never writes a book. One picks up on books that have been written; one places oneself in a phylum. To write a book that wants to be an eternal and universal manual, yes, you're right;

but to write after one thing and before another, that means participating in a chain, in a chain of love as well.

GS: I'd like to return for a moment to what you said about desire and the problems of liberation. I think of people who might profit from that kind of formulation in order to circumvent the question of homosexuality and the specificity of this struggle, by saying that all that is just sexuality and that sexuality alone matters.

FG: I'm very sympathetic to what you say. It's a bit like what they say to us regarding the struggle of the working class. I understand that, but I'd still like to give the same answer: it's up to the homosexuals. I'm not a worker or a homosexual. I'm a homosexual in my own way, but I'm not a homosexual in the world of reality or of the group.

GS: Yes, but the theories one proposes on homosexuality are always important, and they are never innocent. Before writing *Corydon,* Gide read theories. Before writing *La Recherche,* Proust was totally aware of the psychological thought of his time. Even Genet was influenced after the fact by the theories of Sartre. Obviously, it's often writers themselves who are the first to see things that others transform into theories. I'm thinking of Dostoevsky, Proust, and of course, Kafka. You've already begun to use your own theories to study the literature of the past, and they are related perhaps to what may someday be called a "literature of desire." Writers, critics, and homosexuals have the choice of accepting or rejecting these theories, or of playing with them. But they can neither forget them nor ignore the words of moralists, psychoanalysts, and philosophers, certainly not today and certainly not in France.

FG: Right, I completely agree. It's truly a pollution. But in any case, what do you think of the few theoretical propositions I've advanced here? It's my turn to question you.

GS: Judging your position by what you've said here and by what you've written, I think that you and Deleuze have seriously questioned Freud's system. You have turned our attention away from the individual and toward the group, and you have shown to what extent the whole oedipal structure reflects our society's paranoia and has become an instrument for interiorizing social and political oppression. Also, I'd like to quote the following passage from *Anti-Oedipus*: "We are heterosexuals statistically or in molar terms, but homosexuals personally, whether we know it or not, and finally transsexuals elementarily, molecularly." I can't claim to understand fully this or other aspects of your theory, but you do show that the time has come to address ourselves to the question of sexuality in another way, and that's a kind of liberation.

FG: Well, I want to tell those people who say "all that is sexuality" that they must go farther and try to see what in fact is the sexuality not only of the homosexual, but also of the sadomasochist, the transvestite, the prostitute, even the murderer, anyone for that matter, in order not to go in the direction of reassurance. They must see what a terrible world of repression they will enter.

GS: Despite the passage from your work I just quoted, when you speak you often cite groups that are always outside the dominant field of heterosexuality.

FG: For me desire is always "outside"; it always belongs to a minority. For me there is no heterosexual sexuality. Once there's heterosexuality, in fact, once there's marriage, there's no more desire, no more sexuality. In all my twenty-five years of work in this field I've never seen a heterosexual married couple that worked along a line of desire. Never. They don't exist. So don't say that I'm marginalizing sexuality with homosexuals, etc., because for me there is no heterosexuality possible.

GS: Following the same logic there is no homosexuality possible.

FG: In a sense yes, because in a sense homosexuality is counterdependent on heterosexuality. Part of the problem is the reduction of the body. It's the impossibility of becoming a totally sexed body. The sexed body is something that includes all perceptions, everything that occurs in the mind. The problem is how to sexualize the body, how to make bodies desire, vibrate—all aspects of the body.

GS: There are still the fantasies each of us brings. That's often what's interesting in some homosexual writing—this expression of fantasies that are very specialized, very specific.

FG: I don't think it's in terms of fantasies that things are played but in terms of representations. There are fantasies of representations. In desire there are semiotic flows of a totally different nature, including verbal flows. It's not fantasies; it's words, speech, rhythms, poetry. A phantasmal representation in poetry is never the essential thing, no more than is the content. Fantasy is always related to content. What counts is expression, the way expression connects with the body. For example, poetry is a rhythm that transmits itself to the body, to perception. A fantasy when it operates does not do so as a fantasy that represents a content, but as something that puts us in motion, that brings out something that carries us away, that draws us, that locks us onto something.

GS: Aren't there fantasies of form as well?

FG: Fantasies of form, fantasies of expression, become in effect micro-fascistic crystallizations. This implies, for example, in scenes of power of a sadomasochistic character: "Put yourself in exactly this position. Follow this scenario so that it will produce in me such an effect." That becomes a kind of fantasy of form, but what counts there is not the application of the fantasy, it's the relation to the other person, it's complicity! Desire escapes from formal redundancies, escapes from power formations. Desire is not informed, informing; it's not information or content. Desire is not something that deforms but that disconnects, changes, modifies, organizes other forms, and then abandons them.

GS: So, a literary text escapes all categorization as well as any sexuality that can be called one thing or another?

FG: Take any literary work you love very much. Well, you will see that you love it because it is for you a particular form of sexuality or desire, I leave the term up to you. The first time I made love with Joyce while reading *Ulysses* was absolutely unforgettable. It was extraordinary. I made love with Kafka, and I think one can say that, truly.

GS: Proust said it: "To love Balzac; to love Baudelaire." And he was speaking of a love that could not be reduced to any one definition.

FG: Absolutely. And one doesn't make love in the same way with Joyce as with Kafka. If one began to make love in the same way, there would be reason to worry—one might be becoming a professor of literature.

GS: Perhaps! Then literature can be a liberation of desire, and the text is a way of multiplying the sexes.

FG: Certain texts, texts that work. Nothing can be done about those that don't work. But those that do function multiply our functioning. They turn us into madmen; they make us vibrate.

Translated by George Stambolian

1. Cf. "The Poor Man's Couch," *infra.*

8

THE ADOLESCENT REVOLUTION

CHRISTIAN POSLIANEC: How would you describe adolescence?

FÉLIX GUATTARI: In my opinion it's something in adults' minds; something that exists for them on all sorts of levels, as a fantasy, as a segregative social practice, as a collective assemblage, etc. But adolescence as a lived experience can't be defined in terms of age groups. I prefer looking at it as made up of different sorts of "becomings": becoming-child, becoming-woman, becoming-sexual.... These becomings can occur at any time; not necessarily at a fixed age. It is well known that one can become a child again, at the age of seventy-five. One can also never become a child. A twelve-year-old can be an old dotard. One can become a woman, one can become a potted plant. One can become all kinds of things, but I don't think it depends on genetic programming.

CP: So you eliminate all possible reference points from the person you have in front of you. You don't put people into little boxes....

FG: I still have to take them into account because that's what most people do. The little boxes begin in nursery school when the little girl jumping rope has to arrange her body in a certain way and progressively submits to all kinds of behaviors and images. The boxes are everywhere. But on the level of what I call the economy of desire, obviously, there are no boxes. And so, trying to stay close to your question and not be too evasive, I think that adolescence, as far as I can recognize it, constitutes a real micro-revolution, involving multiple components, some of which threaten the world of adults. It is the entrance into a sort of extremely troubled interzone where all kinds of possibilities, conflicts and sometimes extremely difficult and even dramatic clashes suddenly appear. A whole new world opens up when one emerges from the relative equilibrium, the homeostasis or autoregulation of childhood (a category that should be handled with tweezers). But, almost immediately, everthing closes up, and a whole series of institutionalized social controls and the internalization of repressive fantasies march in to capture and neutralize the new virtualities.

So, what would a micro-revolution be? Some obvious, and some not so obvious things. First of all, of course, there is the puberty factor, whose onset breaks up and disorganizes the previous physiological, biological and behavioral *status quo*. This kind of transformation brings about profound modifications, not only of what happens inside of people's heads, on reflexive and conceptual levels, but also on the perceptive level...

CP: And emotional...

FG: Emotional, of course; but I would like to emphasize the perceptive mutations which relate to space, to the body, to time. Proust explored these transformations, which involve synaesthesia, in depth. All of this can lead to a complete topling of behavioral structures, as Merleau-Ponty put it.

CP: And all this occurs during puberty?

FG: No, I am not speaking of a specific phase. You can also have an "adolescent revolution" without considerations of sexual-genital components. What counts in archaic societies are their collective arrangements which serve to integrate the individual into structures of initiation and allow entry into society. Obviously, such initiations do not result automatically from the onset of puberty. Perhaps, conversely, it is the release of the components of puberty which, to some extent, results from the initiation into an age group. Today's social "molting periods" no longer take such collective and spectacular forms. They are much less easy to pinpoint, because they are no longer ritualized in the same way. But they are just as important.

CP: I have mainly worked with young adults or adolescents between the ages of seventeen and twenty-two, and I am tempted by the idea of a "second puberty." Ways of apprehending the world change, particularly through a powerful desire for autonomy in every area: emotional, sexual, financial, intellectual, etc. As if there were a whole internal revolution taking place without the "rich outward signs" which take place during puberty, although I can't exactly say what happens. Does this correspond to something more specific for you than it does for me?

FG: Perhaps you have had experiences that I haven't had. The young men and women with whom I deal are generally much less autonomous than those you describe as going through this "second puberty." It is perhaps even the opposite for psychotics who often lose their autonomy when they enter puberty, which frequently coincides with the onset of pathologies.

I often have the impression that during adolescent periods "imprint phenomena," to take up a term from ethology, are activated. An entire zone of psychic and behavioral disturbances, sometimes of tumultuous richness, expose many adolescents to formidable trials—from which some never escape unharmed. All of this leads to normalization, to characterological difficulties, to neuroses or to all sorts of traumas. It is true that few peo-

65

ple preserve an authentic memory of their adolescence. Writers who know how to describe it, like Andre Gide, are rare.

For girls the ravages are perhaps worse. The capacity for recuperation from the bludgeoning of normative systems frequently takes on frightening forms. Not only because of exterior interventions of explicit repressive attitudes, but also because of internalized systems of punishment that even develop from what seem to be liberating practices. Compare them, for example, to certain groups of homosexuals, who elicit mixed reactions in me since their supposed dimension of emancipation appears above all to be linked to nearly explicit activities of normalization and psychological confinement. In any case, this first adolescent revolution is of the greatest importance in the crystalization of personality. It is no accident that this is where Kraepelin located the origin of *dementia praecox*. It's true that "infantile psychosis" was invented later on, but I'm not sure it's an improvement. In actual terms, clinical descriptions always come back to the period of puberty. Certainly it could be said that a maturation of psychosis may occur before that period, with the revelation, "after the fact," of childhood disorders. But I find these conceptions perplexing. I find it dangerous to speak of psychosis before puberty, because nothing is really crystallized until that point. Imposing an entire etiological program in infantile stages has its risks. Start with the Oedipus complex or much before that according to Melanie Klein—and then an entire chain of distortions and imaginary identifications are inferred.... And you know the rest. Really, I must repeat that serious madness, like serious vocations, comes into being during the *adolescent revolution.*

CP: I thought that everything was already happening in a child at age six! That is what many contemporary pedagogues say....

FG: Yes, I know, but that's really not too sharp. With an idea like that, every kind of passivity, every kind of resignation can be justified. Nothing really starts or ends before or after the age of six. Such schemas of causality should be eliminated. What counts is how people deal with insertion into family, social, sexual, athletic, military, etc., situations. Every such moment concurrently produces both a rupture and possibilities for new beginnings, taking into account sociological, institutional, environmental, collective infrastructural conditions, the mass media.... Paradoxically, entry into the work-place occurs later and later, while the entry into adult semiotics occurs earlier and earlier. In my opinion this results in ever more precocious forms of sexuality and, at the same time, a chronic immaturity in that same sexuality. I'm not against it—but is this what sexual freedom means? It is not at all clear. Because entry into semiotic life means having a job, entering production, the production of models, the production of subjectivity. During the whole of adolescence, there is considerable anxiety concerning the coming of "normal adulthood."

CP: In this issue[1] we have interviewed two "youths" from technical schools who are about to enter into the system of production. As a matter of fact, the anxiety that equates "entering life" to getting a job, to getting shut in, to being productive, to the end of whatever dreams they still may have had, is clearly manifest.

FG: It's where everything ties together. You get your technical diploma, or whatever, you develop your linguistic and performance competencies in the race to get ahead, in areas that depend not only on education or professional training, but also on sexuality. Have you passed your puberty certificate? Are you sure that you're normal? The jury in this kind of competition is often the merciless opinion of your closest buddies, your sweet girlfriend.... It's a dirty deal. And this unhealthy interest is becoming more widespread, not only among psychologists, educators, day-care workers, mothers and all the Ruth Westheimers of the media.

Infantile, adolescent and adult sexuality never cease to be confronted by tests like, "Do you come too soon? Or too late?" "And your orgasm, is it too clitoral?" What an idiotic mess. And see how seriously babies concentrate on the television screen. "That's hard work, poor things." A modelling of perceptive systems also occurs during the stages of infancy. It is clear that this type of childhood has little to do with the rural or proto-capitalistic urban societies of 50 years ago. Now a kind of psychological seriousness is conveyed by the media, through educational games.... "Does my baby suckle at the right time? Does he masturbate when he should? There is something wrong, Doctor, he doesn't masturbate yet. What do you prescribe?" A widespread anxiety accompanies every incident in the development of the child. And it's getting out of hand. For the most part it results from psychoanalytical drivel concerning psychogenesis, all these nameless stupidities that not only postulate stages of intellectual development, but also stages of behavior, and emotional stages. Now isn't this too much already!

CP: Half a century ago youths, in rural areas at least, were freer than those in urban areas. They were not watched over, they were not always under the eyes of adults. This is no longer the case. Now when they leave school they have to return home right away—there are no more haystacks, quiet hideaways, places where one can go in secret. They move from the gaze of adult-teachers to that of adult-parents, to the gaze of the TV. And they are always closed off that way. Whereas in the city, it was the opposite not too long ago. Freedom could be found in basements, in parking lots, in everything that was underground;

that is, in the unconscious of the city, where a certain sexuality in relation to the forbidden, including its unfortunate sexist and violent aspects, would take place. There was something really wild about it. Now it is disappearing because of the control of children's free time.

FG: I would add that it is not only children and adolescents who are under control. The entire society finds itself infantilized, puerilized, under the "panoptic" regime described by Michel Foucault. Because everything you have just described can just as well be applied to the father, to the mother, etc. We are all turned into children by mass media society and various apparatuses producing subjectivity. And maybe "adolescents" are less affected than others, perhaps they are even the most resilient to it. At least up until the moment when they fall apart during an agonizing crisis, unless they make a massive transfer onto a partner, hang on to conjugal life, join the usual circuit.

CP: What you were just saying about that force, the violence that occurs at a given moment—which can be one of the possible definitions of adolescence—could it be considered a political force (in the etymological sense) that can change something, a "hope" even, as the adolescents interviewed say that they put no trust in society, in politics, or even perhaps in any collective organization of any sort at all? They also say that they experience their sexuality in couples, that their sexual life exists as a couple. For me, all these words interfere with each other: security, integration, revolt, etc. Is it clearer for you?

FG: I'm not at all convinced that one can speak so quickly about a return to the couple. A new micropolitics of the couple surely exists, but not necessarily a return. There's another definition, at least in many cases, since, obviously, conservatism is also on the rise and is causing much damage. Whatever it is, I think that the manner in which relations between men and women take place today is very different from what it was two or three generations ago. A careful study would be welcome. This doesn't only happen on the level of daily life, doing the dishes and things like that, or the manifestations of possessiveness or jealousy, etc., but also on the sexual level. It is no longer the same sexuality, because women take charge of their bodies with relatively less dependence on their partner.

And yet there have always been couples. And why not? The myths of sexual communities, with their sometimes half-delirious leaders, to my knowledge, have pretty much fallen apart. But this does not necessarily imply a return to the traditional couple. And I don't see any reason for condemning couples. What matters is how they work. What becomes of the individuals of whom they are composed? What happens to their lives, their emotions, their desires? Analysis presents a similar problem. The question is not whether or not it is necessary to be "two," or alone, or ten, in order to conduct analysis, but to determine what must be done.

A symmetrical answer: it is not true that politics is dead from a social implosion.[2] No doubt, a certain kind of politics and a certain social implosion have occurred. But I believe that there is a collective, unformed search, from above and below, for another kind of politics. This is what I call "micropolitics," and "molecular revolution." It begins with very immediate, daily, individual preoccupations, yet remains connected to what happens at the social level, and even, why not, at the cosmic level. An ecological sensitivity also means a preference for a vision that is at the same time molecular and worldwide in scope. Obviously it is something quite different from the radical socialism of our fathers and grandfathers. But if it is not political, what is it? It is true that its subjects, its objects and its means are no longer the same. Instead of individual subjects, of abstract citizens, there are collective arrangements. It can't be done according to sexual criteria, nor as a political group, nor as an age group. That is what I call a complex multidimensional arrangement. Groups like this, covetous of their autonomy and their singularity can change the nature of human relationships on a large scale, if they can manage to rid themselves of narrow segregationist attitudes. Its objectives are also of another kind. It can't be said that they are ambiguous, but they have multiple facets. They may derive from an immediate pleasure, for example from being together, as well as from more political and social preoccupations that have little to do with everyday wheeling and dealing. So the objects become the whole world, animals, plants, shapes, sounds, humanity....

De Gaulle was completely demoralized in May '68 because he saw that no one even held a grudge against him. It was what he represented that was rejected, and he could remain in power because no credible political alternative was available. He saw that he governed a population of zombies. Perhaps a new kind of '68, of a completely different style, is developing behind the scenes. Your students, your youths, your rockers—their preoccupations are literally imperceptible to "normal" people. Some might say, "People like that don't even know what they want. What they want doesn't make any sense." And since nothing registers in these people's minds, they consider them completely crazy. Except that, from time to time, something does register. Once in a while, from inside the establishment, it turns into Watergate; and on other occasions, from the populace, completely unexpected things come about, like revolts against work, or alarming statistics concerning the fact that people couldn't care less about dying for their country.

When this happens, those in charge ask themselves, "Where did that come from? Who are their ringleaders? Who is putting such ideas into the heads of our youth?" But the way such political situations work is not traditional either. It doesn't happen through social communication, through discourse, programs, *explication de texte* or reference to Great Authors. It has gone over to the side of reflexes, to collective sensibility, to systems of non-verbal expression. Children and adolescents are not aware of their becoming, at least not predominantly in terms of meaningful discourse. They use what I call "a-signifying systems": music, clothing, the body, behaviors as signs of mutual recognition, as well as machinic systems of all kinds. For example, my son is into politics. Not so much through discourse, but with his soldering iron: he sets up "free radios," where technical discourse is hooked right into politics. There is no need to explain the opportunity and the political rationale of free-radio broadcasting; he got it right away. It is the intervention of machinisms—and not only those of communication as means, as political media, which seem fundamental to me. I have confidence in all the techno-scientific categories to which this new political field gives rise.

Translated by Chet Wiener

1. *Sexpol,* "the magazine of sexuality, politics," 1979.
2. Allusion to Jean Baudrillard's "implosion of the social" in *In The Shadow of the Silent Majorities.* New York: Semiotext(e), 1983 [Ed.]

9

POPULAR FREE RADIO

The evolution of the means of mass communication seems to be going in two directions: toward hyper-concentrated systems controlled by the apparatus of state, of monopolies, of big political machines with the aim of shaping opinion and of adapting the attitudes and unconscious schemas of the population to dominant norms; toward miniaturized systems that create the possibility of a collective appropriation of the media, that provide real means of communication, not only to the "large masses," but also to minorities, to marginalized and deviant groups of all kinds.

On the one hand: always more centralization, conformism, oppression; on the other, the perspective of a new space of freedom, self-management, and the fulfillment of the singularities of desire.

How is it that a relatively old technology like radio has set the stage for a breakthrough in this second direction—in Italy and France—through the phenomenon of free radio stations? Why not video, which, not long ago, raised so many expectations? Why not cable? Why not Super 8? It would be very difficult to disentangle all the factors that permitted free radio to take off. But there is one factor which seems to demand particular attention: with video and film, the technical initiative remains, essentially, the object of big industrial enterprise; with free radio, an important part of the technology depends on the improvisational ability of its promoters.

For here as elsewhere, the technical choices always conceal political and micro-political choices. For example, in the domain of television, the technical options have all been centered on family or individual consumption. Hence, a very narrow definition of the broadcast framework (the division of labor between technology, production, and conception of programs; its perpetual reorientation toward boxed-in studios; the national vocation of the programs...) which leads ineluctably to an absolute passivity of the consumer. Yet nothing, at the outset, imposed such a political choice on the technical level. It was possible right away to conceive of technical equipment for the kind of production and consumption that was adapted to "group-subjects" and not to subjugated groups.[1] But with the capitalist and state decision-makers lacking all interest in such an orientation, it's the "heavy duty" means that have triumphed. And today one has a tendency to base the legitimacy of this choice on the nature of things, on the "natural" evolution of the technology.

With free radio, we find ourselves before the same type of technico-political problem. But here, because of the confrontation with power, it's "light weight" technology that assert themselves as if by necessity. In fact, at the present stage, the only way to resist the jamming and the searches is by multiplying the number of transmitters and by miniaturizing the means in order to minimize the risks. (This daily guerrilla warfare of the airwaves is perfectly compatible with the kind of public airing that takes place whenever the balance of powers are poised for it: through public broadcasts, national celebrations, etc.)

But the point the organizers of the popular free radio stations particularly emphasize is that the totality of technical and human means available must permit the establishment of a veritable feed-back system between the auditors and the broadcast team: whether through direct intervention by phone, through opening "studio" doors, through interviews or programs based on listener-made cassettes, etc. The Italian experience in this regard shows us the immense field of new possibilities that is opened up in this way; in particular, the experience of the Bologna group that organized Radio Alice and the journal *A Traverso*.[2] We realize here that radio constitutes but one central element of a whole range of communication means, from informal encounters in the Piazza Maggiore to the daily newspaper—via billboards, mural paintings, posters, leaflets, meetings, community activities, festivals, etc. We are far, very far, from the technocratic conceptions of the French partisans of *local* radio, who insist, on the contrary, that those who express themselves on radio represent their particular interests; or from the conceptions of the traditional left which is concerned above all that nothing more than the party line and certain mobilizing propositions be expressed on their wavelengths. (On Italian free radio, it often happens that very serious debates are directly interrupted by violently contradictory, humorous, or even poetico-delirious interventions.) We are equally far from the conceptions of modernist technicians who declare that what is important today is the content of the broadcasts and the care one brings to the production, and who refer to the entire mythology of the "modern look" and the "new sound." All these "preliminaries," relative to the quality of the spokesman, the content of the messages, and the form of expression, come together here. In effect, the "locals," the militants, and the modernists have this in common: in one way or another, they set themselves up as *specialists*: specialists of contacts, watchwords, culture, and expression.... Yet, to be precise, the way opened up by the free radio phenomenon seems to go against the whole spirit of specialization. What becomes specific here are the collective arrangements of enunciation that absorb or "traverse" specialties.

Of course, such an assumption of direct speech by social groups of all kinds is not without its consequences. It fundamentally endangers traditional systems of social representation, it puts in doubt a certain conception of the delegate, the representative, the authorized spokesman, the leader, the journalist.... It is as if, in some immense, permanent meeting place—given the size of the potential audience—anyone, even the most hesitant, those with the weakest voices, suddenly have the possibility of expressing themselves whenever they wanted. In these conditions, one can expect certain truths to find a *new matter of expression.* Somé time ago Bertrand Boulin launched a broadcast, on *Europe No. 1*, in the course of which children, coming out after school, could express themselves directly by telephone. The result was absolutely surprising and upsetting. Through thousands of testimonies, some aspects of the real conditions of childhood were exposed, the very accent and tone which no journalist, educator, or psychologist could have otherwise revealed. But the names, places, and precise circumstances were also communicated: it created a scandal, a cover-up, and, finally, the cancellation of the broadcast....

In drawing up the *Cahiers de doléances* in 1789, the spokesmen of the Third Estate were literally having to invent a new medium of expression, a new language. Today, the Fourth World is also in search of minor languages to bring problems to light that, in reality, concern society as a whole. It is in this context of experimenting with a new type of direct democracy that the question of free radio is inscribed. Direct speech, living speech, full of confidence, but also hesitation, contradiction, indeed even absurdity, is charged with desire. And it is always this aspect of desire that spokesmen, commentators, and bureaucrats of every stamp tend to reduce, to filter. The language of official media is patterned on the police languages of the managerial milieu and the university; it all gets back to a fundamental split between saying and doing according to which only those who are masters of a licit speech have the right to act. Languages of desire, on the other hand, invent new means and have an unequivocal tendency to lead straight to action;

they begin by "touching," by provoking laughter, by moving people, and then they make one want to "move out," toward those who speak and toward those stakes of concern to them.

One will object that France is not Italy and that there is a big risk involved in letting the cohorts of private, commercial stations and the sharks of advertising rush into the breach made in the monopolies of state. It is through this kind of argument that one denounces free radio and justifies maintaining the monopoly, or adjusting it slightly, so that local radio is driven into the service of the big-wigs and the indirect control of the governors. It takes a heavy dose of bad faith to raise the question of advertising in the context of the development of popular radio. They are clearly two separate problems: on the one hand, there is the question of liquidating the state monopoly as the first condition of expanding free radio and, on the other, there is the bigger question of how to control commercial advertising—but *where ever* it can be found: on walls, in newspapers, on TV, and eventually on free radio itself. Why should raising the question of intoxication by advertising—supposing the left had really committed itself to addressing the issue—imply control, censorship, or the institutional protection of free radio? With lots of money on hand, advertisers are eager to launch numerous private channels. Well! Let's regulate advertising—indeed, prohibit it on all the air waves. It would be very surprising indeed if these people were still prepared to undertake any such venture. Yes, one will say, but the government (not to mention the local big-wigs) secretly supports the advertisers while it represses true free radio stations, as we saw recently with the seizure of materials from "Radio 93," "Paris Free Radio," and "Rocket Radio."

Who will win out in the final analysis? Regulation, underground power maneuvers, or an open balance of power? Let the dozens of existing free radio stations give way to hundreds of new groups and let whole strata of the population, ever larger and more diversified, begin participating, financing, and protecting these new stations and we shall see just how strong the present alliance between the government, local officials, and the private sector is. Monopoly and regulation would not really protect the public from advertising anyway—as we see already on TV. And yet, isn't it up to the masses themselves to organize against the pollutant of advertising? People are not children—and besides, children themselves refuse more and more to be treated as though they were totally irresponsible. They have no need of any protection, despite themselves, against "bad influences" that might carry them off to the trash heap prepared for them by advertisers. The day they can start tuning in to a hundred different stations, they will simply choose what suits them. The prudent attitude (neither here nor there, to say the least) of the parties of the left and of the unions toward free radio reveals an outmoded conception of mass intervention in the social sphere. Texts, petitions, regulations, delegations are one thing, but living, social groups taking real control is another. If one really wants to organize a struggle on a large scale against the advertising blitz, then let's work against all forms of physical and moral billy-clubbing, as well as of domestication (on which not only the power of the state and the employers depends, but also that of the very organizations that claim to fight them). One can only hope in the meantime that the militant bureaucrats will stop bullying those who strive, for better or worse, to create a *real* instrument of struggle against such forms of intimidation and domestication.

Translated by David L. Sweet

1. See Félix Guattari, *Psychanalyse et transversalité* (Paris: Maspéro, 1972).
2. See *Italy: Autonomia. Post-Political Politics. Semiotext(e)*, vol. III, 3, 1980. Edited by Sylvère Lotringer and Christian Marazzi.

10

WHY ITALY?

Why Italy? The first entry is relatively contingent. A number of people responsible for a free Italian radio station in Bologna, Radio Alice, asked me to introduce a French edition of their texts. That interested me because their inspiration was at once Situationist and "deleuzoguattarian," if one can say that.

The second axis is the conjunction between the State apparatus in the traditional sense and the bureaucracies of the worker's movement. We have seen it at work in a spectacular manner in both the USSR and China. The Western democratic tradition, the evolution toward Eurocommunism, and the humanism of the socialist parties made us believe that we weren't exposed to that kind of totalitarianism. It's true that the modes of subjection function differently. Yet there is an irreversible tendency pushing the State to exert its power no longer by traditional means of coercion, like the police or army, but also through every means of negotiation in every domain, from the systematic shaping of children in national education to the immense power of the media, particularly television. This State apparatus is highly visible but often powerless on the national level since real decisions are often taken at the international level. It is on the contrary more and more powerful in its miniaturized interventions.

If one's nose is pressed too close to national realities, the impression is that England is very different from the existing regime in Germany, France or Italy. But stepping back, one can see that a certain kind of totalitarianism is being set up which goes along very well with traditional divisions. The machines of production, formation, and reproduction of the work force imply an immense machinery of State power, and then all kinds of cogwheels in politics, unions, education, sports, etc. In this regard I believe the Italian experience to be the most exemplary, for there we can see the lines of flight and the road that lies ahead. It doesn't lead to an alternative of the English type, or a French popular front, whether on the left or on the right. It amounts to making sure that the Communist Party, mass organizations, and unions will function at full capacity within a national consensus like the Italian political spectrum.

A kind of State regime is now being devised which won't require an October revolution or even a Chinese revolution, but will produce the same result: the people will be controlled by every available means, even if they must be conceded a measure of political and regional diversity.

Why Italy? Because the future of England, France and Germany is Italy. When I got involved with Italy the Common Program of the French left had not yet exploded, but I had already sketched out the idea that it didn't make sense, that things wouldn't happen that way. But integration is inexorable, and the Italian scheme will eventually be reproduced in France.

What I'm saying can only be understood in relation to what I have called the molecular revolution. There is a certain level of desire, violence, and revolt which has become impossible and unbearable in societies such as they have developed at both the technological and social level. Let's take the example of terrorism: throughout the history of the worker's movement, there have been armed actions and acts of terrorism. There have been enormous discussions throughout the communist movement to put into perspective and to situate armed action. Nowadays it's no longer a theoretical problem, but a problem of the collective sensibility as it has been shaped by the State apparatus with its audiovisual tentacles: one doesn't accept any more the idea of death, the idea of violence, the idea of rupture, or even the idea of the unexpected. A general infantilization now pervades all human relationships. If there's a strike at the National Electric Company, be careful. A code of ethics for the strike must be drawn up. Confrontation in Bologna? Be careful, a full negotiation must be made. And if one senses an aberrant factor, if there's a handful of resistors who don't accept the ethical code, it's a black hole. The most beautiful black hole that's been seen was New York during the black-out. When one can no longer see, anything—a great mass, strange fauna—can loom up out of the dark.

A certain type of brutality inherited from capitalist societies of the 19th century was symmetrical with a certain truth of desire. Some people could still free themselves. The progressive tightening up by the Marxist worker's movement has put a stop to that. Today you can't desire rupture, you can't desire revolution, or indeed anything which puts in question the framework and values of contemporary society. Now the control begins in childhood, in the nursery and in school, for everyone must be forced into the dominant redundancies of the system. The repressive societies now being established have two new characteristics: repression is softer, more diffuse, more generalized, but at the same time much more violent. For all who can submit, adapt, and be channeled in, there will be a lessening of police intervention. There will be more and more psychologists, even psychoanalysts, in the police department; there will be more community therapy available; the problems of the individual and of the couple will be talked about everywhere; repression will be more psychologically comprehensive. The work of prostitutes will have to be recognized, there will be a drug advisor on the radio—in short, there will be a general climate of understanding acceptance. But if there are categories and individuals who escape this inclusion, if people attempt to question the general system of confinement, then they will be exterminated like the Black Panthers in the U.S., or their personalities exterminated as it happened with the Red Army Fraction in Germany. Skinnerian conditioning will be used all over.

In no way is terrorism specific to Germany and Italy. In three months France could be crawling with Red Brigades. Considering how power and the media operate, how people are cornered, prisoners in these systems of containment, it's no wonder that some become enraged, and start shooting at people's legs or wherever.

The molecular revolution, however, is produced neither on the level of political and traditional union confrontation, nor on the front of different movements like the Women's Movement, the prostitutes, the Gay Liberation Front, etc., which are often only provisional reterritorializations, even forms of compromise with the State power and the different political forces. There is a miniaturization of forms of expression and of forms of struggle, but no reason to think that one can arrange to meet or wait at a specific place for the molecular revolution to happen.

At a deeper level in contemporary history, it hardly matters anymore whether one lives in Brezhnev's regime of gulags or under Carterism or Berlinguerism, all the powers are intricated in the same bizarre formula. To be sure, there will be contradictions, confrontations, landslides, class struggles in the traditional sense, even wars, but it's actually society as a whole that is now shifting. It won't simply be another bourgeois or proletarian revolution. The gears effected by this shift are so minute that it will be impossible to determine whether it's a class confrontation or a further economic subjugation. I believe that this shift in society, which implies not only a rearrangement of relationships among humans, but also among organs, machines, functions, signs, and flux, is an intrahuman revolution, not a simple re-ordering of explicit relationships. There have been major revolutionary debacles in history before. In the 18th century, ranks, orders, classifications of all kinds suddenly broke down. Today no one or anything seems to be able to semiotize collectively what's happening. Panic creeps in, and people fall back upon State powers more overwhelming and tentacular, ever more manipulative and mystifying. In Italy the Communist Party is often heard saying "let's save Italy," but the more uncertain Italy's future becomes, the more claims there are to save it.

In Italy there is no tradition of State power, no civic spirit, nothing like the French tradition of centralism and hierarchical responsibility. The situation therefore is more favorable for bringing about a number of shifts. Entire regions will be downgraded because of the restructuring of capitalism on the international scale. As for the "Italian miracle," or the French miracle, we'd better forget about it.

I am of a generation which really experienced a deadlocked society. Stalinism then was an institution, a wall blocking the horizon to infinity. I now sense an extraordinary acceleration in the decomposition of all coordinates. It's a treat just the same. All this has to crumble down, but obviously it won't come from any revolutionary organization. Otherwise you fall back on the most mechanistic utopias of the revolution, the Marxist simplifications: at the end of the road lies victory…. It's not the black hole of the 19th century, lots of things have happened since, like the barbarians at the gates. Political superstructures and systems of representation will collapse or crumble down in ridicule and inanity, but there are already an enormous number of things which function, and function remarkably well, whether at the level of science, esthetics, or in the inventiveness of daily life. There is an extraordinary vitality in the machinic processes.

The Italians of Radio Alice have a beautiful saying: when they are asked what has to be built, they answer that the forces capable of destroying this society surely are capable of building something else, yet that will happen along the way. I have no idea what the future model of society or of relationships will be. I think it's a false problem, the kind of false problem that Marx and Engels tried to avoid. We can only do one thing, and that's to acknowledge the end of a society. The revolutionary process won't stem from a rational, Hegelian, or dialectical framework. Instead it will be a generalized revolution, a conjunction of sexual, relational, esthetic, and scientific revolutions, all making cross-overs, markings, and currents of deterritorialization.

On the molecular level, things function otherwise. Looking through the glasses of traditional politics, there is nothing left, for example, of the American radical movement. If one changes glasses, if one peers through the microscope, there is another picture altogether. There is a new sensibility, a new way of relating, a new sort of kindness, all very difficult to define. Historians have a hard time dealing with these objects—history of tenderness. In all sorts of complex ways, through the history of the feminist movement and the history of homosexuality, through relationships in general, this new type of sensibility is also the revolution. If revolutionary glasses don't allow us to see that, then there is no more revolution, it's all finished.

There will be no more October revolutions.

Translated by John Johnston

11

UTOPIA TODAY

[I hate this kind of survey, so I am addressing this answer to you alone; do with it what you like.]

Utopia, today, is to believe that current societies will be able to continue along on their merry little way without major upheavals. Social modes of organization that prevail today on earth *are not holding up,* literally and figuratively. History is gripped by crazy parameters: demography, energy, the technological-scientific explosion, pollution, the arms race.... The earth is deterritorializing itself at top speed. The true utopians are conservatives of all shapes and sizes who would like for this "to hold up all the same," to return to yesterday and the day before yesterday. What is terrifying is our lack of collective imagination in a world that has reached such a boiling point, our myopia before all the "molecular revolutions" which keep pulling the rug out from under us, at an accelerated pace.

I'm just back from Japan. In a few dozen years, a society of "machinic mutants" has come to light—for money *and for the best!* You ask how I see future cities, ideal cities? Somewhat like that. Always more creativity, machinic vitality in the domain of technology, sciences, arts, ways of life and of feeling.

In saying this, I know that I am rubbing the humanist sensibility of many of our friends the wrong way. It's true. I'm crazy about machines, concrete and abstract, and I have no doubt that a fabulous expansion will eventually break down all the conservatisms that "keep us in place" in this absurd and blind society.

You wanted utopia...

Translated by Jeanine Herman

12

A New Alliance is Possible

SYLVÈRE LOTRINGER: There's a lot of talk nowadays about the "end of politics" and the "end of the social." But obviously the social has not evaporated, and politics continue each day to produce its effects. Yet there is a visible and growing disaffection with what until now has constituted the major political and ideological issue: the confrontation between the Eastern and Western blocs. The antagonism is once again hardening up, but it's becoming increasingly clear that politics, in its best acceptation, no longer happens at that level. At what level, then, does it happen? And how can one reformulate political action in a time of decline for Marxism as an instrument of analysis, and in a time of bankruptcy for "real" socialism, as opposed to what some continue to call (optimistically perhaps) "possible" socialism?

FÉLIX GUATTARI: I have never taken seriously the notion that we have outgrown Marxism and that we are now on the verge of a new political era. I have never considered ideas, theories or ideologies as anything but instruments or tools. Whence this expression, which has had a certain success and has since been used by Michel Foucault, that ideas and concepts are all part of a "tool box." As tools they can be changed, borrowed, stolen, or used for another purpose. So what does it mean, "the end of Marxism"? Nothing, or only that certain Marxist tools are no longer working, that others are in need of review, that others continue to be perfectly valid. Hence it would be stupid to junk them all. All the more so in that re-evaluating these concepts means re-examining them—exactly as a re-evaluation of Einstein's theories includes a re-examination of Newton's. One can't say that Newtonianism is totally dead. We are dealing here with a "rhizome" of instruments; certain branches of the rhizome collapse, little sprouts begin to proliferate, etc. For me, Marxism in general has never existed. I have sometimes borrowed or adapted some Marxist concepts I could put to good use. Moreover, I like reading Marx. He's a great writer. As an author he's unbeatable.

SL: And is politics unbeatable?

FG: I've never confused politics with "politicking." So a certain bankruptcy of politicians' politics doesn't upset in any way what I had tried to designate by the concept of "micro-politics." Politics as I understand it, simply cannot be inscribed on the same surface at all. It concerns the relationship of large social groups to what surrounds them, to their own economic set-up, but it also concerns attitudes which run through the individual's life, through family life, through the life of the unconscious, of artistic creation, etc.

SL: The "post-political" era, then, is not the end of politics but rather its inscription on new surfaces.

FG: It obviously does not mean that there's no more politics. In the same way when Jean Baudrillard says that there is an "implosion" of the social, I don't even know what he's talking about. Let's simply say, that the social no longer expresses itself in the usual configuration of forces.

SL: The confrontation no longer involves left and right, or the struggle for power between the workers' movement and the bourgeoisie....

FG: Let's not even talk about the workers' movement! The situation has become much too complex to conceive of it in these terms. We now have to deal with immense masses of people who have nothing to do with any definition of the working class. I don't mean that there are no more relationships of force, simply that the powers of the state, capitalism and Soviet bureaucracy can no longer handle the situation. We are currently in a phase of considerable turmoil, a phase one could call pre-revolutionary, although I'd rather define it as a "molecular" revolution, where virtually no one can control anything anymore.

SL: What exactly do you mean by "molecular revolution"?

FG: Let's take as an example the period of the end of the *Ancien Régime* in France and in Europe. It's very difficult to get a clear picture of the situation. The fall of the Bastille is just the tip of the iceberg. The *Ancien Régime* was, and had been for several decades, a society well along the road to total collapse. A certain way of conceiving the law, religion, the body, filiation, the family, time, literature—all that was moving, changing, bursting at the seams. It took some time for the bourgeoisie to pull themselves together and redefine what could be their new grounds. And it took even more time for the workers' movement to find something around which to gather and to establish itself in a relationship of force.

SL: Now that the bipolar class relationships have ceased for the most part to be operative, and with them a good deal of the Marxist analysis of society, how does one go about recognizing the ways in which the molecular revolution takes form in our society?

FG: First of all we must stop claiming that there is no more "social," that it no longer exists and that nobody gives a damn.

We should at least try to recognize the nature of the phenomena we're dealing with, try to recenter the focus where politics has migrated, where the situation has become critical, difficult to get a grasp on, to attach a meaning to. Secondly, we should put into question all of the so-called political instruments at our disposal, and that goes for the forces of world capitalism as well as for the forces of contestation still striving to establish another kind of society or purpose for life on this planet. What is complicated in all this, it seems to me, is that a sort of complementarity or symmetry has been established between a current of dogmatic Marxists and ossified social-democrats who are incapable of recognizing the radical change in the conditions of contemporary life, and a current that derives largely from the positions of Milton Friedman and others, and which tends to say, with the total fatalism of Voltaire's Candide, that things being as they are, they cannot be otherwise, and that in any case capitalism is a better world—an analysis that can be disastrous in its applications, as we have seen in Chile. As analysis, however, it is not without merit since it implies a re-examination of questions one had thought resolved, to wit that the way the capitalist market works, in spite of all its trash and its horrors, is less catastrophic than certain centralist planification which lead to total failure. We have seen rich agricultural countries collapse into total famine. As far as I am concerned that doesn't mean that we must choose between the two, but that capital itself doesn't go to the end of its potential. It's obviously not a question of making capitalism even more capitalistic but of diverting and orienting in another way the powers of deterritorialization borne by capitalism. I am in favor of a market economy, but not one geared only on profit and its valorization of status, hierarchy and power. I am in favor of an institutional market economy, one founded on another mode of valorization. Instead of being more capitalistic, we want to make an anti-capitalism within capitalism. Thirdly, we should be ready to connect anything that could initiate a new sequence of events: snow-balling sequences, little glimpses of events which right away slap you in the face, like May '68 in France. Since no revolutionary war machine is at present available, and there is no way to get a good grip on reality, then the collective subjectivity is, so to speak, "tripping": from time to time it has "flashes." It sees things, and then it stops. There was the "autonomist" movement in Italy. Today, there is the collective vision of the threat of war facing Europe, of nuclear devastation. And then there is Poland—and we pass on to other things. But it's all going to come back. All these flashes don't mean that there is a total incoherence in this subjectivity, but simply that an effort is being made to perceive something which is not yet registered, inscribed, identified. I believe that the forces which in Europe now rally around the peace movement are the same which, in other phases, will rally around the ecological movement, around regionalist movements, around X number of components of what I call the molecular revolution. What I mean by that expression is not a cult of spontaneity or whatever, only the effort to not miss anything that could help rebuild a new kind of struggle, a new kind of society.

SL: Was the Italian experience only a "flash"?

FG: The Italian experience is linked to the fact that the structure of power in Italy was largely behind the times in relation to the other European nations. The economic integration has become so marked in Europe or in the world that the discrepancy with Italy became more and more striking. With the absence of a state economic policy, and the widespread embezzlement among Italian society, marginal sectors of the economy have paradoxically come to play a considerable role in the economic mechanism, including in the Italian balance of trade. Thus a kind of "society without a State," to use Pierre Clastres' formula, established itself in the middle of structures otherwise controlled from the point of view of state power. On top of that, while the left has slowly withered away in other European countries since the Second World War, a very powerful configuration of forces in favor of the left has maintained itself in Italy—although it has proven incapable of being anything else than an adjacent accomplice of the Christian Democrats.

In the meantime Italy has known an unprecedented cultural effervescence characterized by an immense collective work of publication, of translations—which now make the Italians the most intellectual people on earth. It will take decades before we realize that our Age of Enlightenment is happening not in France nor in the United States or in Germany, but in Italy. And those people have a double-edged intelligence, both theoretical and practical, which consists of trying to grasp the seeds of mutation at work in this society. Instead of considering their situation from a negative point of view, as a step backwards, as a lack to be remedied in the wave of modernization, through the integration of up-to-date industrial techniques, the Italians understood that what used to be considered a social deficiency could become one of the most positive characteristics for the future. After all, why not consider that a certain kind of discipline, of separation between work and leisure, between intellectual and manual work, etc.—has become pointless? Why not envision instead another form of valorization, which they call "auto-valorization"?[1] Of course, they collided immediately headlong with all of the conservative forces. beginning with the most conservative of them all: the Italian Communist Party.

SL: The Italian experience has been rapidly sabotaged by the dogmatic one-upmanship of armed groups. It became easy for the Italian State to eradicate the Autonomia movement by accusing it of having been the "brains" behind the Red Brigades.

FG: These schemes of armed struggle have had a disastrous effect on the movement. They furnished the powers-that-be with a perfect pretext for eliminating those mass structures of somewhat vague outline which constituted "internal colonies" capable of surviving by practicing passive-active modes of resistance such as the "auto-reductions."

SL: Do you think that the autonomist "flash" can resurface elsewhere?

FG: It is bound to, for the need to reformulate the political stakes is felt not only within developed capitalist countries, but everywhere. In France, we've already benefited in small ways from the Italian experience: our fight for free radios took off directly from them. Union leaders in France learned from them that certain demands were no longer in tune with the present struggles.... That the Italian Autonomy was wiped out proves nothing at all. From time to time, a kind of social chemistry provides us with a glimpse of what could be another type of organization, much less molecular, much less atomic, which would result in another type of equilibrium, very different from previous models.

SL: We also see this social chemistry at work in much more ambiguous situations, like in Poland, where paradoxically religion has become a motor for change.

FG: In Poland we are witnessing a violent rejection of bureaucratic society. People cling to religious ideologies—does that make it a religious phenomenon as such? Yes, but we should enlarge the definition somewhat. In other countries like Iran or the Middle East, such phenomena are expressed in other ways. For the moment, there is no common semantic feature through which these movements could recognize and support each other. I believe, however, that we should dare draw an "integral" for these various subjective movements inasmuch as the live forces of society are incapable of having a hold on the inner springs of change.

SL: For the moment, then, there are lots of molecules, but no revolution. And when a revolution occurs, as in Iran, it's once again somewhat "archaic" motives that mobilize the people.

FG: Solidarity isn't an archaic phenomenon, it's a new form of struggle. There aren't many countries where suddenly 10 million unionists arise out of the blue.

SL: Paradoxically, Polish unionism surges up in the East at the very moment the trade union movement in the West is losing steam.

FG: It's not because Solidarity is called a union that it actually is one. It may be an altogether new structure, more apt to take into account everyday problems. If Solidarity had been a regular union Walesa could've worked out a compromise and avoided the mess. But it's a kind of union that cannot be manipulated. The people don't follow. That doesn't mean that it's an anarchistic organization either.

SL: It's a form of unionism which immediately asserted itself on the political level.

FG: On the global level, yes, but also on a micropolitical level. Solidarity takes care of what's happening in the street, in the food lines, etc.

SL: And the other elements of the Polish situation, the self-help aspect for example, doesn't that tie in with certain intuitions of the Italians?

FG: I certainly think so. But, from another angle, that ties in also with those weaknesses adjacent to all such intuitions. There's a lesson to be learned from the events in Iran as well as in Italy or in Poland, if one paradoxically tries to nail down the synchronic traits of these three situations: there won't be any lasting change so long as this type of struggle doesn't go beyond national boundaries. It may prove to be very hard and painful, but I always considered preposterous the idea that the kind of revolution which occurred in Italy could have drastically altered the power situation there.

SL: In a sense, the level of these struggles is always above or below that of national structures—in internal colonies and alternative networks, as in Germany,[2] or bigger, trans-national crystalizations.

FG: Yes, I agree.

SL: How do you think these extremes could connect?

FG: I'm afraid they won't until more drastic situations develop. I'm fairly optimistic about the prospects for political and social action: I find recent revolutionary crises much more mature and promising, much richer in possibilities of expression everywhere. I fear, however, we still have to go through catastrophic crises before we get there. I believe that both the East and the West are going to experience military dictatorships and very hard fascist regimes.

SL: Do you agree with Paul Virilio that we're now confronted with a tremendous growth in military power and a reinforcement of the scientific-military complex at the expense of civil society?

FG: Let's take a closer look at what this analysis seems to apply considering the deep crisis Russia's going through right now. Does it mean, however, that power in Russia is on the verge of falling into a kind of Bonapartism? Does it imply that the disarray of political structures in the USSR is bound to give the military establishment total control over Soviet society? The hypothesis could well be corroborated by spectacular events in Poland, but they are misleading. We're not presently witnessing a take-over by the military establishment, but a whole series of social forces and antagonisms which involve the Church and bureaucracies of all kinds.

SL: Russia has renounced developing its internal consumption for the sake of a protracted arms race—both in conventional and nuclear weapons.

FG: It may well be that the military establishment in the Soviet Union forms a backbone strong enough to withstand current crisis. China presented the same phenomenon with the Lin-Piao line. This line represented the minimal consistency of Chinese society at a time when Maoism was verging on total collapse. So it's true that everywhere, in Africa as well as in Latin America, the role of military establishments has substantially increased. Nevertheless, I don't believe that a mutation in the major developed countries (either capitalism or bureaucratic socialism) will put them simply and squarely under the aegis of military "machines." And therefore I don't believe that international relations will be wholly defined by this antagonism.

SL: But isn't Reagan himself busy dismantling the edifice of the "welfare" State while dramatically reinforcing the American military potential?

FG: In the USA, one thing is for sure: the Kissinger-style conception which envisioned relationships of power in international affairs as a function of local situations, contradictions and specific socio-historical "singularities," is progressively becoming outmoded. It's as if one sort of diplomacy was being phased out to make room for a purely strategic frame-reference—with a peculiar Manicheanism inherent to the cowboy mentality of Reagan and his cronies.

SL: This Manicheanism actually seems to serve everyone.

FG: Exactly. One could conclude that a true symmetry does exist between the two super-powers and that we are presently witnessing a profound change in the international situation. But I don't think so. At present, the movements of social transformation indeed lack coherent and collective political representation, but so does capitalism. International capitalism is undergoing a real trauma as well. It has a hard time coping with the consequences of its own structural crisis. On strictly economic grounds (monetary, oil, etc.) it somehow manages to come up with solutions, however difficult or dangerous they may be, but on the political level, it offers absolutely no perspective. In the final analysis, it has no policy whatsoever concerning the development of Third World countries, in Asia, in Africa, or Latin America. Countless disasters—human, ecological, etc.—now affecting entire countries do not really go in the direction of, nor benefit, an Integrated World Capitalism. International capitalism has not been able to manage the violent crisis which involves whole populations, masses, working classes, farmers, Third and Fourth World countries. As a result I don't believe that the current phase of American capitalism and Soviet antagonisms is anything else but transitory. On the contrary, I foresee in time (in a rather long time) a revival of the American-Soviet complicity and the rise of an international police force.

SL: Do you think that we'll soon witness the negotiation of a new Yalta?

FG: We'll end up with a new distribution of zones of influence, meant to force the planet into a North-South axis and soften the East-West tensions. American capitalism and Soviet bureaucracy have too much to gain by getting along and by compromising. That was also, incidentally, Schmidt's intuition which he shared with the social-democratic tendencies in Europe.

SL: Politics is also a way of avoiding war, or of pursuing war by other means. Human intervention and decision-making power, however, seem more and more incapable of preventing a nuclear holocaust or a generalized conflict.

FG: I love science fiction and *Dr. Strangelove* schemes, but I don't believe at all in the script of a nuclear war. There's going to be a war, yes, but what war? The same war that we've known for thirty years. When you consider the wars in Chad, or in El Salvador, or in Guatemala, from the point of view of human suffering—wounds, torture, deaths from starvation—what is all that but war? Can we hope for a worse outcome? There's going to be wars like these, but everywhere. Fragmented wars, always ambiguous because they deal with local problems while serving the cause of an international police force. The example of Vietnam is spectacular. This interminable war which continues somewhere in Cambodia, at the outset it was a popular war, a war for the liberation of South Vietnam. But like all popular wars, it soon became the arena for the super-powers, and it was China and the Soviet Union who finally profited from it. The final outcome—the Pol-Pot experiment, monstrous, disastrous results for the populations—nowadays these wars are always won by the super-powers.

SL: There are wars that cannot be won, even by superpowers. And that's a new phenomenon which shouldn't be ignored in spite of the increasing number of fragmented wars.

FG: Obviously there is a risk, and the unconscious collective sensibility which permeates peace movements does perceive the danger. But these movements today are quite different from pacifism as it developed during that magnificent period which preceded the First World War. Socialists then advocated the demoralization of the army—of their own army. If such an idea were to spread now, it could work wonders.

SL: We should not underestimate the—so to speak—"positive" effects of the nuclear threat. To begin with, the new movement isn't just backed up by the socialists or even the left. And it's not only fear—the great bourgeois fear—which is being called upon. In Germany the movement is already pulling together many heterogeneous and often conflicting elements—citizen's initiatives, leftists, Christians, ecologists, conservatives and conservationists. I perceive in it the loose contours of an original form of political action expressing in the collective unconscious a still undefinable, but very real, demand for another type of society. Also crucial is the fact that the peace movement, like the ecology movement, can snowball in no time, by-passing purely national boundaries. It took only a few months for the anti-nuclear movement in the USA to reach nationwide stature. The doomsday vision probably ties in to a profound change in the political sentiment of the population at a time when all the avenues of the future appear blocked by the maneuverings of the super-powers and by the muddle of the ideological options we used to depend upon. It's been quite some time since we've witnessed such a mobilization of energies.

FG: I also see emerging there an idea which, if it were to materialize, could yield enormous power—the idea that American missiles don't really protect us against Soviet missiles, and vice-versa. Politicians keep telling us: if you're not protected by the American nuclear umbrella the Russians will come. Let them come! They are already in such a mess in Poland, not to mention Afghanistan, that the extra of Germany, France or Italy would prove fatal. Fantasies keep piling up, and then one says: "Enough is enough."

SL: For the moment, we have very few ways of putting pressure on the USSR. After all, dissidents there are being persecuted, and peaceniks prosecuted. In the Western camp, however, paths of action are not altogether lacking. In spite of appearances, and the policies of the Reagan administration, Europe may not be first on the firing line. Moreover it's not certain that it is in Europe that the peace movement can exert the most effective pressure. If the movement were to gather momentum in the USA—where the military-scientific complex is much more in the open and information on nuclear weapons circulates more freely than anywhere else—if a real political intelligence were to shape up among the American peace movement, that could prove to be of paramount importance.

FG: I entirely agree. That would become possible when people would begin to realize that they have allies in Russia, in Africa, everywhere and that a new alliance is possible because they have common enemies. It's that, I think, which is behind your proposal.

SL: The pacifist movement is actually a mosaic, a collage of many colors which doesn't fit into the traditional political mold, which doesn't follow the logic of partisan politics. That corresponds roughly to what you said about molecular revolutions, even if the modalities are somewhat different. This mosaic in formation keeps moving—elements form in one place, migrate elsewhere, reappear in strange new forms, contradictory forms even.

FG: Let's do a little science fiction also, just for fun. Imagine Russia is in a mess even ten times weaker than in Poland. The relationship of power would change entirely if everyone felt that the political and military-industrial structures of the Soviet Union were beginning to crumble down. Imagine they have two more Polands and two more Afghanistans on their hands....

SL: Do you think this is likely to happen?

FG: The Russians have got themselves stuck in the same wasp's nest as the Americans in Vietnam. It's going to go bad for them. Further, it's not out of the question that an armed conflict erupts in Poland. No Eastern bloc country has yet been exposed to armed resistance. This is a crucial point.

SL: Solidarity always opposed armed resistance. Paradoxically the Church assumes a moderating role with regard to the deep aspirations of the population.

FG: Armed resistance may eventually flare up, and with it a lot of problems. I'm not saying that it's the solution, but we're getting close to the point where the crisis in the Soviet Union will become practically unavoidable.

1. See *Italy: Autonomia*, Semiotext(e), III, 3, 1980. Sylvère Lotringer and Christian Marazzi, eds.
2. See *The German Issue*, Semiotext(e), IV, 2, 1982. Sylvère Lotringer, ed.

13

MACHINIC JUNKIES

We must begin by enlarging the definition of drugs. In my view, all the mechanisms producing a "machinic" subjectivity, everything that contributes to provide a sensation of belonging to something, of being somewhere, along with the sensation of forgetting oneself, are "drugs." The existential aspects of what I call the experience of machinic drugs are not easy to detect. Only the surfaces are visible, in activities like cross-country skiing, piloting ultra-light motorized vehicles, rock music, music videos—all these sorts of things. But the subjective dimension of such influences is not necessarily in an immediate relation to the practice in question. It is how it all works together that is important.

The example of Japan, considered on a large scale, is significant. The Japanese make the best of an archaic, or let's say a pseudo-archaic structure. This is the counterpart to their being on machinic dope, and in this way the society does not dissolve into dust. They have remade a feudal territoriality out of their traditions, by perpetuating the alienated conditions of women, by absorption into repetitive work on machines.... These are also conduits for subjective positioning—well, not really "for," but that is the result: it works! The Japanese structure their universe and order their emotions within the proliferation and disorder of machines, while hanging on to their archaic references. But, above all, they are crazy for machines, for a machinic kind of buzz. For example, did you know that the majority of people

101

who have climbed the Himalayas are Japanese?

"Doping" and drugs, is this a simple analogy? It seems, according to the most recent work in the area, that it is not at all a metaphor. Repeated pain and certain very "engaging" activities incite the brain to secrete hormones, endorphines, which are much "harder" drugs than morphine. Is this not then some sort of self-intoxification? At the La Borde clinic,[1] I observed the extent to which anorexics resemble drug addicts. The same bad faith, the same ways of fooling you by promising to stop.... Anorexia is a major form of "doping." So is sadomasochism, as is any other exclusive passion that induces bursts of endorphines. One "turns oneself on" with the sound of rock-and-roll, with fatigue, with lack of sleep like Kafka, or one knocks one's head against the floor like an autistic child. One can use excitement, cold, repetitive movements, strenuous work, sports, fear. Skiing down a practically vertical slope will transform your notions of personality for you. It is a way of making yourself *be,* of personally incarnating yourself, while the ground of the existential image is blurred.

Again, the result of "dopings" and their social representations have every chance of being out of phase with each other: an intense buzz involves processes that radically elude individual consciousness, bringing about biological transformations whose need is experienced only vaguely, although intensely. A "drug machine" can generate collective euphoria or oppressive gregariousness, but it is nonetheless the response of individual urges. The same thing occurs with minor buzzes. The person who comes home exhausted, spent after a draining day, who automatically turns on his television, evidences another personal reterritorialization by totally artificial means.

I find these phenomena of contemporary doping ambiguous. There are two means of access: repetition, stupidly, like the monomania of pinball and video game addiction, and the intervention of "machinic" processes that are never futile, and never innocent. There is a machinic Eros. Yes, over-driven Japanese youths commit suicide upon completing high school; yes, millions of guys practice their golf swings in unison in concrete parking lots at 6 a.m.; yes, young workers live in dormitories and give up their vacations.... They are machine-nuts. And yet, in Japan, there is a kind of democracy of desire that extends into business. A balance... to doping's advantage?

For us, machinic dope works more in favor of a return to the individual, but it seems nevertheless as indispensible to the subjective stabilization of industrial societies, above all at times of stiff competition. If you don't have at least that pay-off, you really have nothing. Molecular machinic subjectivity fosters creativity, in no matter what area. Believe it. Having been politically destructured after the collapse of opposition movements, this is all that young Italians do—as an "individualist" way of getting by. A society that can't tolerate, that can't manage its intensity doping loses its dynamism, or is out of the picture. For better or for worse, it must even and above all integrate the apparent disorder of doping with what seem to be unproductive outlets. Americans are the champions of doping, they have thousands of ways to do it, and invent new ones every day. It is pretty successful for them. (The Russians on the other hand, don't even have the old dope of Bolshevism.) It is "machinic" subjectivity that fuels great impetuses like Silicon Valley.

And France? French society isn't necessarily out of it. French people are not stupider than others, nor more impoverished libidinally. But they are not "cool." Let's just say that the social superstructures are more "molar." For us, there are hardly any institutions that leave space for processes of "machinic" proliferation. France, as people constantly say, is traditional. And while the whole planet is currently undergoing fantastic changes, France makes faces at the great machinic dope. It is the anti-dope.

France seems to have had a pretty bad start. Europe too. Perhaps machinic processes call for large spaces, large markets or great old royal powers. Also, as Braudel suggests, a concentration of semiological, monetary, intellectual means—knowledge capital—like New York, Chicago, California, with all of America behind them. Or Amsterdam in the seventeenth century. Only this can allow for manageable entities—Mega-machines.

In France, doping belongs to a more or less private club, as a refuge. People subjectivize themselves, and remake their existential territories with dopings, but complementarity between machines and refuge values is not guaranteed. If the buzz aborts, if it fails, the whole thing will implode. There is a critical threshold. If it doesn't bring out a social project, like Japanese enterprise or American mobility, one can die from it. Look at Van Gogh, or Artaud. They could not get out of the machinic process and it destroyed them. Like true addicts. My existence carried away into a process of singularization? Perfect. But if it stops short ("Stop, time's up, turn in your papers!"), catastrophe is immanent for lack of perspective and a micropolitical outlet. It is necessary to make oneself exist "within" the process. Repetition in a doped void is horrible: 60s counterculture. There are plenty of buzzes that have caused much pain when their outmodedness became apparent: Third Worldism, Marxist-Leninism or Rock-and-Roll....

It's either miserable prostration or the creation of an unprecedented universe. Subjective formations concocted by dopings can either get things moving again, or kill them slowly over a low flame. Behind all this there are possibilities for creation, changes of life and scientific, economic and even aesthetic revolutions. New horizons or nothing. I'm not talking about the old story of spontaneousness as a creative factor. That is absurd. But within the grasp of the immense undertakings to stratify and serialize our societies, there are subjective formations roaming about that are capable of getting the power of the process going again and promoting mutant singularities and new minorities. The visibly doped sectors shouldn't merely be defenses of acquired territories; the residual crystals that constitute machinic dope can penetrate the entire planet, re-animate it and relaunch it. A society that has reached the point of being so locked in should open up to this, or it will burst.

Translated by Chet Wiener

1. Cf. "La Borde: A Clinic Unlike Any Other" in Félix Guattari, *Chaosophy* (New York: Semiotext(e), 1995).

14

ENTERING THE POST-MEDIA ERA

B y what means can we hope to accelerate the arrival of what I have called the Post-Media Era? What theoretical and pragmatic conditions can facilitate an awareness of the "reactional" character of the present wave of conservatism, which I don't believe is a necessary evolution of developed societies?

If "organized minorities" are to become the laboratories of thought and experimentation for future forms of subjectivation, how can they structure themselves, and ally themselves with more traditional forms of organization (parties, unions, leftist groups) to avoid the isolation and repression that threatens them, while at the same time preserving their independence and specific traits? The same question holds true for the risks they run of being coopted by the state.

Is it possible to envision a proliferation of "minority becomings" capable of diversifying the factors of subjective autonomy and economic self-management within the social field? Are they, in any case, compatible with modern systems of production and circulation which seem to call for ever more integration and concentration in their decision-making procedures?

Rethinking all the ways that subjectivity is produced requires redefining the unconscious from outside the confining frames of psychoanalysis. The unconscious should no longer be reducible solely in terms of intrapsychic entities or the linguistic signifier, since it must also engage diverse semiotic and pragmatic dimensions that have to do with a multiplicity of

106

existential territories, machinic systems and incorporeal universes. I called it *schizoanalytic* to mark it off from the psychoanalytic unconscious—which, in my opinion, is far too anchored to personological ego formations, transference and identifications, not to mention the way it is irremediably balasted by fixed and psychogenetic conceptions regarding instinctual object. Yet I did not intend to tie it down exclusively to psychoses. Rather, I wished to open it to a maximum variety of schizes, like love, childhood, art, etc. As opposed to Freudian complexes, schizoanalytic arrangements are the sites of both internal transformations and transferences between pre-personal levels (like those Freud describes in *The Psychopathology of Everyday Life*, for example) and the post-personal levels that can be globally assigned to the media-driven world, extending the notion of media to every system of communication, displacement and exchange. From this perspective, the unconscious would become "transversalist," by virtue of the skill with which it traverses the most diverse orders derived from abstract and singular machines, while not clinging to any specific substance of expression, and resisting universals and structuralist mathemes.

Thus, the ego entity, responsible for the essence of the subject and for a person's real and imaginary actions, is only considered as the more or less transitory intersection of arrangements of enunciation varying in size, nature and duration. (Although not present literally, the same inspiration can be found in animist cartographies of subjectivity.)

Analysis must radically change attempts to solve tensions and conflicts that are already "programmed into" the individuated psyche through transference and interpretation. Rather, it will conceive of and transfer enunciations so as to surmount the ever-increasing societal discrepancies, between (a) representations and modes of perception and sensibility having to do with the body, sexuality, social, physical and ecological environments, and with diverse figures of alterity and finitude, shaped by techno-scientific mutations, particularly through information, electronics and images; and (b) social and institutional structures, juridical and regulatory systems, state apparatuses, moral, religious and esthetic norms, etc., which, behind an apparent continuity, are really threatened and sapped from the inside out by deterritorializing tensions from preceding molecular registers, causing every evolutionary process to stop short, to become more and more molar, to hold on to the most obsolete forms, even to the detriment of functional efficiency.

Unlike the transcendental subject of philosophical tradition (the closed-in-on-itself monad that structuralists claim to have opened to alterity solely by virtue of the linguistic signifier), pragmatic enunciative arrangements escape in all directions. Their subjective formations, at the intersections of heterogeneous components, cannot be reduced to a single semiotic entity. For example, the nature of economic subjectivity cannot be equated to aesthetic subjectivity: the quality of the Oedipus complex of a well brought up little boy from New York's Upper East Side is going to be entirely different from that of the initiation into the socius of a *pivete* from a Brazilian *favela*.

The elucidation of the internal composition of various "arrangements," and their reciprocal relationships imply two sorts of logic: (1) those relating to discursive ensembles that determine the relationships between fluxes and machinic systems endo-referring to different types of energetico-spatio-temporal coordinates; (2) those relating to non-discursive organless bodies that determine the relationships between existential territories and endo-referring incorporeal universes.

The introduction into analysis of concepts like endo-reference or auto-organization does not imply a departure from the ordinary fields of scientific rationality, but a break from scientistic causalism. For example, one considers that a schizoanalytic map is not "second" in relation to the existential territories it presents; one cannot even say, properly speaking, that they represent them, because it is the map that engenders the territories.

A related question: does not every esthetic production depend in one way or another on this kind of mapping, which doesn't need any theory of sublimated drives? As soon as unconscious subjectivity is envisaged from the perspective of the heterogeneity of its components, its multiform productivity, its micropolitical intentionality, its tension toward the future instead of its fixations on past stratifications, the focal point of analysis will be systematically displaced from statements and semiotic links toward enunciatory instances. Rather than the analysis of fixed discursive elements, one considers the constituent conditions of the "giver." There will be no point any more chasing nonsense and paradigmatic ramblings in order to pin them down, like butterflies, on interpretive or structuralist grids. Singularities of desire, those unnameable residues of meaning that psychoanalysts thought they could repertory as part-objects—for years they have gone into such arm-waiving ecstacies—will no longer be accepted as the limits of analytical efficiency but will be considered as potential for processual boosts.

For instance, rather than putting emphasis on a symbolic castration lived as post-Oedipian submission, the emphasis will be put on "contingent choices" circumscribing and giving existential consistency to new pragmatic fields. Investigations must give special attention to the singular virtues of semiotic links which support such choices (ritournelles, facial features, becoming-animals, etc.). In parallel to their semiotic functions of signification and designation, they develop an existential function that catalyzes new universes of reference.

Behind the relative non-sense of failed statements, there is no longer a hidden meaning that schizoanalytical pragmatics will force out into the open, nor some latent drive that it will try to liberate. It will focus on unfolding innumerable incorporeal, indivisible materials that, as the experience of desire has taught us, are capable of carrying us far beyond ourselves and far beyond territorial encirclements, towards unexpected, unheard-of universes of possibility. Consequently, the active a-signifying processes of existential singularization will be substituted for the passive insignificance that is the preferred object of hermeneutics.

These high intensity, non-discursive materials, woven into subjective arrangements, only continue to exist by continually deterritorializing themselves into actual and virtual "projectuality," and reterritorializing within real and potential strata such that they can be considered as so many ethico-political options. Every site of desire or reason is within reach of our hands, our wills, our individual and collective choices.... But, in the capitalistic order of things, that is to say the monotheistic, mono-energy-istic, mono-signifying, mono-libidinal, in short, radically disenchanted order of things, nothing can evolve unless everything else remains in place. Subjective productions ("subjectivities") are obliged to submit to the axioms of equilibrium, equivalence, constancy, eternity.... So, what's left for us to reach for? How can we hold on to a lust for life, for creation, or find a reason to die for other horizons?

When everything becomes equivalent to everything else, the only things that count are the ugly compulsions for the abstract accumulation of power over people for various kinds of bonds, and the pitiful exaltation of specular prestige. Under such gloomy conditions, singularity and finitude are necessarily considered scandalous, while "incarnation" and death are experienced as sins rather than part of the rhythms of life and the cosmos. I am not advocating a return to oriental wisdom, which can carry with it the worst sorts of resignation. Nor a rejection of capitalism's great equivalents: energy, libido, information, without cautiously or carefully experimenting with alternatives. Even capital can be reconverted into a dependable instrument of economic writing. All it takes is reinventing its usage; not in a dogmatic and programmatic manner, but through the creation of other "existential chemistries," open to all the re-compositions and transmutations of these "singularity salts" whose secrets art and analysis can deliver up.

Analysis again. But where? How? Well, everywhere possible. Where unskirtable contradictions come to the surface. Where disturbing breaches of meaning trip us up amidst daily banalities, impossible yet perfectly viable loves, all kinds of constructivist passions that mine the edifices of morbid rationality.... It can be individual, for those who tend to lead their lives as if it were a work of art; dual in all possible ways, including, why not, a psychoanalytic couch, as long as it has been dusted off; multiple, through group, network, institutional, and collective practices; and finally, micropolitical by virtue of other social practices, other forms of auto-valorizations and militant actions, leading, through a systematic decentering of social desire, to soft subversions and imperceptible revolutions that will eventually change the face of the world, making it happier. Let's face it, it is long overdue.

Translated by Chet Wiener

15

REGIMES, PATHWAYS, SUBJECTS

Classical thought distanced the soul from matter and separated the essence of the subject from the cogs of the body. Marxists later set up an opposition between subjective superstructures and infrastructural relations of production. How then ought we talk about the production of subjectivity today? Clearly, the contents of subjectivity have become increasingly dependent on a multitude of machinic systems. No area of opinion, thought, images, affects or spectacle has eluded the invasive grip of "computer-assisted" operations, such as databanks and telematics. This leads one to wonder whether the very essence of the subject—that infamous essence, so sought after over the centuries by Western philosophy—is not threatened by contemporary subjectivity's new "machine addiction." Its current result, a curious mix of enrichment and impoverishment, is plainly evident: an apparent democratization of access to data and modes of knowledge, coupled with a segregative exclusion from their means of development; a multiplication of anthropological approaches, a planetary intermixing of cultures, paradoxically accompanied by a rising tide of particularisms, racisms and nationalisms; and a vast expansion in the fields of technoscientific and aesthetic investigation taking place in a general atmosphere of gloom and disenchantment. Rather than joining the fashionable crusades against the misdeeds of modernism, or preaching a rehabilitation of worn-out transcendent values, or indulging in the disillusioned indulgences of postmodernism, we might instead try to find a way out of the dilemma of having to choose between unyielding refusal or cynical acceptance of this situation.

The fact that machines are capable of articulating statements and registering states of fact in as little as a nanosecond, and soon in a picosecond,[1] does not in itself make them diabolical powers that threaten to dominate human beings. People have little reason to turn away from machines, which are nothing other than hyperdeveloped and hyperconcentrated forms of certain aspects of human subjectivity, and emphatically not those aspects that polarize people in relations of domination and power. It will be possible to build a two-way bridge between human beings and machines and, once we have established that, to herald new and confident alliances between them.

In what follows, I shall address the following problem: that today's information and communication machines do not merely convey representational contents, but also contribute to the fabrication of new *assemblages* of enunciation, individual and collective.

Before going any further, we must ask whether subjectivity's "entry into the machine"—as in the past, when one "entered" a religious order—is really all that new. Weren't pre-capitalist or archaic subjectivities already engendered by a variety of initiatory, social and rhetorical machines embedded in clan, religious, military and feudal institutions, among others? For present purposes, I shall group these machines under the general rubric of *collective apparatuses* [equipment] *of subjectification*. Monastic machines, which passed down memories from antiquity to the present day, thereby enriching our modernity, are a case in point. Were they not the computer programs, the "macroprocessors" of the Middle Ages? The neoplatonists, in their own way, were the first programmers of a processuality capable of spanning time and surviving periods of stasis. And what was the Court of Versailles, with its minutely detailed administration of the flows of power, money, prestige and competence, and its high-precision etiquette, if not a machine deliberately designed to churn out a new and improved aristocratic subjectivity—one far more securely under the yoke of the royal state than the seignorial aristocracy of the feudal tradition, and entertaining different relations of subjection to the values of the rising bourgeoisie?

It is beyond the scope of this article to sketch even a thumbnail history of these collective apparatuses of subjectification. As I see it, neither history nor sociology is equal to the task of providing the analytical or political keys to the processes in play. I shall therefore limit myself to highlighting several fundamental paths/voices [*voie/voix*] that these apparatuses have produced, and whose criss-crossing remains the basis for modes and processes of subjectification in contemporary Western societies. I distinguish three series:

First: Paths/voices of *power* circumscribing and circumventing human groupings from the outside, either through direct coercion of, and panoptic grip on, bodies, or through imaginary capture of minds.

Second: Paths/voices of *knowledge* articulating themselves with technoscientific and economic pragmatics from within subjectivity.

Third: Paths/voices of *self-reference* developing a processual subjectivity that defines its own coordinates and is self-consistent (what I have discussed elsewhere under the category of the "subject-group") but can nevertheless establish transversal relations to mental and social stratifications.

(1) Power over exterior territorialities, (2) deterritorialized modes of knowledge about human activities and machines, and (3) the creativity proper to subjective mutations: these three paths/voices, though inscribed in historical time and rigidly incarnated in sociological divisions and segregations, are forever entwining in unexpected and strange dances, alternating between fights to the death and the promotion of new figures.

I should note in passing that the "schizoanalytic" perspective on the processes of subjectification I am proposing will make only very limited use of dialectical or structuralist approaches, systems theory, or even genealogical approaches as understood by Michel Foucault. In my view, all systems for defining models are in a sense equal, all are tenable, but only to the extent that their principles of intelligibility renounce any universalist pretensions, and that their sole mission be to help map real existing territories (sensory, cognitive, affective and aesthetic universes)—and even then only in relation to carefully delimited areas and periods. This relativism is not in the least embarrassing, epistemologically speaking: it holds that the regularities, the quasi-stable configurations, for which our immediate experiences first emerge, are precisely those systems of self-modeling invoked earlier as self-reference, the third path/voice. In this kind of system, discursive links, whether of expression or of content, obey ordinary logics of larger and institutional discursive ensembles only remotely, against the grain, or in a disfiguring way. To put it another way at this level, absolutely anything goes—any ideology, or even religion will do, even the most archaic: all that matters is that it be used as the raw material of existence.[2]

The problem is to situate appropriately this third path/voice, of creative, transforming self-reference, in relation to the first two, modes of power and modes of knowledge. I have said both that self-reference is the most singular, the most contingent path/voice, the one that anchors human realities in finitude, and that it is the most universal one, the one that effects the most dazzling crossings between heterogeneous domains. I might have used other terms. It is not so much that this path/voice is "universal" in the strict sense, but that it is the richest in what may be called *universes of virtuality,* the best endowed with lines of processuality (I ask the reader here not to begrudge me my plethora of qualifiers, or the meaning-overload of certain expressions, or even the vagueness of their cognitive scope: there is no other way to proceed).

The paths/voices of power and knowledge are inscribed in external referential coordinates guaranteeing that they are used extensively and that their meaning is precisely circumscribed. The earth was once the primary referent for modes of power over bodies and populations, just as capital was the referent for economic modes of knowledge and mastery of the means of production. With the figureless and foundationless Body without Organs of self-reference we see spreading before us an entirely different horizon, that of a new machinic processuality considered as the continual point of emergence of all forms of creativity.

I must emphasize that the triad territorialized power–deterritorialized knowledge–processual self-reference has no other aim than to clarify certain problems—for example, the current rise of neoconservative ideologies and other, even more pernicious archaisms. It goes without saying that so perfunctory a model cannot even claim to begin to map concrete processes of subjectification. Suffice it to say that these terms are instruments for a speculative cartography that makes no pretense of providing a universal structural foundation or increasing on-the-ground efficiency. This is another way of saying, by way of a reminder, that these paths/voices have not always existed and undoubtedly will not always exist (at least, not in the same form). Thus, there may be some relevance in trying to locate their historical emergence, and the thresholds of consistency they have crossed in order to enter and remain in the orbit of our modernity.

It is safe to assume that their various consistencies are supported by collective systems for "memorizing" data and modes of knowledge, as well as by material apparatuses of a technical, scientific and aesthetic nature. We can, then, attempt to date these fundamental subjective mutations in relation, on the one hand, to the historical birth of large-scale religious and cultural collective arrangements, and on the other, to the invention of new materials and energies, new machines for crystallizing time and, finally, to new biological technologies. It is not a question of material infrastructures that directly condition collective subjectivity, but of components essential for a given setup to take consistency in space and time as a function of technical, scientific and artistic transformations.

These considerations have led me to distinguish three zones of historical fracture on the basis of which, over the last thousand years, the three fundamental capitalist components have come into being: *the Age of European Christianity* marked by a new conception of the relations between the Earth and power; *the Age of Capitalist Deterritorialization of Modes of Knowledge and Technique*, founded on principles of general equivalence; and *the Age of Planetary Computerization*, creating the possibility for creative and singularizing processuality to become the new fundamental point of reference.

With respect to the last point, one is forced to admit that there are very few objective indications of a shift away from oppressive mass-media modernity toward some kind of more liberating post-media era in which subjective assemblages of self-reference might come into their own. Nevertheless, it is my guess that it is only through "remappings" of the production of computerized subjectivity that the path/voice of self-reference will be able to reach its full amplitude. Obviously, nothing is a foregone conclusion—and nothing that could be done in this domain could ever substitute for innovative social practices. The only point I am making is that, unlike other revolutions of subjective emancipation—Spartacus and other slave rebellions, peasant revolts during the Reformation, the French Revolution, the Paris Commune and so on—individual and social practices for the self-valorization and self-organization of subjectivity are now within our reach and, perhaps for the first time in history, have the potential to lead to something more enduring than mad and ephemeral spontaneous outpourings—in other words, to lead to a fundamental repositioning of human beings in relation to both their machinic and natural environments (which, at any rate, now tend to coincide).

THE AGE OF EUROPEAN CHRISTIANITY

In Western Europe, a new figure of subjectivity arose from the ruins of the late Roman and Carolingian empires. It can be characterized by a double articulation combining two aspects: first, the relatively autonomous base territorial entities of ethnic, national or religious character, which originally constituted the texture of feudal segmentarity, but have survived in other forms up to the present day; and second, the deterritorialized subjective power entity transmitted by the Catholic Church and structured as a collective setup on a European scale.

Unlike earlier formulas for imperial power, Christianity's central figure of power did not assert a direct, totalitarian-totalizing hold over the base territories of society and of subjectivity. Long before Islam, Christianity had to renounce its desire to form an organic unity. However, far from weakening processes for the integration of subjectivity, the disappearance of a flesh-and-blood Caesar and the promotion of a deterritorialized Christ (who cannot be said to be a substitute for the former) only reinforced them. It seems to me that the conjunction between the partial autonomy of the political and economic spheres proper to feudal segmentarity and the hyperfusional character of Christian subjectivity (as seen in the Crusades and the adoption of aristocratic codes such as the Peace of God, as described by Georges Duby) has resulted in a kind of fault line, a metastable equilibrium favoring the proliferation of other equally partial processes of autonomy. This can be seen in the schismatic vitality of religious sensibility and reflection that characterized the medieval period; and of course in the explosion of aesthetic creativity, which has continued unabated since then; the first great "takeoff" of technologies and commercial exchange, which is known to historians as the "industrial revolution of the eleventh century," and was a correlate of the appearance of new figures of urban organization. What could have given this tortured, unstable, ambiguous formula the surfeit of consistency that was to see it persist and flourish through the terrible historical trials awaiting it: barbarian invasions, epidemics, never-ending wars? Schematically, one can identify six series of factors:

First: The promotion of a monotheism that would prove in practice to be quite flexible and evolutionary, able to adapt itself more or less successfully to particular subjective positions—for example, even those of "barbarians" or slaves. The fact that flexibility in a system of ideological reference can be a fundamental asset for its survival is a basic given, which can be observed at every important turning point in the history of capitalist subjectivity (think, for example, of the surprising adaptive abilities enabling contemporary capitalism literally to swallow the so-called socialist economies whole). Western Christianity's consolidation of new ethical and religious patterns led to two parallel markets of subjectification: one involves the perpetual reconstitution of the base territorialities (despite many setbacks), and a redefinition of filiation suzerainty and national networks; the other involves a predisposition to the free circulation of knowledge, monetary signs, aesthetic figures, technology, goods, people and so forth. This kind of market prepared the ground for the deterritorialized capitalist path/voice.

Second: The cultural establishment of a disciplinary grid onto Christian populations through a new type of religious machine, the original base for which was the parish school system created by Charlemagne, but which far outlived his empire.

Third: The establishment of enduring trade organizations, guilds, monasteries, religious orders and so forth, functioning as so many "databanks" for the era's modes of knowledge and technique.

Fourth: The widespread use of iron, and wind and water mills; the development of artisan and urban mentalities. It must be emphasized, however, that this first flowering of machinism only implanted itself in a somewhat parasitic, "encysted" manner within the great human assemblages on which the large-scale systems of production continued essentially to be based. In other words, a break had not yet been made with the fundamental and primordial relation of human being to tool.

Fifth: The appearance of machines operating by much more advanced subjective integration: clocks striking the same canonical hours throughout all of Christendom; and the step-by-step invention of various forms of religious music subordinated to scripture.

Sixth: The selective breeding of animal and plant species, making possible a rapid quantitative expansion of demographic and economic parameters, and therefore leading to a rescaling of the assemblages in question.

In spite or because of the colossal pressures—including territorial restrictions but also enriching acculturations—associated with the Byzantine Empire, then Arab imperialism, as well as with nomadic and "barbarian" powers (which introduced, most notably, metallurgical innovations), the cultural hotbed of protocapitalist Christianity attained a relative (but long-term) stability with respect to the three fundamental poles governing its relations of power and knowledge: peasant, religious and aristocratic subjectification. In short, the "machinic advances" linked to urban development and the flowering of civil and military technologies were simultaneously encouraged and contained. All this constitutes a kind of "state of nature" of the relation between human being and tool, which continues to haunt paradigms of the "Work, Family, Fatherland" type even today.

THE AGE OF CAPITALIST DETERRITORIALIZATION
OF MODES OF KNOWLEDGE AND TECHNIQUE

The second component of capitalist subjectivity begins effectively in the 18th century. It is marked above all by a growing disequilibrium in the relations of human being to tool. Human beings also witnessed the disappearance and eradication of social territorialities that, until then, were thought to be permanent and inalienable. Their landmarks of social and physical corporeality were profoundly shaken. The universe of reference for the new system of generalized exchange was no longer territorial segmentarity, but rather capital as a mode of semiotic reterritorialization of human activities and structures uprooted by machinic processes. Once, a real Despot or imaginary God served as the operational keystone for the local recomposition of actual territories. Now, though, that role would be played by symbolic capitalization of abstract values of power bearing on economic and technological modes of knowledge indexed to newly deterritorialized social classes, and creating a general equivalence between all valorizations of goods and human activities. A system of this sort cannot preserve its historical consistency without resorting to a kind of endless headlong race, with a constant renegotiation of the stakes. The new "capitalist passion" would sweep up everything in its path, in particular the cultures and territorialities that had succeeded to one degree or another in escaping the Christian steamroller. The principal consistency factors of this component are the following:

First: The general spread of the printed text into all aspects of social and cultural life, correlated with a certain weakening of the performative force of direct oral communication; by the same token, capabilities of accumulating and processing knowledge are greatly expanded.

Second: The primacy of steam-powered machines and steel, which multiplied the power of machinic vectors to propagate themselves on land, sea and air, and across every technological, economic and urban space.

Third: The manipulation of time, which is emptied of its natural rhythms by chronometric machines leading to a Taylorist rationalization of labor power; techniques of economic semiotization, for example, involving credit money, which imply a general virtualization of capacities for human initiative and a predictive calculus bearing on domains of innovation—checks written on the future—all of which makes possible an unlimited expansion of the imperium of market economies.

Fourth: The biological revolutions, beginning with Pasteur's discoveries, that have linked the future of living species ever more closely to the development of biochemical industries.

Human beings find themselves relegated to a position of quasi-parasitic adjacency to the machinic phyla. Each of their organs and social relations are quite simply repatterned in order to be reallocated, overcoded, in accordance with the global requirements of the system. (The most gripping and prophetic representations of these bodily rearrangings are found in the work of Leonardo da Vinci, Brueghel and especially Arcimboldo.)

The paradox of this functionalization of human organs and faculties and its attendant regime of general equivalence between systems of value is that, even as it stubbornly continues to invoke universalizing perspectives, all it ever manages to do historically is fold back on itself, yielding reterritorializations of nationalist, classist, corporatist, racist and nationalist kinds. Because of this, it inexorably returns to the most conservative, at times caricatured, paths/voices. The "spirit of enlightenment," which marked the advent of this second figure of capitalist subjectivity, is necessarily accompanied by an utterly hopeless fetishization of profit—a specifically bourgeois libidinal power formula. That formula distanced itself from the old emblematic systems of control over territories, people and goods by employing more deterritorialized mediations—only to secrete the most obtuse, asocial and infantilizing of subjective groundworks. Despite the appearance of freedom of thought that the new capitalist monotheism is so fond of affecting, it has always presupposed an archaistic, irrational grip on unconscious subjectivity, most notably through hyper-individuated apparatuses of responsibility- and guilt-production, which, carried to a fever pitch, lead to compulsive self-punishment and morbid cults of blame—perfectly repertoried in Kafka's universe.

THE AGE OF PLANETARY COMPUTERIZATION

Here, in the third historical zone, the preceding pseudo-stabilities are upset in an entirely different way. The machine is placed under the control of subjectivity—not a reterritorialized human subjectivity, but a new kind of machinic subjectivity. Here are several characteristics of the taking-consistency of this new epoch:

First: Media and telecommunications tend to "double" older oral and scriptural relations. It is worth noting that in the resulting polyphony, not only human but also machinic paths/voices link into databanks, artificial intelligence and the like. Public opinion and group tastes are developed by statistical and modelizing apparatuses, such as those of the advertising and film industries.

Second: Natural raw materials are replaced by a multitude of new custom-made, chemically-produced materials (plastics, new alloys, semiconductors and so on). The rise of nuclear fission, and perhaps soon nuclear fusion, would seem to augur a considerable increase in energy resources—providing, of course, that irreparable pollution disasters do not occur. As always, everything will depend on the new social assemblages' capacity for collective reappropriation.

123

Third: The temporal dimensions to which microprocessors provide access allow enormous quantities of data and huge numbers of problems to be processed in infinitesimal amounts of time, enabling the new machinic subjectivities to stay abreast of the challenges and issues confronting them.

Fourth: Biological engineering is making possible unlimited remodeling of life forms; this may lead to a radical change in the conditions of life on the planet and, consequently, to an equally radical reformulation of all of its ethological and imaginary references.

The burning question, then, becomes this: Why have the immense processual potentials brought forth by the revolutions in information processing, telematics, robotics, office automation, biotechnology and so on, up to now only led to a monstrous reinforcement of earlier systems of alienation, an oppressive mass-media culture and an infantilizing politics of consensus? What would make it possible for them finally to usher in a post-media era, to disconnect themselves from segregative capitalist values and to give free rein to the first stirrings, visible today, of a revolution in intelligence, sensitivity and creativity? Any number of dogmatisms claim to have found the answer to these questions in a violent affirmation of one of the three capitalist paths/voices at the expense of the others. There are those who dream of returning to the legitimated powers of bygone days, to the clear circumscription of peoples, races, religions, castes and sexes. Paradoxically, the neo-Stalinists and social democrats, both of whom are incapable of conceiving of the socius in any terms other than its rigid insertion into State structures and functions must be placed in the same category. There are those whose faith in capitalism leads them to justify all of the terrible ravages of modernity—on people, culture, the environment—on the grounds that in the end they will bring the benefits of progress. Finally, there are those whose fantasies of a radical liberation of human creativity condemn them to chronic marginality, to a world of false pretense, or who turn back to take refuge behind a facade of socialism or communism.

Our project, on the contrary, is to attempt to rethink these three necessarily interwoven paths/voices. No engagement with the creative phyla of the third path/voice is tenable unless new existential territories are concurrently established. Without hearkening back to the post-Carolingian pathos, they must nevertheless include protective mechanisms for the person and the imaginary and create a supportive environment. Surely the mega-enterprises of the second path/voice—the great collective scientific and industrial adventures, the administration of knowledge markets—still have legitimacy: but only on the condition that they redefine their goals, which today remain singularly deaf and blind to human truths. Is it still enough to claim profit as the only goal? In any case, the aim of the division of labor, and of emancipatory social practices, must be redirected toward a *fundamental right to singularity,* toward an ethic of finitude that is all the more demanding of individuals and social entities, because its imperatives are *not* founded on transcendent principles. It has become apparent in this regard that ethicopolitical universes of reference now tend to institute themselves as extensions of aesthetic universes, which in no way authorizes the use of such terms as "perversion" or "sublimation." It will be noted that not only the existential operators pertaining to these ethicopolitical matters but the aesthetic operators as well inevitably reach the point at which meaning breaks down, entail irreversible processual engagements whose agents are, more often than not, incapable of accounting for anything (least of all themselves)—and are therefore exposed to a panoply of risks, including madness. Only if the third path/voice takes consistency in the direction of self-reference—carrying us from the consensual media era to the dissensual post-media era—will each be able to assume his or her processual potential and, perhaps, transform this planet—a living hell for over three quarters of its population—into a universe of creative enchantments.

I imagine that this language will ring false to many a jaded ear, and that even the least malicious will accuse me of utopianism. Utopia, it is true, gets bad press these days, even when it acquires a charge of realism and efficiency as it has with the Greens in Germany. But let there be no mistake: these questions of subjectivity production do not only concern a handful of illuminati. Look at Japan, the prototypical model of new capitalist subjectivities. Not enough emphasis has been put on the fact that one of the essential ingredients of the miracle mix showcased for visitors to Japan is that the collective subjectivity produced there on a massive scale combines the highest of "high-tech" components with feudalisms and archaisms inherited from the mists of time. Once again, we find the reterritorializing function of an ambiguous monotheism—Shinto-Buddhism, a mix of animism and universal powers—contributing to the establishment of a flexible formula for subjectification going far beyond the triadic framework of capitalist Christian paths/voices. We have a lot to learn!

For now, though, consider another extreme, the case of Brazil. There, phenomena involving the reconversion of archaic subjectivities have taken an entirely different turn. It is common knowledge that a considerable proportion of the population is mired in such extreme poverty that it lives outside the money economy, but that does not prevent Brazil's industry being ranked sixth among Western powers. In this society, a dual society if there ever was one, there is a double sweep of subjectivity: on the one hand, there is a fairly racist Yankee wave (like it or not) beamed in on one of the most powerful television transmitting networks in the world, and on the other, an animist wave involving religions like *candomblé,* passed on more or less directly from the African cultural heritage, which are now escaping their original ghet-toization and spreading throughout society, including the most well-connected circles of Rio and Sao Paulo. It is interesting that, in this case, mass-media penetration is preceding capital-ist acculturation. What did President Sarney do when he want-ed to stage a decisive coup against inflation, which was run-ning as high as 400 percent per year? He went on television. Brandishing a piece of paper in front of the cameras, he declared that from the moment he signed the order he held in his hand everyone watching would become his personal rep-resentative and would have the right to arrest any merchant who did not respect the official pricing system. It seems to have been surprisingly effective—but at the price of consider-able regression in the legal system.

Capitalism in permanent crisis (Worldwide Integrated Capitalism) is at a total subjective impasse. It knows that paths/voices of self-reference are indispensable for its expan-sion, and thus for its survival, yet it is under tremendous pres-sure to efface them. A kind of superego—that booming Carolingian voice—dreams only of crushing them and reterri-torializing them onto archaic images. Let us attempt to find a way out of this vicious circle by resituating our three capitalist paths/voices in relation to the geopolitical coordinates—First, Second and Third Worlds—commonly used to establish a hier-archy of the major subjective formations. For Western Christian subjectivity, everything was (and, unconsciously, remains) quite simple: it has no restrictions in latitude and longitude. It is the transcendent center around which everything is deemed to revolve. The paths/voices of capital, for their part, have contin-ued their onward rush—first westward, toward elusive "new frontiers," more recently toward the East, in conquest of what remains of the ancient Asiatic empires (Russia included). However, this mad race has reached the end of the road, from one direction in California, from the other in Japan. The second path/voice of capital has closed the circle; the world has buckled, the system is saturated. Henceforth, the North-South axis will perhaps function as the third path/voice of self-reference. This is what I call "the barbarian compromise." The old walls marking the limits of "barbarism" have been torn down, deterritorialized once and for all. The last shepherds of monotheism have lost their flocks, for it is not in the nature of the new subjectivity to be herded. Moreover capitalism itself is now beginning to shatter into animist and machinic polyvocity. What a fabulous reversal, if the old African, pre-Columbian and aboriginal subjectivities became the final recourse for subjective reappropriation of machinic self-reference! The very same blacks, Indians, even South Sea islanders whose ancestors chose death over submission to Christian and capitalist ideals of power: first slavery, then the exchange economy.

I hope that my last examples are not faulted for being overly exotic. Even in Old World countries such as Italy there has been a proliferation of small family enterprises in symbiosis with cutting-edge sectors of the electronics industry and telematics; this has happened over the last few years in the northeast-center triangle of Italy. If an Italian Silicon Valley develops there, it will be founded on a reconversion of subjective archaisms originating in the country's antiquated patriarchal structures. Some futurologists, who are in no way crackpots, predict that certain Mediterranean countries—Italy and Spain, in particular—will overtake the great economic centers of northern Europe in a few decades' time. So when it comes to dreaming and utopia, the future is wide open. My wish is that all those who remain attached to the idea of social progress— all those for whom the social has not become an illusion or a "simulacrum"—look seriously into these questions of subjectivity production. The subjectivity of power does not fall from the sky. It is not written into our chromosomes that divisions of knowledge and labor must necessarily lead to the hideous segregations humanity now suffers. Unconscious figures of power and knowledge are not universals. They are tied to reference myths profoundly anchored in the psyche, but they can still swing around toward liberatory paths/voices. Subjectivity today remains under the massive control of apparatuses of power and knowledge, thus consigning technical, scientific and artistic innovations to the service of the most reactionary and retrograde figures of sociality. In spite of that, other modalities of subjective production—processual and singularizing ones— are conceivable. These alternate forms of existential reappropriation and self-valorization may in the future become the *reason for living* for human collectivities and individuals who refuse to give in to the deathlike entropy characterizing the period we are passing through.

Translated by Brian Massumi

1. A nanosecond is 10^{-9} seconds; a pico-second is 10^{-12}.
2. The immediate aim of their expressive chains is no longer to denote states of fact or to embed states of sense in significational axes but—I repeat—to activate existential crystallizations operating, in a certain way, outside the fundamental principles of classical reason identity, the excluded middle, causality, sufficient reason, continuity…. The most difficult thing to convey is that these materials, which can set processes of subjective self-reference in motion, are themselves extracted from radically heterogeneous, not to mention heteroclite elements, rhythms of lived time, obsessive refrains, identificational emblems, transitional objects, fetishes of all kinds. What is affirmed in this crossing of regions of being and modes of semiotization are traits of singularization that date—something like existential postmarks—as well as "event," "contingent" states of fact, their referential correlates and their corresponding assemblages of enunciation. Rational modes of discursive knowledge cannot fully grasp this double capacity of intensive traits to singularize and transversalize existence, enabling it, on the one hand, to persist locally, and on the other, to consist transversally (giving it transconsistency). It is accessible to apprehension only on the order of affect, a global transferential grasp whereby that which is most universal is conjoined with the most highly contingent facticity: the loosest of meaning's ordinary moorings becomes anchored in the finitude of being-there. Various traditions of what could be termed "narrow rationalism" persist in a quasi-militant, systematic incomprehension of

129

anything in these metamodelizations pertaining to virtual and incorporeal universes, fuzzy worlds of uncertainty, the aleatory and the probable. Long ago, narrow rationalism banished from anthropology those modes of categorization it considered "prelogical," when they were in reality metalogical or paralogical, their objective essentially being to give consistency to individual and/or collective assemblages of subjectivity. What we need to conceptualize is a continuum running from children's games and the makeshift ritualizations accompanying attempts at psychopathological recompositions of "schizoid" worlds, through the complex cartographies of myth and art, all the way to the sumptuous speculative edifices of theology and philosophy, which have sought to apprehend these same dimensions of existential creativity (examples are Plotinus's "forgetful souls" and the "unmoving motor" which, according to Leibniz, preexists any dissipation of potential).

16

DID YOU SEE THE WAR?

FÉLIX GUATTARI: The Gulf War involved two kinds of war: a material war conducted on the ground (the Middle East), and an immaterial war, which we could call a mass media war. On the ground, no one can deny that the United States got the upper hand, asserting its technological and diplomatic mastery, and an extraordinary ability to manipulate international organizations at the risk of altogether discrediting them. On the second front, the mass media war, which consists of taking over public opinion, the Americans were apparently victorious as well. It provoked reversals of opinion not only in countries like the United States and France—but also in Europe, hesitant or hostile opinions converted to warmongering perspectives. In Arab and Muslim countries, and more generally in Third World countries, this mass-media war proved capable of neutralizing popular response. So the balance seems to weigh very positively on the side of Bush's strategy.

Yet, if we take a little distance and examine these two wars as complex objects, and not as proceeding from a linear causality, the outcome may appear far more catastrophic. Before the conflict, in the Middle East, the balance of forces could evolve through negotiations, along non-military lines. Today, its decomposition could lead to a widespread destabilization of the region.

It may be that some people will benefit from it, like the Kurdish people, but for the others it will end up reinforcing the fundamentalism and fascist tendencies which exist in many forms throughout this region. Economic and democratic progress were never at stake in this war, and we are not witnessing any. It's obvious in the way the Kuwaiti people are treated now. In the entire region the Syrian and Saudi dictators are strengthening their hold. This does not lead to any kind of democratic progress allowing Arab and Muslim subjectivity to evolve a real alternative.

As for the mass media, I myself wonder about the result of this operation. I believe that a passionate position isn't enough. It is important to be passionate, but beyond all the adjectives—scandalous, despicable, infantile—that were applied to it, you have to see what this manipulation of opinion consisted of and to what extent will it be capable of resolving the problems with which the United States has been struggling for quite a number of years.

As Wallerstein emphasized, world polarities are changing: the United States is losing momentum as an economic power and international authority. This operation gave it a kind of shot, some psychic "speed," and with it the illusion that it had gotten past its deficit and could return to a euphoric and conquering period. It is true that international relations, including economic relations, work on this kind of drug. The results are visible in the rise of the dollar. It might help cushion the economic depression the United States is undergoing, so this drug may be effective.

It is very important to me to try to understand how subjective factors can become active causes in economic sectors. For too long we have been reasoning that subjective factors were only limited to the order of superstructures dependent upon economic infrastructures. They have a real effectiveness. It is clear that this war won't allow the United States to make up for their lag in most areas, including the most advanced sectors where it is being eliminated by the Japanese and the

Germans. The United States has considerable internal problems: social, urban, oppressed minorities, a whole Third World inside. So it is difficult to conceive how this kind of "speed," of media "fix" could provide a long-term solution. To pursue Wallerstein's analysis, one could explore what in reality operates within these subjective forces. Phenomena such as those witnessed in Iran with Khomeniism and, in another nonreligious, relatively secular context around Saddam Hussein, are attempts at asserting or giving body to an alternative subjectivity. African and Latin-American subjectivities are mostly eroded by the dominant mass media subjectivity. In Brazil, a station like Globo reaches 80% of the population, an enormous majority of which lives in total poverty. In African countries, including North Africa, Western television exerts a powerful influence. In Arab countries, and more globally, but also less distinctly, in the subjective sphere of the Muslim world, there is a resistance factor. It can have very conservative, reactionary aspects, but is not the less real for it. Eastern countries, on the other hand, have completely collapsed and identified themselves with Western subjectivity. This subjectivity is a snare not only for most populations in the Western sphere but even more so for Eastern, African, or Latin-American countries. It does not allow in any way the reconstitution of a way of life, of a subjectivity capable of answering problems as formidable as the concentration of production and economic means in the affluent countries, the pauperization, systematically enforced, in the poorest countries, demographic problems, ecological problems. There is a kind of race to the abyss involving three quarters of the planet's population.

This snare of Western subjectivity is like a medicine, it works to pacify one's own conscience confronted with the problems posed both at the immediate, molecular level and at the planetary level. In everyday life, one witnesses the total disorganization of the social, familial, and neighborhood fabrics which existed in archaic, pre-capitalist countries. This leads to complete impasses like the debt phenomenon or the incapacity of Third World countries to reconstruct a competitive economy on this planet. Africa's international commerce which, a few years ago, represented 2% of the world's commerce, now only represents 1%. In 1991, some 20 million people will die of starvation in Africa, not counting the 100 million deaths by AIDS in the 25 or 20 years to come. When one speaks of catastrophe, it isn't at all a metaphor.

Q: So, what kind of social polarity could be reconstructed?

FG: It isn't obvious that these new polarities are passing through the Arab countries. They represent resistance factors, but many other resistance factors in the history of contemporary subjectivity, beginning with Nazism and Stalinism, never led to liberating polarizations. The idea that there is only one mode of development, of economic relations, and, finally, of subjectivity, only one mode of control of opinion, sensibility, and formations of the planet, is absolutely false. This leads to a generalized implosion not only on the level of the planet and nations, but also on the level of individuals and social groups.

Q: How will a polarity be able to form again?

FG: This is the question. Today there are only fragmentary and partial answers. In some countries, like Brazil (with the Worker's Party around Lula), resistance exists at all sorts of levels. Struggles are not only situated at the level of economics or of politics, but also at the level of subjectivity, particularly at the level of the mass media. It is important to initiate an entry into a post-media era through aesthetic reappropriation of the production of images, of audiovisual production. It is through this kind of redefinition of the struggle, of post-media social practices that other types of alternative polarities will begin to crystallize. Otherwise neither the left, nor even the ecological movements as they presently are, will be able to advance on this area.

Q: How do you see the role of intellectuals in this recomposition?

FG: It's an illusion to talk like that about intellectuals. Intellectuals are like everybody else. There are only preformed, pre-modeled surfaces of mass-media inscription. The answers are programmed through the questions, otherwise they are neither aired, nor broadcast. There is nothing to expect from those who adapt to this mass-media economy. This does not mean that there isn't also an immense intellectual stratum that reflects and works on it. But the concept of the intellectual should be thought anew. Who is an intellectual? Technicians are intellectuals, teachers, all the people who work in every kind of discipline are intellectuals. We should speak about the intellectual function, and not about intellectuals. The intellectual function is called on to occupy productive and social practices of every kind. This extension of the intellectual function is something worth thinking about. It is too easy to accuse workers in the media, or journalists. They are caught in the gears of the production of subjectivity like everyone else. They have to organize, reinvent an ability to express themselves assertively. But the same thing occurs in psychiatry, education, urban affairs, etc.

So, how to recompose collective set-ups of enunciation effectively so that intellectual functions are in a position to foil the traps constantly set by the powers-that-be? And when I say powers, I mean not only the big powers, like state powers, but also molecular power which creates in public opinion the need to be reassured, infantilized, to systematically mask and exclude everything singular, anything that has to do with danger, pain, death and desire. It is these behaviors of avoidance, this lamination of the means to produce subjectivity, this kind of one-dimensionality that we have to turn around. This is what, in my terminology, I called the *homogenesis of subjectivity*. There is a relationship which is increasingly functional between individuals and goals, like revenue, prestige, things that turn individuals into zombies of the dominant value-system. This is quite obvious in American subjectivity where the dollar has a thoroughly affective value. Fortunately, there are areas of potential resistance to this one-dimensionality of subjectivity— what I call a possible *heterogenesis of subjectivity*. Childhood is one of these areas which, at least temporarily, "gels" different- ly, escapes, manages to mobilize a wide range of semiotizations to enrich existence. It is also everything that provokes crisis in individuals. Media crises, neurotic and psychotic crises can be a will to creation and an existential affirmation. Peoples and social categories resist as well. In the United States, African Americans clearly are a factor of subjective recomposition. In the ghetto, in different sectors of life, through song, dance and music, they partly escape this leveling. The recomposition of the historical subject is also achieved through the recomposi- tion of subjectivity on the molecular, individual level.

All the new psychological practices or new religions, which are the rage in the United States, are spreading every- where. This amuses journalists and investigators, but it is not so funny. Using whatever means available, people gather residual instruments, crumbs to resituate themselves, put them- selves back on the map, regain a foothold in existence. This explains the tremendous rise in irrationalism, which we are witnessing just about everywhere. Isn't there another path this subjective recomposition could take to avoid falling back on racism, male chauvinism, loneliness, and, finally, a culture of anguish? Is there no possible junction, no transversal path, between these practices of the heterogenesis of subjectivity?

Subjectivity is sensitivity, social relations, a pathic approach to the other. It's something else than an ideology: it's ideas. You have to admit that ideology matters little for subjectivity. When it matters, it means that it is involved in the production of subjectivity. Ideology functions like rational, discursive statements meant to understand and analyze situations; repetitive statements like the binary rhythm of rock music give you a relation to time, make you feel that you belong somewhere. Most of the time, ideology works like a refrain, a function whose aim is not ideological, but perverse—just as the psychiatrist has a perverse pleasure at being a small, local despot over the pitiful, wretched realm which is what most of the psychiatric services still are in France today. You also have to refrain from judging in simple terms this kind of perverse pleasure for fear of getting started off on a war of good against evil, or virtue against perversity. In any case, there is an ethical, political responsibility which is not global and massive, but a partial one. There are partial objects over which you can have a hold, and then there are immense constraints, immense sectors where you can't intervene.

Q: How to initiate a revival of affirmation, a resumption of control?

FG: It's very tricky. Each of us has a piece of ethico-political responsibility in this sector. And then there are all the opportunities, the carelessness, worries, neuroses, inhibitions and also, eventually, the perverse pleasure of finding one's little thrill there in spite of everything else.

There exist relations of suggestion—subjects are literally transferred onto the apparatus. They become adjacent to the discourse they hear, images, phrases, pieces of music. At that point, there is a kind of dispossession of subjectivity, an infantilization and a lessening of responsibility, which is like the consumption of all the sleep-inducing chemical therapy for the anxiety-ridden and others. This is not a metaphor, it is exactly of the same order. It involves the same functional and biological processes. You can't start with a simple vectorization, a place from where subjectivity is manipulated, and then move to a wretched victimized population. Obviously it is a victim, but an agent as well in this matter. We all have the media and chemiotherapy that we deserve in a certain sense. Therefore the more Western subjectivity is decomposed, the more it will be infantilized, and the more media there will be to meet its expectations. Thus the necessity of recomposing subjectivity, which I keep reasserting, even at the most molecular level, and of recomposing this heterogenesis by which subjectivity is being produced. It is important to watch TV, it is important as well to watch the stars at night, and to confront one's own finitude, age, sex, a thousand things like poetry, music, creation. If a recomposition of this type doesn't occur, then one is caught in an infernal circle.

One shouldn't forget that the levels of resistance are different. Maybe there is more to expect from the Third World, where intense centers of subjective heterogenesis, it seems, have been preserved. So here I am waiting as if in a dream, a utopic dream, that ways of recomposing subjectivity will find an anchor, a center in the South. This will be due to its considerable demographic expansion and the pressure it will exert on the North. Maybe they will bring about more ideological, more militant recompositions capable of reorienting relations of force, transforming international relations, creating other roads to resolution, and not just in terms of economic conflicts....

Q: In the Gulf War, isn't the Western media more aggressive and more powerful than all the other processes of subjectivity put together?

FG: I believe so. And I believe it more and more, because

the media intervenes at a nearly physiological, neurological level. Take the phenomenon of war. In 1914, there were all these images of collective jubilation, exchanges—before WWI, not after. Whereas today this festive character has been evacuated. Remember the images of London during the bombings? There was a real social interaction around the war. I lived through the war of 1940; we heard about it on the radio, and in the newspapers but very little; mostly we talked about it among ourselves. The war was something that inhabited my environment. Whereas in the Gulf War, another type of relation to war was established. One waits, one sees the percussion of a shell on a target. We are told about the war, but it's within ourselves. There's a solipsistic relationship to war, and many people experienced it like a total intrusion, in complete anguish. For some, it triggered reactions of incredible panic; they stockpiled, bought a rifle, things like that. For others, it was a little like waking up. "Hey, something is finally happening when usually it's always the same thing." For the more psychotic, it was an entirely noteworthy event, like a good memory. This sort of dates something in this world where nothing ever happens. Generally, it had a fearsome effect, it was a profound intervention in the subjectivity, perhaps more profound than other military ordeals. All the more so it had little to do with anyone. There were a few dead among the foreign legion. Nothing to get worked up about. It's another type of relationship that's being implemented here.

Q: I don't understand why we're only speaking about TV, you of all people....

FG: I watch TV like everybody else. I'm just as dumb, no question about it. From August to January, I didn't believe a word about this war story. I took it to be a photomontage, propaganda. I have to recognize that, for once, I really appreciated an article Baudrillard published in *Libération* two days before the operations started, with the title "The war will not take place." There was something very courageous about it because three lines from the end, he said: "Maybe it will take place anyway, but it shouldn't have taken place." Everything had been set up and programmed in international relations so that it could be avoided. This seemed to me totally obvious. Precisely, the event is that it took place in spite of the fact that it shouldn't have taken place. We witnessed a kind of springing up, of awakening, a stroke of incredible madness. This stroke of monstrous passion led to the extermination of hundreds of thousands of Iraqis. On the other side, among the coalition, there were a few dozen or hundred victims; and to pass all this off as war. In a sense, Baudrillard was not wrong when he said "The war did not take place." What war, what are they talking about? There was a massacre, at least the equivalent of what happened at Hiroshima and Nagasaki, or Dresden. Except that this time there was no war. It's as if they had sent A-bombs without a war. The secret services, the political and military chiefs-of-staff knew the situation perfectly well, and public opinion could sense it as well. And then no. It had to be war.

It's something of that kind that happened, completely astounding, the same kind of surprise I had during the suppression of the extreme left in Italy. The Italian government declared: "This is war. Yes, yes, it is war!" And it was war because there were about three or ten dozen Red Brigades who were doing a few terrorist attacks. It was war! It's as if there was a need to erect the paradigm of war, with the whole range of resonances back to the Hundred Years War, in order to justify this kind of monstrous orgy, this sort of incredible erection displayed on all the grinning faces of journalists, military experts, all the leaders. "The planet is in danger, so we're supporting the President!" It's scary. It's an event which has the look of a pseudo-event because of its media dressing, but it's still with this kind of event today that one makes history, as pitiful as it may seem.

Q: Have you thought about the news? At the beginning of the war, they told us: "There's Iraq, 4th army in the world, weapons of massive destruction, chemical weapons, ready for war because they tackled the Iranians for ten years." And you end up with this, an aggression, a massacre. Why did they say that? The coalition's information systems knew the reality of Iraq's strength. But the TV never put these facts in parallel, never put Iraq's alleged power and the actual massacre together.

FG: It's as if one had opened fire with a machine gun on a high-school uprising. This is about the nature of it. There was an obvious and manifest disproportion and at the same time one could tell, and there were ways to know, that the violent talk of Saddam Hussein's and of the Iraqi leaders was largely fictional. Among other things there were 5,000 hostages at the beginning of this operation and Hussein liberated them. If he had been that Machiavellian, he would have kept them, which would perhaps have altered the way they handled the bombardment on the civilian population. This hijacking of all the news at the same time indicates a racism such as there has, perhaps, never been in history. It proves that Arabs are not weighed with the same scale, they are not accounted for the same way Western populations are.

Q: Was there not a displacement of the public's sensibility linked to the massacre of the Jewish people during WWII? The Scud missile, falling on Israel, the German-made gas…. It was some sort of deliberate amalgamation that provoked a real hijacking of History.

FG: Just think of these hysterics over the Scud missile

falling on Israel; it was as if they were exterminating the Israeli people. Expressions like this, which could be considered Machiavellian, simply indicated an incredibly racist subjectivity. The worst example occured three days before the cease fire, when Saddam Hussein asked for an armistice, a first armistice. Bush responded: "This is a scandal. This is a hoax! He dares ask for an armistice!" What was so scandalous about that I have never understood. Maybe they had to see the extermination to the end and kill the tens, maybe hundreds, of thousands of soldiers who were fleeing Kuwait towards Iraq.

We are already in a period of planetary mutation. It is proceeding at considerable speed. It has become impossible to highlight, grasp and record the speed with which these technoscientific and biological discoveries are progressing. It's unprecedented. Claude Valeski's machine records childbirth second by second, but it's impossible to pinpoint the large mutations of the world economy that Wallerstein evoked. One cannot do without a minimum of social, cosmological, and geopolitical representation, so one rewrites History. One erases the Vietnam War, one returns to the conquering spirit and all-powerfulness America displayed during the last World War. One makes this kind of collage, of amalgam, a forced and permanent redundancy between all these periods. That Palestinian children, meanwhile, are being massacred for months in the Intifadas doesn't provoke anything, doesn't show at all anywhere, activates nothing. Nothing's happening.

Translated by Andrea Loselle

17

A CINEMA OF DESIRE

The history of desire is inseparable from the history of its repression. Maybe one day a historian will try to write a history of "cinemas of desire" (the way one tells an audience who express their sentiments too excitedly to "stop their cinema"). But, at the very least, he would have to begin this history with classical antiquity! It could start with the opening of the first big theater of international renown, a theater for captive cinephiles: Plato's cave. It would have to describe the 2000 years or so of the Catholic church's monopoly of production and distribution, as well as the abortive attempts of dissident societies of production, such as the Cathar cinema of the 12th century, or the Jansenist cinema of the 17th, up to the triumph of the baroque monopoly. There would be color film in it: with 10th century stained-glass windows would be the silent cinema of the "bepowdered" and the Pierrots. A special place should be reserved for the big schools that transformed the economy of desire on a long-term basis, like that of courtly love, with its four hundred troubadours who managed to "launch" a new form of love and a new kind of woman. It would have to appreciate the devastating effects of the great consortia of romanticism and their promotion of an infantilization of love, while awaiting the saturation of the market by psychoanalytical racketeering with its standard shorts for miniaturized screens: the little cinema of transference, Oedipus, and castration.

Power can only be maintained insofar as it relies on the semiologies of signification: "No one can ignore the law." This

143

implies that no one can ignore the meaning of words. Linguists like Oswald Ducrot insist on the fact that language is not simply an instrument of communication, but also an instrument of power.[1] The law, as the culmination of sexual, ethnic, and class struggles, etc., crystallizes in language. The "reality" imposed by the powers-that-be is conveyed by a dominant semiology. Therefore, one should not go from a principled opposition between pleasure and reality, between a principle of desire and a principle of reality, but rather, from a *principle of dominant reality* and a *principle of licit pleasure.* Desire is forced to maintain itself, as well as can be expected, in this space between reality and pleasure, this frontier that power jealously controls with the help of innumerable frontier guards: in the family, at school, in the barracks, at the workshop, in psychiatric hospitals and, of course, at the movies.

Thus, desire is so ruthlessly hunted down that it usually ends up renouncing its objects and investing itself and its guardians on these boundaries. The capitalist eros will turn into a passion for the boundary, it becomes the cop. While bumping on the all-too-explicit signs of the libido, it will take its pleasure from their hateful contemplation. "Look at this filth." It will become the gaze, the forbidden spectacle, the transgression, "without really getting into it." All the morals of asceticism and sublimation consist, in fact, of capturing the libido in order to identify and contain it within this system of limits. I don't mean, here, to oppose centralism with spontaneism, or the disciplines necessary for organizing the collectivity with the turbulence of the "natural" impulses; nor is it a matter of reducing this question to a simple case of morality or ideological strategy of dominant powers in order to better control the exploited.... The dualities morality/instinct, culture/nature, order/disorder, master/slave, centrality/democracy, etc., appear to us to be insufficient as a way of accounting for this eroticization of the limits, at least in its contemporary evolution.

The development of productive forces in industrialized societies (it is true both for capitalism and bureaucratic socialism) involves an increasing liberation of the energy of desire. The capitalist system does not function simply by putting a flux of slaves to work. It depends on modelling individuals according to its preferences and, for this purpose, to propose and impose models of desire: it puts models of childhood, fatherhood, motherhood, and love in circulation. It launches these models the same way the automobile industry launches a new line of cars. The important thing is that these models always remain compatible with the axiomatic of capital: the object of love should always be an exclusive object participating in the system of private ownership. The fundamental equation is: enjoyment = possession. Individuals are modelled to adapt, like a cog, to the capitalist machine. At the heart of their desire and in the exercise of their pleasure, they have to find private ownership. They have to invest it with ideality: "production for production's sake." They can only desire the objects that the market production proposes to them; they must not only submit to the hierarchy, but even more, love it as such. To conjure up the dangers of class struggle, capitalism has tried hard to introduce a bourgeois owner into the heart of each worker. It is the prerequisite of his integration. Traditional models that attached the worker to his job, to his quarter, to his moral values, indeed to his religion (even if it be socialism) have all collapsed. The paternalistic model of the boss is no longer compatible with production, no more than that of the *pater familias* with the education of children. One now needs a deterritorialized worker, someone who does not freeze into professional experience, but who follows the progress of technology, indeed, who develops a certain creativity, a certain participation. Moreover, one needs a consumer who adapts to the evolution of the market.

For this reason, the problem raised is the transformation of traditional relations of production and other relations—familial, conjugal, educational, etc.... But if one relaxes the brakes too abruptly, then it is the machines of desire that risk flying off the handle, and breaking not only through the outdated frontiers but even the new ones the system wants to establish. The relations of production, formation, and reproduction oscillate between immobilist temptations and archaic fixations. The capitalist "solution" consists in pushing models that are at once adapted to its imperatives of standardization—i.e., that dismantle traditional territorialities—and that reconstitute an artificial security; in other words, that modernize the archaisms and inject artificial ones. In conditions such as these, from the angle of production, the worker will be deterritorialized; from the angle of relations of production, formation, and reproduction, he will be reterritorialized.

Cinema, television, and the press have become fundamental instruments of forming and imposing a dominant reality and dominant significations. Beyond being means of communication, of transmitting information, they are instruments of power. They not only handle messages, but, above all, libidinal energy. The themes of cinema—its models, its genres, its professional castes, its mandarins, its stars—are, whether they want to be or not, at the service of power. And not only insofar as they depend directly on the financial power machine, but first and foremost, because they participate in the elaboration and transmission of subjective models. Presently, the media, for the most part, functions in the service of repression. But they could become instruments of liberation of great importance. Commercial cinema, for example, entertains a latent racism in its Westerns; it can prevent the production of films about events like those of May '68 in France; but the Super-8 and the video-tape recorder could be turned into means of writing that are much more direct and much more effective than discourses, pamphlets, and brochures. As such it could contribute greatly to foiling the tyranny of the *savoir-écrire* that weighs not only on the bourgeois hierarchy but which operates also among the ranks of what is traditionally called the worker movement.

Beyond the signifier, beyond the illusion of a permanent reality. It's not a speculative option, but an affirmation: all reality is dated, historically and socially situated. The order of the real has nothing to do with destiny; one can change it. Let us consider three modern currents of thought, vehicles of three systems of signification: totalitarian systems, psychoanalysis, and structuralism. In each case, there is a certain keystone on which the organization of the dominant reality converges. A signifier dominates every statement of a totalitarian power, a leader, a church, or God. By right, all desire must converge upon it. No one can remain with impunity across "the line" or outside the church. But this type of libidinal economy centered on a transcendent object no longer corresponds exactly to the necessities of modern production, and it tends to be replaced by a more flexible system in developed capitalist countries. In order to form a worker, one must start in the cradle, discipline his Oedipal development within the family, follow him to school, to sports, to the cinema, and all the way to the juke-box.

Psychoanalysis, while borrowing its own model from this traditional type of libidinal economy, has refined and "molecularized" it. It has put to task new types of less obvious objects —objects that anyone can buy, so to speak. These objects are supposed to over-code all the *énoncés* of desire: the phallus and the partial objects—breast, shit, etc.... From then on, the despotism of the signifier no longer tends to concentrate on a leader or a God and to express itself on the massive scale of an empire or a church, but on that of the family itself reduced to a state of triangularity. The struggle between the sexes, generations, and social classes, has been reduced to the scale of the family and the self. The machine of familial power, rectified by psychoanalysis, functions by means of two primary parts: the symbolic phallus and castration, instruments of the alienation of woman and child. One recalls the tyrannical interrogation of Little Hans by his father under the supervision of Professor Freud. But before that, the mother's resistance must be subdued, compelling her to submit to psychoanalytical dogma. In fact, it never crosses her mind to object to her son's coming to join her in bed whenever he wants. The mother becoming the agent of phallic power, the attack on childhood is concentrated on the question of masturbation. One does not accuse him directly of masturbating; one imposes upon him the good, "castrating" explanation with regard to this question. One forces him to incorporate a particular system of signification: "What you desire—we know this better than you—is to sleep with your mother and to kill your father."

The importance of submitting the child to the Oedipian code—and this at an early age—does not result from a structural or signifying effect, separate from history or society. It depends on capitalism's inability to find other ways of providing the family with an artificial consistency. In archaic societies, the child was relatively free in his movements until his initiation. But in a capitalist society, initiation begins with the pacifier: the mother-child relationship tends to be more and more strictly controlled by psychologists, psychoanalysts, educators, etc. In its older formulation, power was maintained as a paradigmatic series—father-boss-king, etc., culminating in a discernible, incarnate, and institutionalized God. In its present formulation, incarnation is deterritorialized and decentered. It is everywhere and nowhere, and it depends on family models to arrange a refuge for it. But in their turn, the diverse psychoanalytic models of Oedipal triangulation appear too territorialized with regard to parental images and partial objects. Much more abstract, much more mathematical models of the unconscious have to be proposed.

Structuralism in psychoanalysis—as in other domains—

can be thought of as an attempt to substitute a nameless God for the God of the church and the family. It proposes a transcendent model of subjectivity and desire that would be independent of history and real social struggle. From that moment, the conflict of ideas tends to be displaced anew. It leaves the psychoanalytical terrain of the family and the self for that of the semiotic and its applications in mass media. I cannot undertake here a critical analysis of structuralism; I only want to point out that, to my mind, such a critique should start by questioning the syncretic conception of the diverse modes of encoding. It seems to me indispensable, first of all, to avoid absorbing "natural" encodings, such as the genetic code, into human semiologies. One entertains the illusion that the "natural" order as well as that of the social arrangements (like structures of kinship) would be structured "like languages." Thus, one confuses the modes of encoding that I call *a-semiotic*—like music, painting, mathematics, etc.—with those of speech and writing. Second, it seems necessary to distinguish between the pre-signifying semiologies—for example, of archaic societies, the insane, and children—and fully signifying semiologies of modern societies that are all over-coded in the writing of social and economic laws. In primitive societies, one expresses oneself as much by speech as by gestures, dances, rituals, or signs marked on the body. In industrialized societies, this richness of expression is attenuated; all *énoncés* have to be translatable to the language that encodes dominant meanings.

It is also important to expose and insist on the independence of an a-signifying semiotics. It is this, in fact, that will allow us to understand what permits cinema to escape the semiologies of meaning and to participate in the collective arrangements of desire.[2]

If structuralism refuses to consider this independence, there can be no question of leaving the domain of signification—i.e., the signifier-signified duality. It tries, moreover, to systematically inject meaning into all signifying regimes that tend to escape it. (It will invent "relational significations" for science or, for the cinema, the unities of "iconomatic" significations, etc.) In putting the signifier and the signifying chains in the forefront, it substantiates the idea of keeping the contents at a secondary level. But in fact, it secretly transfers the normalizing power of language onto the signifier. Hence, in masking the possible creativity of a-signifying semiotic machines, structuralism plays into an order tied down to dominant significations.

When it is exploited by capitalist and bureaucratic socialist powers to mold the collective imaginary, cinema topples over to the side of meaning. Yet, its own effectiveness continues to depend on its pre-signifying symbolic components as well as its a-signifying ones: linkages, internal movements of visual images, colors, sounds, rhythms, gestures, speech, etc. But unlike the speech and writing that, for hundreds, indeed, thousands of years, has remained pretty much the same as a means of expression, cinema has, in a few decades, never ceased to enrich its technique. In this way, to catch up with these effects, the powers-that-be have tried to increase the control they exercise upon it. The more it enlarges its scale of aesthetic intensities, the more the systems of control and censure have tried to subjugate it to signifying semiologies.

As an a-signifying semiotic, how does cinema go beyond the structure of signifying semiologies? Christian Metz explains it better than I can; he shows that cinema is not a specialized language and that its *matter of content*[3] is undefined: "the breadth of its semantic fabric is a consequence of two distinct causes whose effects are cumulative. On the one hand, cinema encompasses a code—language, in the talkies—whose presence itself would be enough to authorize semantic information of the most varied type. Second, other elements of the filmic text, for example, images, are themselves languages whose matter of content has no precise boundaries."[4] Its matter of content extends so much more effectively beyond traditional encodings, since the semiotic alloy that composes its matter of expression is itself open to multiple systems of external intensities.

Its matters of expression are not fixed. They go in different directions. Christian Metz enumerates some of them, emphasizing that each has an intrinsic system of pertinent features:

—the phonic fabric of expression, that refers to spoken language (signifying semiology);

—the sonorous but non-phonic fabric that refers to instrumental music (a-signifying semiotic);

—the visual and colored fabric that refers to painting (mixed, symbolic, and a-signifying semiotic);

—the non-colored, visual fabric that refers to black and white photography (mixed, symbolic, and a-signifying semiotic);

—the gestures and movements of the human body, etc. (symbolic semiologies).

Umberto Eco had already pointed out that cinema does not bend to a system of double articulation, and that this had even led him to try to find a third articulation. But, doubtless, it is preferable to follow Metz who believes that cinema escapes all systems of double articulation, and, in my opinion, all elementary systems of significative encoding. The meanings in cinema are not directly encoded in a machine of intersecting syntagmatic and paradigmatic axes—they always come to it, secondarily, from external constraints that model it. If silent film, for example, had succeeded in expressing the intensities of desire in relation to the social field in a way that was much more immediate and authentic than that of the talkies, it was not because he was less expressive, but *because the signifying script had not yet taken possession of the image* and because, in these conditions, capitalism had not yet seized all the advantages it could take from it. The successive inventions of the talkies, of color, of television, etc., insofar as they enriched the possibilities of expressing desire, have led capitalism to take possession of cinema, and to use it as a privileged instrument of social control.

It is interesting, in this respect, to consider the extent to which television has not only not absorbed cinema, but has even subjected itself to the formula of commercial film, whose power, for this very reason, has never been so strong. In these conditions, the stakes of liberalizing pornographic film seems secondary to me. One remains here at the level of a sort of "negotiation" with the contents that do not really threaten the established powers. On the contrary, these powers find it expedient to release the ballast on a terrain that does not threaten the foundations of established order. It would be completely different if the masses were at liberty to make the kind of film they wanted, whether pornographic or not. The miniaturization of material could become a determining factor in such an evolution.[5] The creation of private television channels by cable should be a decisive test; in fact, nothing guarantees us that what will develop, from the standpoint of the economy of desire, will not be even more reactionary than what is broadcast by national television. Whatever it is, it seems to me that all that tends toward limiting micropolitical struggles of desire to an eros cut off from all context is a trap. And this doesn't just hold true for the cinema.

The capitalist eros, we said, is always invested on the limit between a licit pleasure and a codified interdiction. It proliferates alongside the law; it makes itself the accomplice of what is forbidden; it channels the libido to the forbidden object that it only touches on superficially. This economy of transgression polarizes the desiring production in a game of mirrors that cut it from all access to the real and catches it in phantasmic representations. In this way, desiring production never ceases to be separated from social production. Fantasized desire and the capitalist real which convert desire to "useful" work involve, apparently, two different types of arrangements. In fact, they involve two politics of desire that are absolutely complementary: a politics of re-enclosure on the person, the self, the appropriation of the other, hierarchy, exploitation, etc., and a politics of passive acceptance of the world such as it is.

Against the notions of eros and eroticism, I would like to oppose that of desire and desiring energy. Desire is not, like eros, tied down with the body, the person, and the law; it is no more dependent on the shameful body—with its hidden organs and its incestuous taboo—than to a fascination with and to myths about the nude body, the all-powerful phallus, and sublimation. Desire is constituted *before* the crystallization of the body and the organs, *before* the division of the sexes, *before* the separation between the familiarized self and the social field. It is enough to observe children, the insane, and the primitive without prejudice in order to understand that desire can make love with humans as well as with flowers, machines, or celebrations. It does not respect the ritual games of the war *between* the sexes: *it is not sexual,* it is trans-sexual. The struggle for the phallus, the threat of an imaginary castration, no more than the opposition between genitality and pre-genitality, normality and perversion, fundamentally concern it. Nothing essential leads to the subjugation of the child, the woman, or the homosexual. In a word, it is not centered on dominant significations and values: it participates in open, a-signifying semiotics, available for better or worse. Nothing depends here on destiny, but on collective arrangements in action.

In conclusion, I must say of the cinema that it can be both the machine of eros, i.e., the interiorization of repression, and the machine of liberated desire. An action in favor of the liberty of expression should therefore not be centered a priori on erotic cinema, but on what I will call a cinema of desire. The real trap is the separation between erotic themes and social themes; all themes are at once social and transsexual. There is no political cinema on the one hand and an erotic cinema on the other. Cinema is political whatever its subject; each time it represents a man, a woman, a child, or an animal, it takes sides in the micro-class struggle that concerns the reproduction of models of desire. The real repression of cinema is not centered on erotic images; it aims above all at imposing a respect for dominant representations and models used by the power to control and channel the desire of the masses. In every production, in every sequence, in every frame, a choice is made between a conservative economy of desire and a revolutionary breakthrough. The more a film is conceived and produced according to the relations of production, or modelled on capitalist enterprise, the more chance there is of participating in the libidinal economy of the system. Yet no theory can furnish the keys to a correct orientation in this domain. One can make a film having life in a convent as its theme that puts the revolutionary libido in motion; one can make a film in defense of revolution that is fascist from the point of view of the economy of desire. In the last resort, what will be determinant in the political and aesthetic plane is not the words and the contents of ideas, but essentially a-signifying messages that escape dominant semiologies.

Translated by David L. Sweet

1. Cf. J. L. Austin, *How to Do Things With Words* (Oxford: Clarendon Press, 1962).
2. One must address in detail the role of a-signifying components vis-à-vis analogical ones: the fact, in particular, that the functioning as machines of deterritorialized signs "breaks" the effects of signification and interpretation, thwarts the system of dominant redundancies, accelerates the most "innovative," "constructivist," "rhizomatic" components.
3. Cf. Louis Hjelmslev, *Essais Linguistiques* (Paris: Editions de Minuit, 1971) and *Prolégomènes à une théorie du langage* (Paris: Minuit, 1971).
4. Christian Metz, *Language and Cinema* (The Hague: Mouton, 1974); *Film Language, A Semiotic of the Cinema* (New York: Oxford University Press, 1974).
5. The recent development of free radios on miniaturized FM transmitters would seem to confirm this tendency.

18

THE POOR MAN'S COUCH

Psychoanalysts are always a little suspicious of film, or rather, they have always been attracted to other forms of expression. But the reverse is not true. The covert advances of film into psychoanalysis have been innumerable, beginning with Mr. Goldwyn's proposition to Freud: $100,000 to put the famous loves on screen. This asymmetry is due, no doubt, not only to matters of respectability; it is tied, even more fundamentally, to the fact that psychoanalysis understands nothing of the unconscious processes involved in cinema. Psychoanalysis has sometimes tried to seize on the formal analogies between dream and film—for René Laforgue, cinema is a sort of collective dream; for René Lebovici, a dream to make spectators dream. Psychoanalysis has tried to absorb filmic syntagms into the primary processes, but it has never figured out its specificity and for a good reason: a normalization of the social imaginary that is irreducible to familialist and Oedipal models, even on those occasions when it puts itself deliberately at their service. Psychoanalysis now inflates itself in vain with linguistics and mathematics; yet it also continues trotting out the same generalities about the individual and the family, while film is bound up with the whole social field and with history. Something important happens in cinema where fantastic libidinal charges are invested—for example, those clustered around certain complexes that constitute the racist Western, Nazism and the Resistance, the "American way of life," etc. Sophocles no longer holds his own in all this. Film has become a gigantic machine for modelling the social libido, while psychoanalysis will forever remain a small cottage industry reserved for selected elites.

One goes to the cinema to suspend the usual modes of communication for a while. All the constitutive elements of this situation lead to this suspension. Whatever alienating character the content or form of expression of a film may have, it aims fundamentally at reproducing a certain type of behavior that, for lack of a better term, I will call cinematographic performance.[1] Because film is capable of mobilizing the libido on this type of performance, it can be used to serve what Mikel Dufrenne has called a "house unconscious."[2]

Considered from the standpoint of unconscious repression, the cinematographic performance and the psychoanalytical performance ("the analytical act") perhaps deserve to be compared. For too long, belle époque psychoanalysis has persuaded us it was liberating the instincts by giving them a language; in fact, it never intended loosening the vice of the dominant discourse except insofar as it reckoned on achieving even greater success than ordinary repression had ever done: to control, to discipline, to adapt people to the norms of a certain type of society. In the end, the discourse that is proffered in the analytical session is no more "liberated" than that served up in movie theaters. The so-called liberty of free association is only an illusion that masks a certain program, a secret modelization of statements (énoncés). As on the film screen, it is understood in analysis that no semiotic production of desire should have any effect on reality. The little playhouse of analysis and the mass analysis of film both proscribe the passage to action, to "acting out." Psychoanalysts, and even, in a way, filmmakers, would like to be considered as special beings beyond time and space: pure creators, neutral, apolitical, irresponsible… and in a sense, they may be right, they hardly have a hold on the process of control of which they are the agent. The grid of the psychoanalytical reading belongs today as much to the analyst as to the analysand. It is tailor-made for all and sundry—"hey, you made a Freudian slip"—it integrates itself with intersubjective strategies and even perceptive codes: one proffers symbolic interpretations like threats, one "sees" the phallus, the returns to the maternal breast, etc. The interpretation is so obvious that the best, the most assured strategy, for an alerted psychoanalyst, continues to be silence, a systematically sanctioned silence: pure analytical *écoute,* floating attention. In truth, the emptiness of the *écoute* answers here to a desire emptied of all content, to a desire for nothing, to a radical powerlessness, and it is not surprising, under such conditions, that the castration complex has become the constant curative reference, the punctuation of every sequence, the cursor that perpetually brings desire back to the bottom line. The psychoanalyst, like the filmmaker, is "carried" by his subject. What one expects from both is the confection of a certain type of drug that, though technologically more sophisticated than the ordinary joint or pipe, nonetheless functions by transforming the mode of subjectivity of those who use it: one captures the energy of desire in order to turn it against itself, to anaesthetize it, to cut it off from the external world in such a way that it ceases to threaten the organization and values of the dominant social system. Yet, the psychoanalytic drug and the cinematographic drug are not the same; overall, they have the same objectives, but the micropolitics of desire they involve and the semiotic arrangements they rely on are completely different.

One could assume that these criticisms only aim at a certain type of psychoanalysis and are not concerned with the present structuralist current, insofar as it no longer affirms the reliance of interpretation on paradigms of content—as was the case with the classic theory of parental complexes—but rather on an interplay of universal signifiers, independent of any meanings they may carry. But can one believe structuralist psychoanalysts when they claim to have renounced shaping and translating the production of desire? The unconscious of orthodox Freudians was organized in complexes that crystallized the libido on heterogeneous elements: biological, familial, social, ethical, etc. The Oedipal complex, for example, apart from its real or imaginary traumatic components, was founded on the division of the sexes and age groups. One would think it was a matter, then, of *objective bases* in relation to which the libido had to express and finalize itself, with the consequence that, even today, questioning the "evidence" appears completely inappropriate to some. And yet, everyone knows about numerous situations in which the libido refuses these so-called objective bases, where it eschews the division of the sexes, where it ignores prohibitions linked to the separation of age groups, where it mixes people together, as if for the sake of it, where it tends to systematically avoid exclusive oppositions of subjective and objective, self and other. Orthodox psychoanalysts believe that it is only a matter of perverse, marginal, or pathological situations requiring interpretation and adaptation. Lacanian structuralism was originally founded in reaction to these "abuses," to this naive realism, particularly regarding questions about narcissism and psychosis. It intended to radically break with a curative practice uniquely centered on reshaping the self. But in denaturalizing the unconscious, in liberating these objects from an all-too-constraining psychogenesis, in structuring them "like a language,"[3] it hasn't succeeded in breaking its personological moorings or opening up to the social field, to cosmic and semiological flows of all kinds. One no longer submits these productions of desire to the whole battery of junk room complexes, yet one still claims to interpret each connection through the unique logic of the signifier. One has renounced summary interpretations of content ("the umbrella means...") and the stages of development (the famous "returns" to oral, anal stages, etc.). It is no longer a question of the father and the mother. Now one talks about the "name of the father," the phallus, and the great Other of the symbolic castration, yet without getting one step nearer to the *micropolitics of desire* on which is founded, in each particular situation, the social differentiation of the sexes, the alienation of the child. As far as we are concerned, the struggles of desire should not just be circumscribed in the domain of the signifier—even in the case of a "pure" signifying neurosis, like obsessional neurosis. They always overflow into somatic, social, and economic domains, etc. And unless one believes the signifier is found in everything and anything, one may as well admit that the role of the unconscious has been singularly restrained in order to consider it only from the angle of the signifying chains it activates. "The unconscious is structured like a language," Lacan tells us. Certainly. But by whom? By the family, the school, the barracks, the factory, the cinema, and, in special cases, by psychiatry and psychoanalysis. When one has fixed it, succeeded in crushing the polyvocity of its semiotic modes of expression, bound it to a certain type of semiological machine, then yes, it ends up being structured like a language. It remains fairly docile. It starts speaking the language of the dominant system, which is, moreover, not everyday language, but a special, sublimated, psychoanalyzed language. Not only has desire come to accept its alienation within the signifying chains, but it keeps demanding more and more signifier. It no longer wants to have anything to do with the rest of the world and its modes of semiotization. Any troubling problem will find there, if not its solution, at least a comforting suspension in the interplay of the signifier. Under such conditions, what becomes, for example, of the age-old alienation of women by men? For the signifier, as it is conceived by linguists, only neutral and innocent traces such as the opposition of *masculin/feminin,* and for the psychoanalysts, the mirages that play around the presence/absence of the phallus. In fact, for each type of linguistic performance, for each "degree of grammaticality" of an *énoncé,* there is a corresponding formation of power. The structure of the signifier is never completely reducible to pure mathematical logic; it is always partly bound by diverse, repressive social machines. Only then can a theory of universals, both in linguistics and economics, in anthropology and psychoanalysis be an obstacle to any real exploration of the unconscious, i.e., *all kinds* of semiotic constellations, connections of flows, power relations and constraints that constitute the arrangements of desire.

Structuralist psychoanalysis doesn't have much more to teach us about the unconscious mechanisms mobilized by film at the level of its *syntagmatic organization* any more than orthodox psychoanalysis has at the level of its *semantic contents*. On the contrary, film could perhaps help us to better understand the *pragmatic of unconscious investments* in the social field. In fact, the unconscious does not manifest itself in cinema in the same way it does on the couch: it partially escapes the dictatorship of the signifier, it is not reducible to a fact of language, it no longer respects, as the psychoanalytical transfer continued to do, the classic locutor-auditor dichotomy of meaningful communication. A question arises as to whether it is simply bracketed or whether there is any opportunity for re-examining the entirety of relations between discourse and communication. Communication between a discernible locutor and auditor is perhaps only a particular case, an extreme case, of the discursive exercise. The effects of de-subjectivation and de-individuation produced by the *énoncé* in cinema or in such arrangements as drugs, dreaming, passion, creation, delirium, etc., are perhaps not as exceptional as one would think in relation to the general case that "normal" intersubjective communication and "rational" consciousness of the subject-object relationship is supposed to be. It's the idea of a transcendent subject of enunciation that is being questioned here, as well as the opposition between discourse and language (*langue*) or, even more, the dependence of diverse types of semiotic performance in relation to a so-called universal semiological competence.

The self-conscious subject should be considered a particular "option," a sort of normal madness. It is illusory to believe there exists only *one* subject—an autonomous subject, centered on one individual. One never has to do with a multiplicity of subjective and semiotic modes of which film, in particular, can show how they are orchestrated, "machinated," and infinitely manipulated. But if it is true that the machinic expansion, the exaltation of the cinematographic unconscious, does not protect it—far from it—from contamination by the significations of power, the fact remains that, with it, things do not happen in the same way as with psychoanalysis or with even better-policed artistic techniques. And this all depends on the fact that it manifests itself through semiotic arrangements irreducible to a syntagmatic concatenation that would discipline it mechanically, structure it according to a rigorously formalized pattern of expression and content. Its montage of a-signifying semiotic chains of intensities, movements, and multiplicities fundamentally tends to free it from the signifying grid that intervenes only at a second stage, through the filmic syntagmatic that fixes genres, crystallizes characters and behaviorial stereotypes homogeneous to the dominant semantic field.[4]

This "excess" of the matters of expression over the content certainly limits a possible comparison between cinema and psychoanalysis with respect to repressing the unconscious. Both fundamentally lead to the same politics, but the stakes and the means they resort to are quite different. The psychoanalyst's clientele acquiesces to the whole enterprise of semiotic reduction, while cinema must permanently stay attuned to the social imaginary's mutations just to "stay in the race." It also has to mobilize a real industry, a multiplicity of institutions and powers capable of getting the better of the unconscious proliferation it threatens to unleash. Spoken language itself does not function in film the same way it does in psychoanalysis; it isn't the law, it constitutes but one way among others, a single instrument at the core of a complex semiotic orchestration. The semiotic components of film glide by each other without ever fixing or stabilizing themselves in a deep syntax of latent contents or in the transformational system that ends up with, on the face of it, the manifest content. Relational, emotive, sexual significations—I would prefer to say intensities—are constantly transported there by heterogeneous "traits of the matter of expression" (to borrow a formula that Christian Metz himself borrowed from Hjelmslev). The codes intertwine without one ever succeeding in dominating the others; one passes, in a continual back and forth, from perceptive codes to denotative, musical, connotative, rhetorical, technological, economic, sociological codes, etc....

Commercial cinema is nothing else but a simple, inexpensive drug. Its unconscious action is profound. More perhaps than that of psychoanalysis. First of all at the level of the session. Cinematographic performance affects subjectivity. It affects the personological individuation of enunciation and develops a very particular mode of conscience. Without the support of the other's existence, subjectivation tends to become hallucinatory; it no longer concentrates on *one* subject, but explodes on a multiplicity of poles even when it fixes itself on one character. Strictly speaking, it doesn't even concern a subject of enunciation in the usual sense—what is emitted by these poles is not simply a discourse, but intensities of all kinds, constellations of features of faciality, crystallizations of affects.... It reaches the point where one no longer knows who is speaking or who is who.

The roles are much better defined in psychoanalysis, and the subjective transitivity much better controlled. In fact, one doesn't stop using the *discourse of the analyst:* one says what one thinks someone would like to hear, one alienates oneself by wanting to be worthy of the listener. In cinema, one no longer speaks; *it* speaks in one's place: the cinematographic industry uses the kind of speech it imagines one wants to hear.[5]

A machine treats you like a machine, and the essential thing is not what it says, but the sort of vertigo of abolition that the fact of being "machinized" provides for you. With people dissolving and things passing unwitnessed, one abandons oneself to a guilt-free world. While on the couch one pays to have a witness (preferably someone distinguished, someone of clearly higher standing than oneself) invest and control your most intimate thoughts and sentiments, at the movies one pays to be invaded by subjective arrangements with blurry contours in order to give in to adventures that, in principle, have no lasting effects. "In principle," because the modelization resulting from this cheap sort of vertigo is not without telltale traces: the unconscious finds itself populated by cowboys and indians, cops and robbers, Belmondos and Monroes.... It's like tobacco or cocaine; one cannot trace its effects (even if that were possible) unless one is already completely hooked.

But wasn't the psychoanalytical cure instituted precisely to avoid such promiscuity? Wasn't the function of interpretation and transfer to saturate and select the good and the bad in the unconscious? Isn't it the point that the patient be guided, helped by a safety net? Certainly. But in reality this net is more alienating than any other system of subjectivity-control. Upon leaving the movie-house, one has to wake up and quietly put on one's own film reel (the entire social reality is devoted to it), while the psychoanalytic session, becoming interminable, overflows into the rest of life. Going to the movies, as one says, is an entertainment, while the analytical cure—and it is true even for neurotics—tends to be a sort of social promotion: it is accompanied by the sentiment that in the end one will be a specialist of the unconscious—a specialist, moreover, as bothersome for the whole entourage as any other specialists whatsoever, beginning with those of film.

Alienation by psychoanalysis depends on the fact that the particular mode of subjectivation that it produces is organized around a subject-for-an-other, a personological subject, over-adapted, over-indebted to the signifying practices of the system. The cinematographic projection, for its part, deterritorializes the perceptual and deictic coordinates.[6] The semiotic taste buds of the unconscious haven't even been titillated before the film, as a manufactured work, starts conditioning them to the semio-logic paste of the system. The unconscious, as soon as it is exposed, becomes like an occupied territory. Cinema, in the end, has taken the place of ancient liturgies. Its function is to renovate, adapt, and assimilate the ancient gods of bourgeois familialism. The religion it serves borrows the language of "normal" communication that one finds in the family, at school, or at work. Even when it seems to give the "normal" character, a man, woman, or child a chance to speak, it is always, in real-ity, a reconstitution, a puppet, a zombie-model, an "invader" who is ready to be grafted onto the unconscious in order to dominate it. One doesn't go to the cinema with one's ego, one's childhood memories, the way one goes to a psychoanalyst. One accepts in advance that it robs us of our identity, our past and our future. Its derisive miracle is to turn us, for a few moments, into orphans: single, amnesiac, unconscious, and eternal. When, upon leaving, we take up our "daily" reflexes again, when we find the faces of our loved ones closed in on them-selves again, we may be tempted to prolong the impression pro-duced by the film, if it has touched us. It is even possible for a film to upset our whole existence. In truth, a film that could shake itself free of its function of adaptational drugging could have unimaginable liberating effects, effects on an entirely dif-ferent scale from those produced by books or literary trends. This is due to the fact that cinema intervenes directly in our relations with the external world. And even if this exterior is contaminated by dominant representations, a minimal aperture could result from this intervention. Psychoanalysis suffocates us—with considerable luxury, it is true—it shuts off our relation to the external world in what is most singular, most unpredictable, by projecting the cinema of interiority onto it. Whatever its stereotypes, its conformisms, cinema is overflowing with the richness of its expressive means. In this regard, everyone knows how the work of film is prolonged, sometimes directly, in that of the dream (I have shown that this interaction was all the stronger the weaker the film seemed to be).

Commercial cinema is undeniably familialist, Oedipian, and reactionary. But it is not intrinsically so, the way psychoanalysis is. It is so "on top of everything else." Its "mission" is not to adapt people to outdated and archaic elitist Freudian models, but to those implied by mass production. Even, it should be stressed, when they reconstitute archetypes of the traditional family. While its "analytic" means are richer, more dangerous, because more fascinating than those of psychoanalysis, they are, in fact, more precarious and more full of promise. And if one can imagine another film praxis being constituted in the future, a cinema of combat attacking dominant values in the present state of things, one can hardly see how a revolutionary psychoanalysis could possibly emerge.

In fact, the psychoanalytic unconscious (or the literary unconscious, since they derive one from the other) is always a secondhand unconscious. The discourse of analysis is shaped by analytical myths: individual myths themselves have to adapt to the framework of these reference-myths. Cinematic myths do not have at their disposal such a meta-mythic system, and the gamut of semiological means they do mobilize directly connects with the spectator's processes of semiotization. In a word, the language of cinema and audio-visual media is alive, while that of psychoanalysis has, for a long time now, spoken a dead language. One can expect the best or the worst from cinema. From psychoanalysis, nothing but a soothing yet hopeless purring. In the worst commercial circumstances, good films can still be produced, films that modify the arrangements of desire, that "change life," while, for quite some time now, there have been no worthwhile psychoanalytic sessions, discoveries, books.

Translated by Gianna Quach

1. One could speak here of "film viewing-acts" in symmetry with the "speech-acts" studied by John Searle.
2. "One offers you beautiful images, but in order to entice you: at the same time that you believe that you are having a treat, you absorb the ideology necessary to the reproduction of the relations of production. One dissimulates historical reality for you, one camouflages it under a similitude of convention that is not just tolerable, but fascinating: so much so that you no longer even need to dream, nor have the right to do so, because your dreams could be nonconformist: one gives you the kind of packaged dream that disturbs nothing: tailor-made fantasies, an agreeable phantasmagoria that puts you in tune with your unconscious, for it is understood that your consconcious must be given its due, from the time when you are knowledgeable enough to draw upon it and beg for it. Cinema today puts at your disposal a house unconscious perfectly ideologized." Mikel Dufrene in *Cinema, Theory and Reading* (Paris: Klincksieck, 1973).
3. With his theory of the little object *a*, Lacan came to treat partial objects as logico-mathematic entities ("There is a mathème of psychoanalysis").
4. One should take up again the analysis of Bettini and Cassetti, who distinguished the notion of iconicity from that of analogism: the filmic syntagmatic, in some way, "analogizes" the icons which are transported by the unconscious. See "La sémiologie des moyens de communications audio-visuels," *Cinéma* (Paris: Klincksieck, 1973).
5. The psychoanalyst is somewhat in the position of the spectator at the cinema: he assists in the unfolding of a montage that one fabricates especially for him.
6. With television, the effect of deterritorialization seems attenuated, but perhaps it is still more underhanded: one bathes in a minimum of light, the machine is before you, like an amicable interlocutor, it's a family affair; in the Pullman car, one visits the abyssal profundities of the unconscious, then one switches to advertising and the news. The aggression is, in fact, even more violent than anywhere else; one bends unconsciously to the socio-political coordinates, to a type of modelization without which capitalist industrialized societies probably could not function.

19

CINEMA FOU

ÉLIX GUATTARI: What seems interesting to me with regard to this film, *Badlands* [1973, by Terence Malick], is that it shows us a story of *amour fou*, which is precisely what the critics did not see. I think that this makes people nervous. There are color elements, of blue, that are really agonizing throughout. It is a film about mad love and people refuse to accept these two dimensions of love and madness in combination. If there weren't all the murders, everything that makes one compare the film to *Billy the Kid, The Wild Bunch, Bonnie and Clyde,* etc., this would be an avant-garde film and it wouldn't get shown anywhere. In fact, the story is only there to support a schizophrenic journey. At every turn, we are on the edge of madness. It is this constant crossing of borders that seems perfectly conveyed to me. What the critics retained, in short, was the idea that this guy gets unhinged by dint of imitating James Dean. But things don't happen like that at all. The first thing that one has to realize is that the boy, Kit, should never be separated from the girl, Holly. They make up a sort of double arrangement. Certain behaviors of Holly belong to the schizo-process of Kit, although she herself is not schizophrenic. Conversely, certain behaviors of Kit belong to the completely average, normal world of Holly. Hence, it's absolutely impossible to separate the normal and the pathological. What is paradoxical is that the entire film is built around the idea that the guy is not really mad. The proof is that he goes to the electric chair. And yet, his madness, the fact that he has a screw loose, etc., is constantly alluded to. For her part,

Holly is presented as a steady girl. For example, she says: "I'll never let myself get carried away with another dare-devil again." Second negation after madness: love. We are shown a love story which is totally beyond stereotypes, a kind of extraordinary schizo love. For example, when Kit has just killed Holly's father, she says to him, "Don't worry," and gives him a small slap that is both nagging and reassuring. Or again when they fuck for the first time, Kit pretends to smash his hand, a typical schizo act. She tells him: "You're making fun of me, you don't care how I feel." But his indifference is only apparent; one senses he is so sure of his love that it never occurs to him to doubt her. It is only at the end of the film, when she ends up leaving him, that there is this very beautiful scene in which he angrily threatens to shoot her. But finally, he makes an imaginary rendezvous with her knowing full well he'll not see her again.

There are two ways of considering the world of schizo-desire: the infra-personal level of desiring machines—how the world is organized with systems of intensity—of colors, impressions, appearances—and the supra-personal level, in direct contact with the *socius*.

I picked out several elements in these two categories. The moment when he hits a can of food in the street, the moment when he's in love, and the moment when he listens to seashells and sees Holly coming as a white form. All this remains sort of "normal." But there is also the moment when he shoots at the fish, or shoots at the balloon, or shoots at the tires, and a series of completely bizarre behaviors such as the theme of the stones that one finds throughout the film. There are also explicitly crazy acts, acts of agony: when he kills Holly's father and puts his body in the basement, he takes up a toaster that reappears several times in the film; when he puts Cato's body in a cool place and begins turning round and round in a sort of military march with completely discordant gestures; and finally, when he makes a record and then burns it.

There are also scenes of schizo humor. At one moment he says: "We could have stopped the train by putting the car in front." And then there is this incredible scene when he locks up the two guys who come into Cato's house by accident. He shoots twice and says: "You think I got 'em? I don't want to know." Another high point of the film, in my opinion, is when, refering to the owner of a villa whom he has shut up with a deaf person, he says: "They were lucky, these two." At that point one realizes that, in fact, he remembers every detail, that he is not at all confused.

Another very important theme is the loss of objects. It begins in the closed off family circle, and then assumes a cosmic perspective when some objects float toward the sky in a balloon, when he buries other objects in the ground so that they can be found a few hundred years later. When things begin to go badly for him, Kit looks at other objects that he has kept in a suitcase and says to someone: "You can take them." He keeps a children's book. At the end of the film, he gives away his pencil, his pen, etc. It is like an expanding universe. It goes in every direction, this really is a schizo thing. All the coordinates, all the values explode all over the place. This starts with the fire which is a kind of schizo *jouissance* as well, a desire for annihilation.

Now, let us take some examples in the domain I called the supra-personal level, in direct contact with the *socius*. The characters, for example, make reflections of the kind: "You see, we've made waves, the two of us." It is clear that what they are aiming at, then, is the stupidity of society, the stupidity of the police. It is the whole James Dean dimension, the whole paranoid dimension. He dumps on us all the trash about bounty hunters, the Commies, the atomic bomb.... Same thing when he reconstructs a camp, like one in Vietnam, when he speaks in the cassette recorder: one must follow the elders, etc. Completely reactionary....

Q: You say "he is schizo," you say "he is reactionary."

FG: Schizo or paranoid, it's of little importance; he is reactionary as soon as he enters the field of dominant significations. At the level of intensities, where you don't know if you are man, woman, plant, or whatever, you stand directly in relations of desire, the relations of love with Holly. One no longer knows who is who, or who speaks to whom. Everything becomes an inter-relational fabric—the eyes, the machines, the gestures. At the level of a-signifying connections that escape the everyday world, one identifies something, one says to oneself: "Here is a funny thing; yes, well, I didn't see it," and then one goes on to something else. At the level where significations solidify—"I am a cop; I am a man; you are a woman, hence you do not drive; you are a cop, I shoot you face to face; you are a bounty hunter, I shoot you from behind"—there are double-entry tables that serve to classify all people and roles. At this moment he is completely reactionary. He organizes his whole life in exact symmetry with the girl's father; he is as much of a bastard as the girl's father or the police. The schizo is an individual who can be in direct contact with the unconscious in the social field, but who can also function in a paranoid mode, openly seeing through the stupidity of the police: "You are so proud to have arrested me, you think you're heroes." He understands immediately. He is in the unconscious of others. He deciphers American society. Because in reality, he does not take himself at all for James Dean. It is the police, in fact....

Q: Yes, twice, he is compared to James Dean. It is the girl at the beginning who says: "I liked him because he made me think of James Dean." It is the cops in the end, after having arrested him, who say: "You are like James Dean."

FG: Yes, his favorite hero is I don't remember who.

Q: He wants to be Nat King Cole. It is not at all the same as James Dean.

FG: He wants to sing. That is the world of crystallized people. They are grimacing, like TV stars. But as soon as you go beyond that, then it is a marine or airy world, a world of intensities. One goes there because the air is purer; it is the sand, the colors, the caresses. They say (the critics) that he treats her like an animal. That's wrong, it's an absolutely marvellous love story.

Q: There's another aspect of the film we have to talk about, the political aspect. The young cop who arrests him acts exactly like him.

FG: Exactly. He arrests him, then he shoots at him just to be mean, to scare him.

Q: It's the same type of stupidity. At a given moment, society becomes completely crazy. Because they are on the run, sheriffs accompany the kids to school; troops guard the central bank because there are rumors that they were going to attack it. Holly says: "It's as if we were Russians." It's a critique of American society.

FG: In *Night of the Living Dead* there was the same mass phenomenon. Good Americans all go out with their guns and end up shooting this poor black guy who had nothing to do with anything.

Q: At first, one doesn't have to see this guy as being crazy.

FG: He is no more crazy at the beginning than at the end, or he is crazy all the time, it's just the way you look at it. *Amour fou* is madness no matter what. He says: "Me, I can lay all the girls, I have no problem, but you are something else"; or he says: "Besides, fucking, fucking, who cares? Yeah, yeah, it was very good." He doesn't give a shit for stories about fucking. No, it is really the story of a great love. A love that goes right through people. The father's on his back? Good, well, he shoots him. Too bad, he shouldn't have been there!

Q: It's not like that, you're rigging the story a little. At the beginning, this guy is normal.

FG: Absolutely not normal.

Q: He's a poor bum, a garbage collector, and he is not so proud of it. Besides, when the girl asks him what he does, he says: "I'm afraid to get up early in the morning, so I work as a garbage collector," and then afterwards he's fired from his garbage job and works on a farm. He accepts the first job the employment agency offers him; he's the kind of guy who'll take anything, not a rebel in any way. He goes out with a girl and the father doesn't want him to go out with her because she shouldn't go out with a guy of his social class. Already there, society blunders. The father prevents him from seeing the girl. They see each other anyway. Then the father kills the girl's dog to punish her. This is the first act of madness in the film. It is the father who commits it. That's what the guy is up against. So what does he do, he goes to see the father and says to him: "Sir, I've a lot of respect for your daughter. I don't see why you won't let me see her, and if one day, she no longer wants to see me, I'll let her go, I promise you, etc." and the father tells him to piss off. Then, at that point, he goes to see the girl. No one is home, he ends up entering the house, but really by chance....

FG: No, not at all. He says: "I figured everything out."

Q: He thinks the girl is there.

FG: He is armed, and he says, "I figured everything out."

It triggers a kind of infernal machine of which he is the prisoner. It ends up going badly, but he already had figured it might go badly, because of taking the risk of entering the girl's house, of packing up and leaving and all that....

Q: They all have guns in this film. That's where I really see the thing about American madness. There isn't a single guy who isn't armed. If he kills the father, it's in self-defense, because the father says to him: "You entered my house. I'm handing you over to the police for armed robbery." It's twenty years; he's got to kill the father.

FG: I'm sorry, I don't agree with you. Let's be precise. He's as crazy at the beginning as at the end, neither more nor less. Madness coincides with the schizo journey, with *amour fou*. From the moment he sees the girl, a machine of *amour fou* is triggered. He manages to get fired from his job. He wants to see her again, but because she tells him, "I don't hang out with garbage collectors," he comes back with a proper job.

Q: He doesn't improve. He goes to work and his boss tells him, "You're fired!"

FG: Yes, but—you understand—it's one thing if the general framework unleashes behaviors of panic, of agony, of typical madness. It's a way of making clear what is already apparent from the beginning. Remember how he behaves at the beginning: "You want shoes? A dollar! You want to eat the dead dog? Give me a cigarette?" He says this to the guy with whom he picks garbage. Is all this nothing? Is it normal? All this is of no consequence. Remember, all of a sudden, he leaves: "Oh, shit. I've worked enough for today," etc. He is crazy all the time, if one looks closely. And Holly certainly knows it. Before agreeing to leave with him, she says to herself: "I love him, but he's totally crazy! How he treats me, he's weird."

Q: Yes, she often says it. She says it to the rich guy; she says it to the girl he's going to kill....

FG: At the beginning, all this is of no consequence because nobody's bothering him. When passion and repression come along, it's a catastrophe, it's as if he had been put in an asylum. You take a guy who is a bit mad, you put him in an asylum, either you or me, and he becomes completely crazy!

Q: We are shown the kind of society that makes this guy totally crazy. He's crazy and he makes the society crazy, and at the same time, he's the perfect cop, he is respectful of the established order.

FG: There, I'm sorry, one must avoid a major misinterpretation. A paranoiac is not necessarily a reactionary.

Q: Why is a paranoiac not a reactionary?

FG: Because a guy who starts talking to you about Hitler, Joan of Arc, or whoever, he borrows, let's say, semiotic elements in the social field. He is no more reactionary than a kid who says: "I'll pull the head off my little brother," or "I'll kill mum," or who will do anything to annoy you. One cannot say that he is reactionary. The paranoiac-libido is so entangled in its molecular elements with the schizo-libido that it makes no sense to divide people into good or bad, reactionary or progressive. Kids in neighborhood gangs who wear Hitlerian insignia on their backs are not fascists; fascists are White Suprematists, they are structured organisms. It's a fact that representations of the *socius*, reactionary representations, are conveyed both in one and in the other. You find unconscious, reactionary elements of the *socius* in your dreams. Sometimes you also have disgusting dreams. You look for what is most rotten in the *socius*, but what you select are semiotic chains that are all put together outside. This does not mean that you are a fascist or that the dream is fascist, it proves nothing.

Q: There is their madness, when one presses them. The father is not dead and the girl says: "Let's call the doctor." Then he says: "No, forget it." She says: "Yes, and I'll tell 'em what happened"—implying, of course, that if one tells what happened, nothing will happen, because when the others find out the way things happened, they'll realize he isn't guilty. And he replies: "That won't do," i.e., in any case they won't believe it. It's the system; it doesn't quite fit your interpretation.

FG: Yes, but I was careful to say at the beginning...

Q: ...that the story was only there to make you accept the rest....

FG: ...because there is something that doesn't fit. Kit, after all, is a guy who's pretty together. In various circumstances, he shows that he's an excellent organizer. He panics at the scene of the first murder—that of the father—because he'd planned everything in order to leave with the girl. He took a gun, but hadn't foreseen that it might turn out like that. But then later he thinks things out in detail. There is always a bit of improvisation, but as far as the essential is concerned, nothing is left to chance. It is there that, in my opinion, the film blunders. The way the character has been defined, it's not at all obvious that he would end up shooting guys around like this, systematically. The second time with Cato is still understandable, because he is scandalized that Cato talks nonsense to him (the story of gold pieces buried in the fields, etc.). He is terribly angry, a shot is fired as happened with Holly's father. He is infuriated by all the bullshit. The other murders seem really forced to fit the story.

Q: You don't say it's a film about a schizo. You say it's a schizo film.

FG: It's a schizo film. I think critics don't tolerate things like this. They have to put this somewhere.

Q: There is an interview with the author.

FG: An interview? Where?

Q: Here, in *Positif*. I don't think he mentions the word "schizo" even once.

FG: There isn't a sentence where he says the guy is crazy? He doesn't realize it himself?

Q: I don't think so. He says: "I thought of him and the girl as the sort of children you find in fairy tales; you see them in *Huckleberry Finn*, *Swiss Family Robinson*, and *Treasure Island*. They're lost in nature, they only know how to react to what is inside themselves. They do not communicate with the external world, they do not understand what others feel. Which doesn't mean they have no emotions, or that they are insensitive."

FG: Yes, it's really stupid, it's terrible.

(He takes *Positif* and glances through it.)

FG: This interview is really revolting. Yuk! It makes me puke!

Translated by David L. Sweet

20

NOT SO MAD

Q: What do you make of the new interest that the media, and particularly film, bring to the problem of madness?

FÉLIX GUATTARI: I don't think that this interest is completely new. Numerous films in the history of cinema have tackled this "problem." But the audience of these films, perhaps, has expanded. For example, the audience for *Asylum* has been substantial and has indirectly revealed an anti-psychiatric current. The same was already true of *Family Life*.

Q: Where does this expanded audience come from, and what does the public want?

FG: There are perhaps two sets of phenomena. First, a certain taste for a morbid aspect—not of madness, but of what one thinks of as madness: this is part of the same "modelling" system, the "popular" taste that one finds in detective or certain porno flicks. So, from this angle, nothing new. But one can also put forth the hypothesis that society is presently being racked by a whole series of "molecular" disturbances that are not yet visible on a large scale; it is shaped by transformations that effect basic institutional systems—schools, prisons, couples, women, immigrants, the mentally ill, homosexuals.... Long before certain spectacular uprisings occurred—as in the university in 1968 or in prisons—a whole underground was operating, a whole new sensibility was searching for itself. I get the impression that the general crisis in psychiatry—before it expressed itself on a large scale—started to shape opinions at all levels. It was in this context that filmmakers began to get interested in it.

Q: What do you think of the fact that *Fous à délier* [*Not So Mad*] came out when the second round of meetings of the International Anti-Psychiatry Network were being held?

FG: The "Bastille Day" team came asking us what sort of film we would like to have shown during these international meetings. The film of the Parma and Bellochio teams corresponded so well to the whole orientation of the Network that it served in some ways as an introduction for us. What's it all about? Until now, criticisms of psychiatry had come from madness "professionals": from psychiatrists, nurses, or less often, ex-patients. But often the language of these "specialists" was incomprehensible to the public at large, and sometimes, it must be said, it was counter-dependent upon the system itself. What is extraordinary about *Fous à délier* is that it is the people involved who really get the opportunity to speak. Its success is a credit to the "cinema of combat." I even think they expressed themselves better here than they could have done using some other mode of communication. I don't know how the Bellochio team succeeded in working so well with the different groups that speak in *Fous à délier:* children, educators, psychiatrists, militant groups; they always give the best of themselves. It's a small miracle; for once one does not have the feeling one is being presented with another "documentary"; people speak here in a way one is not used to hearing.

Q: How is such a result possible?

FG: I don't know. But there is obviously a whole new technology that is being experimented with, and this at all levels of production. Members of the Bellochio team explained, for example, that each sequence, each shot, was collectively discussed during the editing. It's up to the film people to answer your question. But it seems to me that what was achieved in this film goes far beyond the problems of psychiatry. Until now, cinema of mass distribution, or commercial cinema, has functioned like an enterprise of mystification, of enlistment, that consists in making people absorb, willingly or by force, dominant representations. But here, all of a sudden, one has the impression it is just the reverse, that a cinema of the masses can become a form of expression and struggle that is even more effective than discourses, meetings, pamphlets....

Q: After having seen *Fous à délier,* I wonder if it isn't abnormal to want to return such patients to work, since it is work, in fact, that alienates.

FG: You are right. In France today, certain organizations attempt to "re-adapt by work" (according to American methods of conditioning) the mentally retarded, the insane, the handicapped. At Sainte-Anne's Hospital, "scientific" methods of conditioning are also experimented with. There is a major danger here: to think that work as such can be therapeutic is absurd. What is at issue in *Fous à délier* is completely different. The workers of Parma express themselves very clearly on this point: they don't believe that work is the issue, but the fact that all these marginal types have the chance to become people like everyone else. It is not the work that allows them to be this way, it is the relations they succeed in establishing with the workers. It is the human warmth of these relations that is so well conveyed in the film.

Q: Does cinema appear to you to be a minor art?

FG: Yes, if one specifies that a "minor" art is an art that serves people who constitute a minority, and that it is not at all pejorative. A major art is an art at the service of power. Hence, I wonder if a certain number of films like *Fous à délier*, *Ce gamin-là*, *Coup pour coup*, *La Ville bidon*, *Paul's Story*, *Asylum* do not announce a new era in the history of cinema. A minor cinema for minorities, in one form or another, and for the rest of us, too: we all participate in one of these minorities, more or less. Perhaps now a potential public exists that could encroach on the terrain of cinematographic distribution controlled by the big industry. Some spectacular successes have shown that the public wants more than what it is habitually presented with. Perhaps a large proportion of the public would be attracted to a new cinema, but only on condition that filmmakers manage to get away from an elitist style, a language either completely cut off from the public, or completely demagogical.

Translated by Gianna Quach

21

LIKE THE ECHO OF
A COLLECTIVE MELANCHOLIA

In many ways the film *Germany in Autumn* will leave its mark in the history of the cinema or, rather, of "engaged" cinema. First, because it is a collective work which presents not a juxtaposition of sequences made by different filmmakers but rather the fruit of discussions and elaborations in common. Next, because it was made in the heat of the moment, immediately after the events of Autumn 1977, which allowed for the creation of a remarkably authentic atmosphere. One feels, even when the sequences are acted out, that the actors and directors (who sometimes play themselves) are still under the sway of these events in such a way that a truth passes directly, with no visible break between the elements of reporting, fiction, and documentary.

This attempt, call it analytic, to go beyond auteur cinema suggests to me a new possibility for grasping collective emotional elements through film. This kind of "analysis" occurs around two poles.

The first involves the manipulation of events by the mass media. Schleyer's death, the skyjacking to Mogadishu, and the deaths of the inmates of Stammheim prison have been transformed into an emotional charge placed entirely at the disposal of social control and repression. The reference to Sophocles' *Antigone* becomes a key to the film, the events in Germany that autumn taking on the proportions of ancient drama. In this light, the deaths of Hans Martin Schleyer and of the RAF prisoners would function as an outlet or an exorcism in two acts, a double sacrifice meant to internalize a collective guilt that goes back to Nazism and beyond that in a violence supposedly essential to the German mentality.

The other pole of the film consists in the authors' attempts to counteract this collective intoxication by the media, to obstruct the "infernal machine" of guilt inducement—to paraphrase here Jean Cocteau on Oedipus. It is essentially a matter of getting out of the RAF-West Germany confrontation, of the repression-reprisals cycle, of the quasi-symmetrical simplification of ideologies in opposition. For the most part, the filmmakers manage to keep their own reactions on the most immediate level: on the level of what they felt and what they saw camera in hand; they film their squabbles with their peers, they stage their own fantasies. On such a serious topic, in such a dramatic context, that takes guts. And yet the result is no less serious. And no doubt much more truthful than any other means of inquiry or reporting, or propaganda film. Through each sequence, we are witnessing the proliferation of the escape routes, sometimes minor, laughable, or bizarre, that personally enabled the authors to become disengaged, to a certain extent, from this Manicheaen drama. The very personal behavior which in any event defies current political classifications—Fassbinder embracing a friend, a young woman professor starting out with a shovel over a frozen field, a child watching in astonishment the burial of the Stammheim prisoners, a young man remaining seated near the gravediggers and the police after the procession's departure, a young woman and her little daughter on the road home—constitutes so many elements of life, elements of survival, so many flashes, escapes from the so-called "tragic destiny" of the German people. This in no way implies that the problematic of repressive power is left aside, nor that of social control, of the media's role in daily fascism. In this respect, the film is quite explicit in its descriptions and denunciations. But its main objective lies elsewhere. On these points, opinions are already crystallized, and one explanation more or less will hardly make a noticeable difference. What is questioned here is the collective emotional context in which these opinions take shape, that is, one of the essential components in the massive foundation of any opinion that becomes law.

In this domain, the real consequence of "terrorist" actions of the RAF/Red Brigades type does not at all seem to have been taken into account by the leaders of these movements. Schematically, two positions come face to face on this question of armed struggle, in the heart of the European far left. The first, close to that of the RAF, considering that current social struggles go beyond the national and onto the international scale, and especially those between German-American imperialism and the Third World, deems it appropriate to destabilize the bastions of capitalism by all available means, beginning with armed underground warfare, and to reveal the intrinsically fascist nature of their democratic bourgeois regimes, while waiting for the avant-garde of the working classes, together with the oppressed masses of the Third World, once more to grasp hold of the old torch of the struggle for socialist revolution. The second position, which can be compared to that of the so-called "spontaneist" tendency, represented in the film by Horst Mahler, former "terrorist" practicing his self-criticism, consists on the contrary in denouncing, and rightly so, a "politics of the worst" which would only lead away from its initial objectives.

But this second view quickly plunges one into social-democratic, humanist reappropriation and ends by condemning all violent acts in the name of a morality that accommodates itself to even greater acts of violence perpetrated in its own name. It promotes the idea that the only means of social transformation are those sanctioned by the law.

In its own way, each of these two positions seems to mask the true meaning of the new forms of underground action which are developing all over Europe and which seemingly are becoming one of the specific features of the blocked political situation characteristic of capitalist regimes.

What a film like *Germany in Autumn* brings to light, in an original way, is that the intense emotional charge associated with the "terrorist phenomenon" has become a fundamental given of current political strategies. Like it or not, politics today has become inseparable from the collective affects molded and transmitted by the media, which constitutes a means of subjection crossing over classes and nations, and at the heart of which it is very difficult to separate the manipulated fantasies from socio-economic realities.

All formations of power, at whatever level, are the object and/or agent of this manipulation of the media "material." Thus when young men and women rush headlong down the road of "terrorism," they don't do so only because of ideological systems, but also as delegates or sacrificial offerings of a subjective movement that surpasses them on all sides. Their actions, their feelings are "in touch" with those who approve of them, but also with all those layers of militants, of young revolutionaries, who have found no end to the struggles they have led for fifteen years. Furthermore, it is the passivity of the "swine," of the meek who comprise public opinion, which is worked on from within by their spectacular and desperate gestures. They, in return, manipulate the information and images transmitted by the media, and use their prestige to force the hand of those with whom they rub elbows.

In my view, what should be questioned is not the principle of armed struggle, nor its methods which are a part of all revolutionary movements, but, at the heart of each specific situation, its real influence on the totality of anticapitalist struggles. Clearly, the liquidation of a leader like Schleyer could never derail the functioning of the system. Instead, by providing power with the opportunity to fully deploy its police brigades and its media arsenals, it helped to further ensnare millions among the exploited. In other words, the real drama is not that a man was killed, but that these actions were conducted in a way that simply does not break free of the repressive bourgeois system, fascist assassinations, or kidnappings carried out by unofficial police gangs, and that in the final account, their only result will have been to echo the collective melancholy that has present-day Germany in its grip. As far as I am concerned, I know of nothing more sinister or odious than those photos of Schleyer or Moro,[1] with their little placards on their chests. While I refuse to judge whether or not their executions were well-founded—to judge their judges—I cannot stand this type of operation; for it is this sort of image, propelled across the media, which leads to a legitimate feeling of pity for those who are its objects and of disgust and revulsion toward those who are its authors.

Capitalism has only managed to consolidate those very bastions that the RAF and the Red Brigades claim to shake, insofar as it has managed to develop a majority consensus founded on social ultra-conservatism, the protection of acquired advantages and the systematic misinterpretation of anything that falls outside of corporate or national interests. And whatever works toward the isolation of individuals, what-ever reinforces their feelings of impotence, whatever makes them feel guilty and dependent on the state, on collective agen-cies and their extensions—which the unions and traditional leftist parties are fast becoming—feeds this consensus. To claim to lead a revolutionary movement without attacking these phenomena of mass manipulation is an absurdity. While the secret war conducted by the industrial powers along the north-south axis to keep the Third World in tow is indeed the main issue, it should not make us forget that there is another north south axis, which encircles the globe and along which conflicts of an equally essential nature are played out, involving the powers of the state and oppressed nationalities, immigrant workers, the unemployed, the "marginals," the "non-guaranteed"[2] and the "standardized" wage-earners, the people of the cities and of the barrios, of the favellas, the ghettoes, the shanty-towns, engaging the opposition of races, sexes, classes, age-groups, etc. To conduct this other war, to insure its social and mental control over this whole everyday, desiring world, capitalism mobilizes tremendous forces. To ignore this kind of opposition or to consider it of secondary importance is to condemn all other forms of social struggle led by the traditional Workers' Movement to impotence or reappropriation. Like it or not, in today's world, violence and the media work hand in glove. And when a revolutionary group plays the game of the most reactionary media, the game of collective guilt, then it has been mistaken: mistaken in its target, mistaken in its method, mistaken in its strategy, mistaken in its theory, mistaken in its dreams....

To express complete solidarity with the victims of capitalist repression—with all of the victims—in no way implies exonerating the aberrations that led to the unconscionable spectacles of the skyjacking to Mogadishu or the supposed People's Courts that deliberated in a cellar! The inane reproduction of the state's model of "justice" and repression, the revolting use of the media, the narrow-minded sectarianism, the manipulation of the "fellow travellers" are not questions of secondary importance. The merit of a film like *Germany in Autumn* is that it helps us to see these problems in their entirety. It not only gives us a virulent critique of German society, but also initiates an examination of underground armed struggle on its own terms. In this last matter, its criticisms still remain too timid and unfocused. Again one feels the weight of the event and the fear of reappropriation by the powers that be.

But it does touch on the main point, which is the morbid dramatization spawned by the altogether absurd confrontation between a monstrous state power and pitiful politico-military machines. The authors of this film are not shooting with a P.38, but with a most singular expression of desire, the right to an unrestrained word, regardless of the pressures, regardless of the dramatic, or rather tragic, character of the situation today is an essential prerequisite of any effective revolutionary advance.

Translated by Mark Polizzotti

1. Aldo Moro, President of the Christian Democrats, was kidnapped by the Red Brigades and executed in Rome on March 16, 1978. [Ed.]
2. By the term "Guaranteeism" is meant all the victories achieved by traditional proletarian struggles on the level of wages, job security, working conditions, social services. Cf. *Autonomia: Post-Political Politics*, Semiotext(e), III, vol. 3, 1980. Edited by Sylvére Lotringer and Christian Marrazzi. [Ed.]

22

MARXISM AND FREUDIANISM
NO LONGER DISTURB ANYONE

Question: How, in your opinion, can or should the works of Freud and Marx complement one another?

FÉLIX GUATTARI: Can or should... The problem is that they have effectively done so. At least in the university, where the concoction of "cocktails" mixing the two in various proportions seems to be the guarantee of an "appropriate" political affiliation. Reread Marx, return to Freud, promote their peaceful coexistence... a whole program. And then isn't it marvellous to be able to serve the people this way, on the sole front of "theoretical combat" without having to leave our lecturehall or our office?

No, definitely, this kind of question makes me very suspicious. Freudo-Marxism is the busy work of the Victor Cousin type of academics of our time. The academician always returns to the same devices for shunning reality, by taking refuge behind the exegesis and interpretation of texts. But behind Marx and Freud, behind "Marxology" and "Freudology," there is the shitty reality of the Communist movement, of the psychoanalytic movement. That's where we should start and that's where we should always return. And when I speak of shit, it is hardly a metaphor: capitalism reduces everything to a fecal state, to the state of undifferentiated and unencoded flux, out of which each person in his private, guilt-ridden way must pull out his part. Capitalism is the regime of generalized inter-changeability: anything in the "right" proportions can equal anything else. Take Marx and Freud for example, reduced to a state of dogmatic mush; they can be introduced into the system without presenting any risk to it. Marxism and Freudianism, carefully neutralized by the institutions of the worker's move-ment, the psychoanalytic movement, and the university, not only no longer disturb anyone, but have actually become the guar-antors of the established order, a demonstration via reduction to the absurd, that it is no longer possible to seriously unsettle that order. One might object that these theories shouldn't be blamed for deviations in their application; that the original message has been betrayed; that precisely it is necessary to return to the sources, review the faulty translations, etc. That's the trap of fetishism. There is no comparable example in any scientific domain of a similar respect for the texts and formu-lae pronounced by great scientists. Revisionism is the rule here. The process of relativizing, dissolving, and dislocating these established theories is permanent. Those which resist are constantly under attack. The ideal thing would not be to mum-mify them, but to leave them open to other constructs, all equally temporary, but better strengthened by such experimen-tation. *What counts in the long run is the use one makes of a theory.* Therefore, we cannot disregard the pragmatic imple-mentation of Marxism and Freudianism. We must start from existing practices in order to retrace the fundamental flaws of these theories insofar as, in one way or another, they lend themselves to distortions of that kind.

Theoretical activity escapes only with difficulty the propensity of capitalism to ritualize and retrieve any minimally subversive practice by cutting it off from its libidinal invest-ments; only by confronting real struggles can theoretical activ-ity hope to leave its ghetto. The primary task of a theory of "desire" must be to discern the possible ways in which it can invade the social field, rather than guarantee the quasi-mystical exercise of psychoanalytical eavesdropping such as it has evolved since Freud. Correlatively, any theoretical development bearing upon class struggle at this time should be concerned primarily with its connection with libidinal production and its impact on the creativity of the masses. Marxism, in all its versions, excludes desire, and loses its guts with bureaucracy and humanism, while Freudianism, from its very beginning, has not only been alien to class struggle, but moreover has continued to distort its first discoveries about desire by trying to lead it back, handcuffed, to the familial and social norms of the establishment. The refusal to confront these fundamental deficiencies, the attempt to mask them, lead one to believe that the internal limits of these theories are actually insurmountable.

There are two ways to absorb these theoretical statements; the academic one, which takes or leaves the text in its integrity, and the revolutionary one, which takes and leaves it at the same time, doctoring it for its own use in order to elucidate its own co-ordinates and guide its practice. The only question is to try to make a text work. And, from this point of view, what has always been alive in Marxism and in Freudianism, in their initial stages, is not the coherence of their statements, but the fact that the very act of enunciating them represents a breaking off, a way of telling Hegelian dialectics, bourgeois political economy, academic psychology, and psychiatry of the time, etc., to go to hell.

Even the idea of the possible coupling of these two separate bodies, Marxism and Freudianism, falsifies the perspective. Some bits of a "dismembered" Marxism can and should converge with a theory and practice of desire; bits of a "dismembered" Freudianism can and should converge with a theory and practice pertaining to class struggle. Even the idea of a separation between a private exercise of desire and public struggles involving opposite interests, leads implicitly to integration into capitalism. Private ownership of the means of production is intrinsically bound up with the appropriation of desire by the individual, the family, and the social order. One begins by neutralizing the worker's access to desire, through familial castration, the lures of consumption, etc., in order to appropriate his capacity for social work. To sever desire from work: such is the primary imperative of capitalism. To separate political economy from libidinal economy: such is the mission of those theoreticians who serve capitalism. Work and desire are in contradiction only in the framework of relations of production, of well-defined social and familial relations: those of capitalism and bureaucratic socialism.

There is no alienation of desire, no psychosexual complexes that may be radically and permanently separated from repression and psychosocial complexes. For example, to tell the present-day Chinese that their Maoism would continue to depend upon a universal Oedipus would be the same as considering Maoism itself as something eternal, always being reborn from its own ashes. But, of course, history just doesn't work like that. A revolutionary in France after May '68, with regard to desire, is of a completely different race than his father in June '36.[1] There is no possible Oedipal relationship between them. Neither rivalry, nor identification. No continuity in change. And if it is indeed true that the rupture is that radical, theoreticians of society and those of psychoanalysis would do well to prepare themselves for a serious recycling.

Translated by Janis Forman

1. The "Popular Front" of June 1936, which put Léon Blum at the head of a socialist government, is another major landmark of the French Left. [Ed.]

23

BEYOND THE PSYCHOANALYTICAL UNCONSCIOUS

Individual and collective behavior are governed by multiple factors. Some are of a rational order, or appear to be, like those that can be treated in terms of power relations or economics. Others, however, appear to depend principally on nonrational motivations whose ends are difficult to decipher and which can sometimes even lead individuals or groups to act in ways that are contrary to their obvious interests.

There are numerous ways to approach this "other side" of human rationality. One can deny the problem, or fall back on the usual logic regarding normalcy and proper social adaptation. Considered that way, the world of desires and passions leads to nothing in the end, except to the "jamming" of objective cognition, to "noise" in the sense that communication theory uses the term.[1] From this point of view, the only course of action is to correct these defects and facilitate a return to prevailing norms. However, one can also consider that these behaviors belong to a different logic, which deserves to be examined as such. Rather than abandon them to their apparent irrationality they can be treated as a kind of basic material, as an ore, whose life-essential elements, and particularly those relating to humanity's desires and creative potentialities, can be extracted.

According to Freud, this is what the original task of psychoanalysis was supposed to be. But to what extent has it achieved this objective? Has it really become a new "chemistry" of the unconscious psyche, or has it remained a sort of "alchemy" whose mysterious powers have waned with time, and whose simplifications and "reductionism" (whether in its orthodox currents or structuralist offshoots) are less and less tolerable?

After years of training and practice, I have come to the conclusion that if psychoanalysis does not radically reform its methods and its theoretical references it will lose all credibility, which I would find regrettable on several counts. In fact, it would hardly matter to me if psychoanalytic societies, schools, or even the profession itself were to disappear, so long as the analysis of the unconscious reaffirms its legitimacy and renews its theoretical and practical modalities.

The very first thing which must be thought anew is the conception of the unconscious itself. Today the unconscious is supposed to be part of everone's essential baggage. No one doubts its existence. It is spoken about in the same way as memory or will, without anyone wondering about what it really is. The unconscious is supposed to be something at the back of the head, a kind of black box where mixed feelings and weird afterthoughts accumulate; something that should be handled with care.

Certainly professional psychoanalysts are not content with such a vague consideration. Explorers or guardians of a domain they consider to be their own, covetous of their prerogatives, they consider that access to the world of the unconscious can only be made after long and costly preparation, with a sort of strictly controlled asceticism. In order to succeed, didactic analysis, like ordinary analysis, demands much time and the use of a very particular apparatus (e.g., transference between analyst and analysand, controlling anamneses, exploring identifications and fantasies, lifting resistances through interpretation, etc.).

No one seems to wonder why this unconscious, supposedly loged at the core of every person, and referred to in connection with a great variety of domains like neuroses, psychoses, daily life, art, social life, etc., is the exclusive concern of specialists. So many things that seemed to belong unquestionably to everyone, like water, air, energy and art, are now about to become the property of new industrial and commercial branches. So why not fantasies and desire as well?

I am interested in a totally different kind of unconscious. It is not the unconscious of specialists, but a region everyone can have access to with neither distress nor particular preparation: it is open to social and economic interactions and directly engaged with major historical currents. It is not centered exclusively around the family quarrels of the tragic heroes of ancient Greece. This unconscious, which I call "schizoanalytic," as opposed to the psychoanalytic subconscious, is inspired more by the "model" of psychosis than that of neurosis on which psychoanalysis was built. I call it "machinic" because it is not necessarily centered around human subjectivity, but involves the most diverse material fluxes and social systems. One after the other, the old territories of Ego, family, profession, religion, ethnicity, etc., have been undone and deterritorialized. The realm of desire can no longer be taken for granted. This is because the modern unconscious is constantly manipulated by the media, by collective apparatuses and their cohorts of technicians. It is no longer enough to simply define it in terms of an intrapsychic entity, as Freud did when he was conceiving his different topics. Would it suffice to say that the machinic unconscious is more impersonal or archetypical than the traditional unconscious? Certainly not, since its "mission" is precisely to circumscribe individual singularities more closely, in order to tie them down more strictly to social relations and historical realities of the "machinic age." Simply put, the questions raised by the unconscious no longer fall squarely within the realm of psychology. They involve the most fundamental choices for both society and desire, "existential choices" in a world which is criss-crossed by a myriad of machinic systems that expropriate the processes of singularization and fold them back over standardized—real as much as imagined—territorialities.

This model of the unconscious is not opposed point by point to the old psychoanalytic model. It takes up some of its elements, or, at least, reshuffles them as variants or exemplars. Actually, an unconscious pattern really does exist within an intrapsychic "familialized" space where certain mental materials elaborated during early stages of psychic life are tied together. No one can deny that such a place where hidden and forbidden desires, a sort of secret kingdom, a state within the state exists, which seeks to impose its law over the whole psychism and its behaviors. But this formula, a private individualized and Oedipal unconscious, assumes premier importance in developed societies where most of their power depends upon systems of guilt and internalizations of norms. Still, I repeat, a new kind of analysis must discover and promote what could only be a variant to the notion of the unconscious, realigned according to other possiblities.

The Freudian model of the unconscious, one recalls, obeyed a double movement: (1) repulsing "representative drives" that the unconscious and the preconscious could not tolerate (utterances, images and forbidden fantasies); (2) attracting those which originate in always already repressed psychic formations (originary repression). Thus forbidden contents had first to travel through the conscious and the unconscious before falling into something like an "unconscious-discharge" governed by a particular syntax called the "primary processes" (for example the condensations and displacements at the heart of dreams). This double movement did not allow for creative processes that would be specific to the unconscious. (Freud:

"The dream-work is never creative.") Everything there was played out in advance, every possible path marked out: the psychoanalytic unconscious was programmed like destiny.

Instead of relying on such a binary mechanism—a system of repression proper and a system of originary repression—the schizoanalytic unconscious implies a proliferation made up not only of typical "part-objects" —the breast, the feces, the penis; or mathemes like Lacan's "a-object" —but also a multitude of singular entities, fluxes, territories and incorporeal universes, making up *functional arrangements* that are never reducible to universals.

To recapitulate some characteristics of the machinic unconscious:

1. It *is not* the exclusive seat of representative contents (representations of things or representations of words, etc.). Rather it *is* the site of *interaction between semiotic components and extremely diverse systems of intensity*, like linguistic semiotics, "iconic" semiotics, ethological semiotics, economic semiotics, etc. As a consequence, it no longer answers to the famous axiom formulated by Lacan, of being "structured like a language."

2. Its different components *do not depend upon a universal syntax*. The configuration of its contents and its systems of intensity (as these may be manifested in dreams, fantasies and symptoms) depend upon *processes of singularization* which necessarily resist reductive analytic descriptions, like castration or Oedipus complexes (or intrafamilial systematizations). Collective arrangements that relate to specific cultural or social contexts account for such machinic instances.

3. *Unconscious inter-individual relationships do not depend on universal structures* (like those that the disciples of Lacan try to base on a sort of "game theory" of intersubjectivity). Both imaginary and symbolic interpersonal relations obviously occupy a nodal point at the heart of unconscious

arrangements, but they don't account for them all. Other, no less essential dispositions, come from systems of abstract entities and concrete machines that operate outside human identifications. The machinic unconscious is like a department store—you can find whatever you want there. This explains both its subservience to consumer society, its rich creativity and openness to innovation.

4. The unconscious can fall back on a nostalgic imaginary, *open up to the here and now*, or take chances on the future. Archaic fixations on narcissism, the death instinct and the fear of castration can be avoided. They are not, as Freud assumed, the rock bottom of the whole edifice.

5. The machinic unconscious is not the same all over the world: *it evolves with history*. Obviously, the economy of desire of Malinowsky's Trobrianders is different from the inhabitants of Brooklyn, and the fantasies of Precolumbian Teotihuacans has little to do with those of contemporary Mexicans.

6. The structures of unconscious analytic enunciations do not necessarily require the services of the corporation of analysts. *Analysis can be pursued individually or collectively.* The notions of transference, interpretation and neutrality, based on a "typical cure," should also be revised. They are only admissible in very particular cases, within a very limited range of circumstances.

No matter what upheavals of history or technological and cultural transformations may be in store, isn't it inevitable that structural elements will always be found within unconscious transformations? Don't the oppositions self/other, man/woman, parent/child, etc., criss-cross in such a way as to constitute a kind of universal mathematic grid of the unconscious? But why should the existence of such a grid preclude the possibility of a diversity of unconsciousnesses? Even the people who are most open to a "schizoanalytic revision" sometimes come back to these kinds of questions. I should therefore emphasize several of the reasons that lead me to reject "universals" of expression as much as universals of content as bases for the unconscious.

One of Freud's major discoveries was to bring to light the fact that there is no negation in the unconscious, at least not the kind of negation that is found in the logic of consciousness. It is a mental world where rigid oppositions don't have to apply, where self and other, man and woman, parent and child can—and actually do—exist simultaneously in the same person. What matters then, is not the existence of reified, polarized entities, but rather processes that Gilles Deleuze and I have called "becomings." Becoming-women, becoming-plants, becoming-music, becoming-animals, becoming-invisible, becoming-abstract.... The "primary processes" of the Freudian unconscious (whose reductionist interpretations, based on normalized noetic structures patterned on dominant coordinates and significations we cannot condone) only gives us access to a universe of transformations of an incorporeal nature: when everything appears to be stratified and definitively crystalized, it introduces virtualities of meaning and praxis that are extrinsic to the opposition reality/representation.

For example, if it happpens that a patient tells his analyst about a problem concerning his boss or the President of the Republic, one can be sure that only mechanisms of paternal identification will be called forth. Behind the woman post–office official, or the female television announcer, will loom the maternal imago, or a universal structural matheme. More generally, behind all the forms that come to life around us, the different analytical schools only locate sexual symbols and references to symbolic castration. But in the long run, such a one-track reading obviously loses its appeal.

If the symbolic father is often lurking behind the boss—which is why one speaks of "paternalism" in various kinds of enterprises—there also often is, in a most concrete fashion, a boss or hierarchic superior behind the real father. In the unconscious, paternal functions are inseparable from the socio-professional and cultural involvements which sustain them. Behind the mother, whether real or symbolic, a certain type of feminine condition exists, in a socially defined imaginary context. Must I point out that children do not grow up cut off from the world, even within the family womb? The family is permeable to environmental forces and exterior influences. Collective infrastructures, like the media and advertising, never cease to interfere with the most intimate levels of subjective life. The unconscious is not something that exists by itself to be gotten hold of through intimate discourse. In fact, it is only a rhizome of machinic interactions, a link to power systems and power relations that surround us. As such, unconscious processes cannot be analyzed in terms of specific content or structural syntax, but rather in terms of enunciation, of *collective enunciative arrangements*, which, by definition, correspond neither to biological individuals nor to structural paradigms. Unconscious subjectivity engendered by these arrangements is not "ready made." It locates its processes of singularization, its subjective ensemble, within orders which differ greatly from each other (signs, incorporeal universes, energy, the "mechanosphere," etc.), according to open configurations, in the way that we speak today of opening up creative possibilities in the visual arts, in materials, substances, forms....

The customary psychoanalytical family-based reductions of the unconscious are not "errors." They correspond to a particular kind of collective enunciative arrangement. In relation to unconscious formation, they proceed from the particular micropolitics of capitalistic societal organization. An overly diversified, overly creative machinic unconscious would exceed the limits of "good behavior" within the relations of production founded upon social exploitation and segregation.

This is why our societies grant a special position to those who specialize in re-centering the unconscious onto the individuated subject, onto partially reified objects, where methods of *containment* prevent its expansion beyond dominant realities and significations. The impact of the scientific aspirations of techniques like psychoanalysis and family therapy should be considered as a gigantic industry for the normalization, adaption and organized division of the socius.

The workings of the social division of labor, the assignment of individuals to particular productive tasks, no longer depend solely on means of direct coercion, or capitalistic systems of semiotization (like monetary remuneration based on profit, etc.). They depend just as fundamentally on techniques modeling the unconscious through social infrastructures, the mass media and different psychological and behavioral devices. The deterritorialization of the libido by productive forces that support World Integrated Capitalism (WIC) effectively develops a kind of collective anguish, as a counterpoint to the scope of science and technology, resurrecting factors like religious ideologies, myths, archaisms, etc. It is more than probable to expect that despite the amplitude of subjective operations reterritorializing the socius and the imaginary by diverse forces of WIC (like capitalist regimes, socialist bureaucracies, Third World dictatorships, etc.), the machinic integration of humanity will continue. What we don't know yet are its eventual modalities. Will it continue to move at counter-currents to the creative lines of desire and the most fundamental human ends? Just consider the immense physical and moral misery that reigns over the greater part of this planet. On the other hand, will the economy of desire be able to harmonize itself to technical and scientific progress? Only a profound transformation of social relationships at every level, an immense movement by machines of desire to "get their hands on" technical machines, a "molecular revolution" correlative to analytical practices and new micropolitics, will enable such a readjustment. Even the outcome of the class struggle of the oppressed—the fact that they constantly risk being sucked into relations of domination—appears to be linked to such a perspective.

An analytic and micropolitical approach towards collective formations of desire should constantly renew its methods, diversify and enrich itself through contact with every domain of creation, so that it can become "everybody's business." In short, it must do everything that the psychoanalytic profession of today does not do.

Translated by Chet Wiener

1. In communication theory, "noise" is an element of anti-communication, like "static." [Ed.]

24

CAPITAL AS THE INTEGRAL OF POWER FORMATIONS

Capital is not an abstract category, it is a semiotic operator at the service of specific social formations. Its function is to record, balance, regulate and overcode the power formations inherent to developed industrial societies, power relations and the fluxes that make up the planet's overall economic powers. One can find systems of capitalization of power in the most archaic societies. These powers can assume multiple forms: capital of prestige, capital of magical power embodied in an individual, a lineage, an ethnic group. But only, it seems, in the capitalist mode of production has a general procedure of semiotization of such a capitalization became autonomous. It developed according to the two following axes:

—a deterritorialization of the local modes of semiotization of powers, which become subjected to a general system of inscription and quantification of power;

—a reterritorialization of the latter system onto a hegemonic power formation: the bourgeoisie of the Nation-states.

Economic capital, expressed in monetary, accounting, stock-market or other languages, always rests in the final analysis on mechanisms of differential and dynamic evaluation of powers confronting each other on a concrete terrain. An exhaustive analysis of a capital, whatever its nature, would therefore have to take into account extremely diversified components, dealing with services that are more or less monetarized, for instance sexual or domestic (presents, acquired advantages, "secondary benefits," pocket money, lump sums, etc.) as well as to gigantic international transactions, which, in the guise of operations of credit, investment, industrial implantations, cooperations, etc., are in fact nothing else than economico-strategic confrontations. In this regard, any overemphasis on Capital as a general equivalent, or as currencies tied down to systems of fixed parity, etc., can only mask the real nature of capitalist processes of subjugation and subjection, which involve social and micro-social power relations, power slippages, advances and withdrawals of one social formation in relation to another, or collective attitudes of inflationistic anticipation meant to conjure any loss of ground, or also, of imperceptible take-overs which, ultimately, will only be revealed in broad daylight. The standards of reference have no other function than that of calculation or relative identification, transitory regulation. A genuine quantification of powers could only rest on modes of semiotization directly plugged on to power formations and productive agencements (material as well as semiotic) tied down to local social coordinates.

I. MACHINIC LABOR AND HUMAN LABOR

The value of labor sold on the capitalist market depends on a quantitative factor—work-time—and on a qualitative factor—the average qualification of labor. In this second aspect of machinic subjection,[1] it cannot be circumscribed in individual terms. First, because the qualification of a human performance is inseparable from a particular machinic environment. Second, because its competence always depends on a collective agency of formation and socialization. Marx frequently speaks of work as resulting from a "collective worker"; but for him, such an entity remains a statistical one: the "collective worker" is an abstract character resulting from a calculation based on "average social labor." This operation allows him to overcome individual differences in the calculation of the work-value, which thus finds itself indexed to univocal quantitative factors such as the work-time required for a production, and the amount of workers concerned. From there, this value can be broken down into two parts:

—a quantity corresponding to the labor which is necessary to the reproduction of labor;

—a quantity constitutive of surplus-value, which is identified with the extortion of surplus-labor by capitalism.[2]

Such a conception of surplus-value may correspond to an accounting practice of capitalism, but certainly not to the way it really functions, especially in modern industry. This notion of "collective worker" should not be reduced to an abstraction. Labor-power always manifests itself through concrete agencements of production, intimately combining social relations with the means of production, and human labor with the labor of the machine. Hence the schematic character of the organic composition of Capital, which Marx divides into constant capital (Capital tied down to means of production) and variable capital (Capital tied down to means of work), should be put into question.

Marx distinguishes the composition in value of Capital (constant and capital) from its technical composition by comparing the real mass of means of production engaged in the valorization of Capital and the objective quantity of work which is socially necessary for their implementation. One goes from a sign-value to material and social power relations. With the advances in mechanized labor, the capitalist mode of production ineluctably leads to a relative diminishment of variable capital in relation to the constant capital. From this, Marx deduces a law of tendential lowering of the profit rate, which would be a kind of historical destiny of capitalism. But in the real context of the arrangements of production, the Marxist mode of calculation of absolute surplus-value, based on the quantity of average social labor—a part of which would be, in some sense, stolen by capitalists—is far from obvious. This time factor, in fact, is only one among many parameters of exploitation. It is known today that the administration of the capital of knowledge, the degree of participation in the organization of labor, the corporate spirit, and collective discipline, etc., can also take on determining importance in the productivity of Capital. In this respect, the idea of a social average for an hourly output in a given sector doesn't make much sense. It is teams, workshops, and factories, wherever a local reduction of "productive entropy" appears for x reasons, which drive things forward, and actually direct this kind of average in a branch of industry or in a country, while collective worker resistance, organizational bureaucracy, etc., slow it down. In other words, it is complex arrangements—training, innovation, internal structures, union relations, etc.—which circumscribe the magnitude of capitalist zones of profit, and not a simple levy on work-time. Actually Marx himself had perfectly pinpointed the growing discrepancy between machinic, intellectual, and manual components of labor. In the *Grundrisse,* he had emphasized that the totality of knowledge tends to become an "immediate productive power." He then insisted on the absurdity and the transitional character of a measure of value based on work-time.

Let us note in passing the fragility of this parallel: indeed, if today it appears that the absolute rule of the measure of work-time is on the verge of vanishing, the same does not hold with the law of exchange-value. It is true that if capitalism seems to be able to do without the former, it is unimaginable that it could survive the disappearance of the latter, which could only be the result of revolutionary social transformations. Marx believed that the removal of the leisure-work opposition would coincide with the control by workers over surplus labor.[3] Unfortunately it is perfectly conceivable that it is capitalism itself which would loosen up the measure of work-time, and practice a politics of leisure and formation all the more "open" that it would better colonize it (today how many workers, employees, and high-level staff spend their evenings and week-ends preparing for promotions!). The recasting of the quantification of value based on work-time won't be, as Marx assumed, the privilege of a classless society. And indeed, through modes of transportation, of urban, domestic, married life, through the media, the leisure industry and even the dream industry, it does seem that one cannot escape from the grip of Capital for one second.

One does not pay wages to a worker for the pure duration of "average social labor," but for putting the worker at one's disposal; one compensates the worker for a *power* which exceeds that which is exercised during the worker's presence in the factory. What counts here is filling a position, a power game between the workers and the social groups which control the arrangements of production and social formations. The capitalist does not extort a surplus of time, but a complex qualitative process. He doesn't buy labor-power but power over productive arrangements. Labor which is the most serial in appearance, for example pressing a lever or keeping watch on a security blinker, always presupposes the prior formation of a semiotic capital with multiple components—knowledge of language, customs, rules and hierarchies, mastery of processes of increasing abstraction, itineraries, and interactions which are inherent to productive arrangements.... Work is no longer, if it ever was, a mere ingredient, mere raw matter of production. In other words, the portion of machinic subjection entering into human labor is never quantifiable as such. On the other hand, subjective subjugation, the social alienation inherent in a work position or any other social function certainly is. That is in fact the function assigned to Capital.

The two problems concerning, on the one hand, work-value and its role in surplus-value, and on the other, the effect of the rise of productivity through increased mechanization over the profit rate, are irredeemably linked. Human time is increasingly replaced by *machinic time.*

As Marx says, it is no longer human labor which is made to fit mechanized labor. It does indeed seem that the assembly line and the various forms of Taylorism, in the most modern branches of the economy, are about to become far more dependent on general methods of social subjugation than on processes of subjection which are specific to productive forces.[4] This Taylorist alienation of work-time, these neo-archaic forms of subjugation to the work position, in principle, remain measurable in terms of a general equivalent. The control of average social labor, in theory, can always be incarnated in an exchange-value of powers (one could thus compare the formal alienation time of a Senegalese peasant to that of a civil servant in the Ministry of Finance or an I.B.M. worker.) But the real control of machinic times, from the subjection of human organs to productive arrangements, cannot legitimately be grounded on such a general equivalent. One can measure a time of work presence, a time of alienation, a time of incarceration in a factory or a prison; one cannot measure their consequences on an individual. One may quantify the apparent labor of a physicist in a laboratory, but not the productive value of the formulas that he elaborates. Marxist abstract value over-coded the whole of human labor, which was concretely assigned to the production of use-values. But the present movement of capitalism tends to turn all use-values into exchange-values; all productive labor is defined by mechanized labor. The poles of the exchange themselves have passed over to the side of mechanized labor; computers dialogue across continents, and dictate the terms of the exchanges to the managers. Automatized and computerized production no longer draws its consistency from a basic human factor, but from a machinic phylum which traverses, bypasses, disperses, miniaturizes, and coopts all human activities.

These transformations do not imply that the new capitalism completely takes the place of the old one. There is rather coexistence, stratification, and hierarchalization of capitalisms at different levels, which involve:

—on the one hand, *traditional segmentary capitalisms,* territorialized onto nation-states, and deriving their unity from a monetary and financial mode of semiotization;[5]

—and on the other, *a World-Wide Integrated Capitalism,* which no longer rests on the sole mode of semiotization of financial and monetary Capital, but more fundamentally, on a whole set of technico-scientific, macro- and micro-social, and mass media procedures of subjection.

The formula of Marxist surplus-value is essentially linked to segmentary capitalisms. It does not account for the double movement of globalization and miniaturization which characterizes the current evolution. For example, in the extreme case of an entirely automatized branch of industry, one cannot see what becomes of this surplus-value. If one rigorously stuck to Marxist equations, it should completely disappear, which is absurd. Should one then ascribe it solely to machinic labor? Why not? One could set forth a formula according to which a machinic surplus-value would correspond to surplus labor "required" from the machine, beyond its upkeep and replacement costs. But trying to rearrange the quantitativistic side of the problem would certainly not take us very far. In reality, in such a case—but also in all the intermediate cases of strong reduction of variable capital in relation to constant capital—the extraction of surplus-value for the most part evades the corporation and the immediate manager-employee relation, and refers back to the second formula of integrated capitalism.

The double equation posited by Marx, setting as equivalent "the real degree of exploitation of labor," the rate of surplus-value, and the time of surplus labor tied down to variable capital, cannot be accepted as such.

Capitalist exploitation tends to treat humans like machines and pay them like machines, in a purely quantitativistic mode. But exploitation, as we have seen, goes beyond that. Capitalists extract many other surplus-values, many other profits tied down as well to the standard of Capital. Capitalism is just as interested in the "social" as the exploited are. But while for it, the machinic precedes the social and must control it, for them, conversely, the machinic should be subservient to the social. What essentially separates humans from machines is the fact that humans don't let themselves be exploited passively. One may admit that, in the present conditions, exploitation concerns machinic arrangements at first—man and his faculties having become an integral part of these arrangements. From this absolute exploitation, secondly, social forces enter into a struggle for the dividing-up of the *machinic product.* As the survival criterion of the worker has become relative—how indeed could we appreciate the "minimum subsistence," the portion of value corresponding to the labor which is necessary for the reproduction of labor?—all the questions of allotment of economic and social goods have essentially become political matters. But the concept of the political has to be broadened to include the whole of the micropolitical dimensions involving the various styles of living, experience, speaking, projecting the future, memorizing history, etc.

After pointing out that the subjugation of the worker only involves the quantitative factor of "average social labor" marginally, I have tried to "lift" the exploitation rate from the Marxist surplus-value rate. By doing this, I implicitly lifted it away from the profit rate, which in Marx is a close relative of the latter.[6]

This distinction is confirmed by the fact, which has become frequent in sectors subsidized by the State, that corporations "selling at a loss," despite a theoretically negative surplus-value, according to the Marxist formula, nevertheless generate considerable profits. Profit today may depend on fac-

tors which are not only outside the corporation, but also outside the nation, as the Third World is exploited "from a distance," by means of the international market of raw materials.

Let us note, lastly, that the alleged law of tendential lowering of the profit rate could not be sustained in the present
politico-economic field. Trans-national mechanisms have
acquired so much importance that it is no longer conceivable
to determine a local rate of surplus-value tied down to a local
growth rate of mechanical labor in terms of constant capital.[7]

II. THE ORGANIC COMPOSITION OF
WORLD-WIDE INTEGRATED CAPITALISM

Unlike what Marx thought, Capital was able to disengage
itself from a formula that would have enclosed it in a blind
mode of quantification of exchange values (that is, controlling
the whole of the modes of circulation and production of use-
values).[8] Capitalist valorization still has not caught the
machinic cancer which, from the tendential lowering of the
profit rate to crises of over-production, should have led it to a
dead end, and what is more, forced capitalism into total isolation. The semiotization of Capital now has more and more
means to locate, quantify, and manipulate the concrete valorizations of power, and thereby not only survive but proliferate. Whatever appearance it may give itself, Capital is not rational, it is hegemonistic. It does not harmonize social formations;
it enforces socio-economic disparities. It is a power operation
before being a profit operation. It cannot be deduced from a
basic mechanism of profit, but imposes itself from above.
Previously based on what Marx called "the total social Capital
of a country,"[9] today it relies on a World-Wide Integrated
Capital. Capital has always relied on a general movement of
deterritorialization of all sectors of the economy, of science and
technology, of mores, etc. Its semiotic existence is systemati-

cally grafted onto all the technical and social mutations, which it diagrammatizes and reterritorializes onto the dominant power formations. Even at the time when it seemed to be solely centered on an extraction of monetary profit from commercial, banking and financial activities, Capital—as the expression of the most dynamic capitalist classes—was already practicing a politics of destruction and restructuring: deterritorialization of the traditional peasantry, constitution of an urban working class, expropriation of the old commercial bourgeoisie and the old crafts, liquidation of the regional and separatist "archaisms," colonial expansionism, etc.[10]

It is therefore not sufficient here to evoke the politics of Capital. Capital as such is nothing but the political, social, and technico-scientific elements, related to each other. This general diagrammatic dimension appears more and more clearly with the growing role of State capitalism, as a relay to the globalization of Capital. Nation-States manipulate a multi-dimensional Capital: monetary masses, economic indices, quantities necessary to bring some social category "into line," fluxes of inhibition to keep people in place, etc. One witnesses a sort of collectivization of capitalism—whether it is circumscribed in a national framework or not. But this does not mean that it is about to degenerate. Through the continuous enrichment of its semiotic components,[11] beyond wage labor and monetarized goods, it takes control of multitude of quanta of power which previously had remained contained in the local economy, both domestic and libidinal. Today, each particular operation of capitalist extraction of profit—in money and in social power—involves power formations across the board. Notions such as the capitalist corporation and the salaried position have become inseparable from the whole of the social fabric, which itself is directly produced and reproduced under the control of Capital. The very notion of the capitalist corporation should be broadened so as to include collective equipments, and the notion of work position, as well as most non-salaried activities. In a way, the housewife occupies a work position in her home, the child holds a work position at school, the consumer at the supermarket, and the television viewer in front of the screen…. Machines in the factory seem to be working all by themselves, but in fact it is the whole of society which is adjacent to them. It would be quite arbitrary today to consider corporate salaries independently from the multiple systems of deferred wages, benefits, and social costs, which affect the reproduction of the collective labor-power more or less closely, move out of the monetary circuit of the corporation, and are taken on by multiple institutions and collective equipments. Let us add to all this an essential point about which more will be said: not only does capitalism exploit salaried workers beyond their work-time, during their "leisure" time, but moreover, it uses them as relay-points in order to exploit those who are subjugated in their own sphere of action: their subalterns, their unsalaried kin, wives, children, old people, dependents of all kinds.

We always come back to this central idea: through the wage system, capitalism aims above all at controlling *the whole of society*. And in a recurring way, it appears that in any circumstance, the play of exchange-values has always been dependent on social relations, and not the reverse. Mechanisms such as inflation illustrate the constant intrusion of the social in the economic. What is "normal" is inflation, and not price equilibrium, since the issue is to adjust power relations which are in permanent evolution (buying power, investment power, the various social formations' international exchange power). As economic surplus-value is irrevocably tied to surplus-values of power which have to do with labor, machines, and social spaces, the redefinition of Capital as the general mode of capitalization of the semioses of power (rather than as an abstract, universal quantity) therefore implies a redefinition of its technical composition. The latter no longer rests on two basic givens—living labor and labor crystallized in the means of production—but on at least four components, four set-ups which are irreducible to one another:

1) *The capitalist power formations,* through which Capital maintains order, guarantees property, social stratifications, and the allotment of material and social goods. (The value of a good, whichever it might be, being inseparable from the credibility of the repressive equipments of law and police... and also from the existence of a certain degree of popular consensus in favor of the established order).

2) *The machinic arrangements* of productive forces, which constitute a fixed capital (machine, factory, transportation, storage of raw materials, capital of technico-scientific knowledge, techniques of machinic subjection and training, laboratories, etc.). This is the classic realm of productive forces.

3) *Collective labor-power and the whole of social relations which are subjugated by capitalist power.* Collective labor-power is no longer considered here in terms of machinic subjection, but of social alienation. It is subjugated to the bourgeoisies and the bureaucracies; at the same time, it is a factor of subjugation of other social categories (women, children, immigrants, sexual minorities, etc.). This is the realm of relations of production and social relations.

4) *The network of equipments, apparatuses of State and para-State power, the media.* This network, both ramified on the micro-social and on the planetary scale, has become an essential element of Capital. It is through this network that it can extract and integrate the sectorial capitalizations of power inherent to the three preceding components.

Capital, as the semiotic operator of all the power formations, thus deploys a deterritorialized surface of inscription on which these four components will evolve. But I will emphasize the fact that it is not just a stage where something would be *represented,* a sort of parliamentary theater where the various points of view would be confronted with one another. It will also be a directly *productive* activity, inasmuch as Capital participates in the ordering of machinic and social arrangements, and in an entire series of prospective operations concerning them. The specific diagrammatic functions of Capital—that is, functions of inscription which are not exclusively representational but operational—"add" something essential to what would be otherwise a mere accumulation of the various components mentioned above. The elevation of the level of semiotic abstraction corresponding to this level of diagrammatism may evoke what Bertrand Russell described in his theory of logical types, that is, that a fundamental discontinuity exists between a set and its components. But with Capital, discontinuity is not just logical but machinic, in the sense that it does not only emanate from fluxes of signs, but also from material and social fluxes. In fact, the reduction-ratio power of the diagrammatism proper to Capital is inseparable from the deterritorializing "dynamism" of the various concrete arrangements of capitalism. This makes reformist political perspectives grounded on intra- or inter-capitalist contradictions irrelevant, and this holds true to those which emphasize its humanization in response to the pressure of the masses. It is futile, for instance, to "play" multi-national corporations off against national capitalism, or Germano-American Europe against the Europe of fatherlands, "Western" liberalism against the social capitalism of the USSR, North against South, etc. Capital thrives on these contradictions; they are just so many tests promoting deterritorialization. A revolutionary alternative, if such does exist, can certainly not be established on such bases.

III. CAPITAL AND THE FUNCTIONS
OF SUBJECTIVE ALIENATION

The exercise of power by means of the semioses of Capital proceeds concurrently with a control from above of social segments, and by a constant subjugation of each individual's life.

Even though its enunciation is individuated, there is nothing less individual than capitalist subjectivity. The over-coding by Capital of human activities, thoughts, and feelings makes all particularized modes of subjectivation equivalent and resonant with each other. Subjectivity, so to speak, is nationalized. Values of desire are reordered in an economy grounded on a systematic dependence of use-values in relation to exchange-values, to the point of making this opposition meaningless. Strolling "freely" down a street, or in the country, breathing fresh air, or singing a bit loudly have become quantifiable activities from a capitalistic point of view. Squares, natural parks, and free movement have a social and industrial cost. Ultimately, the subjects of capitalism—like the subjects of the king—only assume the portion of their existence that is accountable in terms of general equivalency: Capital, according to the expanded definition I am proposing here. The capitalist order claims that individuals should only live for an exchange system, a general translatability of all values so that their slightest desire is felt to be asocial, dangerous, and guilty.

Such an operation of subjugation, meant to cover the whole social field, while "targeting" accurately its minutest disparities, cannot be satisfied with exterior social control. The general market of values deployed by Capital will at once proceed from within and from without. It will not only be concerned with economically identifiable values, but also mental and affective values. It will be up to a multi-centered network of collective equipments, State, para-State, and media apparatuses to make the junction between this "without" and this "within." The general translatability of the local modes of semiotization of power does not only obey central commands, but "semiotic condensators" which are adjacent to State power, or directly indentured to it. One essential function is to make sure that each individual assumes mechanisms of control, repression, and modelization of the dominant order.[12]

In the context of World-Wide Integrated Capitalism, one may hold that the central powers of Nation-States are at once everything and nothing. Nothing, or not much, with regard to real economic efficiency; everything, or almost everything, with regard to modelization and social control. The paradox is that, up to a point, the network of State apparatuses, equipments, and bureaucracies itself tends to escape State power. In fact, often it is the network which guides and manipulates the State by remote control, its actual interlocutors being "social partners," pressure groups, and lobbies. The reality of the State thus tends to coincide with the State and para-State structures which occupy a very ambiguous position in relations of production and class relations, since on the one hand they control real executive positions and effectively contribute to maintaining the dominant order, and on the other, they themselves are the object of capitalist exploitation, on the same basis as the various components of the working class.

Marx held that a school-master was a productive worker since he prepared his pupils to work for the bosses.[13] But today's school-master has multiplied infinitely. Through this capitalistic network, it generates training and sociability, to such a point that it would be quite arbitrary to break down the conglomerate of "collective arrangements" into autonomous spheres of material production, socius, and modes of semiotization and subjectivation.

The same ambiguity and the same ambivalence between production and repression which characterizes technocracies can be found among the working masses: workers "work" on themselves at the very time as they are working towards the production of consumption goods. In one way or another, all participate in the production of control and repression. In fact, as we saw before, one individual never stops shifting roles in the same day: exploited at the workshop or office, he in turn becomes the exploiter in his family or in the couple, etc. At all levels of the socius, one finds an inextricable mixture of vectors of alienation. For example, the workers and the unions of an advanced sector will passionately defend the position their industry occupies in the national economy, and will do so regardless of its consequences for pollution, or whether fighter jets will be used to strafe the African populations…. Class borders, "fronts of struggle," have become blurred. Could one say that they have disappeared? No. But they have multiplied infinitely, and even when direct confrontations come forth, most often they take on an "exemplary character," their first aim being to draw the attention of the media, which in turn manipulates them at will.

At the root of the mechanisms which model the force of labor, at all the levels where ideology and affects keep overlapping, one discovers the machinic tentacles of capitalistic equipment. I would like to emphasize that they don't make up a network of ideological apparati, but rather a megamachine encompassing a multitude of scattered elements which concerns not just workers, but all those "involved in production," permanently and everywhere, women, children, the elderly, the marginals, etc. Today, for example, from birth through family, television and social services, a child is "set to work" and is engaged in a complex process of formation, with a view of adapting the child's various modes of semiosis to upcoming productive and social functions.

Today assessments of industrial maintenance in the management of enterprises is of paramount importance. Is it enough to say that the State is assuming the role of general "social maintenance"? To me, this would be completely insufficient. Both in the East and in the West, the State is directly hooked on the essential components of Capital—in this respect one has the right to speak of two modes of State capitalism, on condition that one simultaneously modifies the definition of the organic composition of Capital and that of the State. The function of the network of Capitalist equipment (which includes, up to a point, the media, unions, associations, etc.) is to *make Capital homogeneous* with exchange values and the social Capital of power values. It manages collective attitudes, patterns of conduct, referents of every sort compatible with the "good behavior" of the system, as well as legal and financial means distributing the power of purchase and investment between the various social and industrial zones, or again, financing huge military-industrial complexes which serve as a back-bone on an international scale.

It is essential to not isolate each of these domains into foolproof categories. In each occasion, in the last analysis, we find the same Capital manipulated by socially dominant formations: Capital of knowledge, of adaptation and submission of labor-power to the productive environment, and more generally the entire population to the urban-rural environment, the Capital of unconscious introjection of models of the system, the Capital of repressive and military force. All these ways of semiotizing power fully participate in the organic composition of contemporary Capital.

Thus the development of a general market of capitalist values, the proliferation of multicentered capitalist and State equipments which sustains it, far from contradicting powers centered on the Nation-States—which generally tend to reinforce it—in fact complement it. In reality, what is thereby capitalized is much more a power exerted as *the image of power* than a true power in the areas of production and of the economy. In the most diverse ways, the State and its countless ramifications tend to recreate a minimum of coordinates and spare territories, in order to allow the masses to more or less artificially adjust their everyday life and social rapport. By contrast, the true axes of decisionality are elsewhere: they traverse and dodge the ancient and new modes of territorialization, being increasingly dependent on a system of capitalist networks integrated on a world scale.[14]

The spaces of contemporary capital no longer adhere to local turf, castes, ethical, religious, corporative, "precapitalist" traditions, and less and less to metropolises, industrial cities, to class relations and bureaucracies of segmented capitalism from the era of the Nation-States. Spaces are constructed on planetary as well as micro-social and physical scales. The feeling of "belonging to something" itself seems to result from the same sort of asembly-line as "life-design." It is easier to understand, under these conditions, why State power can no longer afford to sit on the throne of the social pyramid, legislating from a distance, but that it has to intervene endlessly in order to shape and recompose the social texture, constantly reshuffling its "formulas" of hierarchization, segregation, functional prescriptions, specific qualifications. Global Capitalism is moving forward in a dizzying race. It has to make use of everything and no longer affords the luxury of national traditions, legislative texts, or the independence, even formal, of institutions like magistracy, which might limit in any way its freedom.

IV. CAPITAL AND THE FUNCTIONS OF MACHINIC ENSLAVEMENT

To the traditional systems of direct coercion, capitalist power keeps adding control mechanisms requiring, if not the complicity of each individual, at least its passive consent. But such an extension of the means of action is only possible inasmuch as those involve the inner springs of life and human action. Miniaturization of these means goes far beyond machinic techniques. It bears down on the basic functioning of the perceptive, sensorial, affective, cognitive, linguistic, etc., behaviors grafted to a capitalist machinery, of which the "invisible" deterritorialized part is probably the most fearfully efficient. We cannot accept the theoretical explanations of subjugation of the masses in terms of ideological deceit or a collective masochistic passion. Capitalism seizes individuals from the inside. Alienation by means of images and ideas is only an aspect of a general system of enslavement of their fundamental modes of semiotization, both individual and collective. Individuals are "equipped" with modes of perception or normalization of desire just as they are with factories, schools, territories. The expansion of the division of labor to planetary levels implies, on the part of global Capitalism, not only an attempt to integrate productive forces of every social category, but moreover a permanent recomposition, a re-invention of this collective work-force. The ideal of Capital is no longer to bother with individuals endowed with passions, capable of ambiguity, hesitation and refusal as well as enthusiasm, but exclusively human robots. It would rather deal with only two types: the salaried and the subsidized. Its aim is to erase, neutralize, if not suppress, any categorization founded on something other than its own axiomatic of power and its technological imperatives. When, at the close of the chain, it "rediscovers" men, women, children, the old, rich and poor, manual laborers, intellectuals, etc., it pretends to recreate them by itself, to redefine them according to its own criteria.

But, precisely because it intervenes on the most functional levels—sensorial, affective and practical—the capitalist machinic enslavement is liable to reverse its effects, and to lead to a new type of machinic surplus-value accurately perceived by Marx (expansion of alternatives for the human race, constant renewal of the horizon of desires and creativity).[15] Capitalism claims to seize the force of desires borne by the human race. It is by means of machinic enslavement that it settles in the heart of individuals. It is doubtlessly true, for example, that social and political integration of workers' elites is not only based on material interests, but also on their involvement, sometimes very profound, with their profession, their technology, their machines.... More generally, it is clear that the machinic environment secreted by capitalism is far from being indifferent to the great masses of people, and this is not only due to the seduction of advertisement or the internalization by individuals of objects and ideas of the consumer society. Something of the machine seems to belong to the essence of human desire. The question is to know of which machine, and what it is for.

Machinic enslavement does not coincide with social subjugation. While enslavement involves full-fledged persons, easily manipulated subjective representations, machinic enslavement combines infrapersonal and infrasocial elements, because of a molecular economy of desire more difficult to "contain" within stratified social relations.[16] Directly involving perceptive functions, affects, unconscious behaviors, capitalism takes possession of labor-power and desire, which extends far beyond that of the working class, sociologically speaking. Accordingly, class relations tend to evolve differently. They are less bi-polarized, and increasingly rely on complex strategies. The fate of the French working class, for example, does not solely depend upon its direct bosses, but also on those from the State, Europe, the Third World, multinationals, and in another area, immigrant workers, women's labor, precarious and provisional work, regional conflicts, etc.

The bourgeoisie's nature has changed. It is no longer as vigorously engaged, at least in its modernist parts, in defending the personal possession of means of production—either individual or collective. Today its problem is to collectively and globally control the basic network of machines and social equipment. Its power, not only monetary, but social, libidinal, cultural, etc., comes from there. It is on this terrain that it defends itself against expropriation. And, in this regard, it is necessary to recognize that it showed a surprising capacity for adaptation, renovation, in particular for regeneration in the social-capitalist regimes of the East. It loses ground on the side of private capitalism, but gains ground on the side of State capitalism, collective equipment, media, etc. Not only does it incorporate new sectors of the State, bureaucracy and apparatus, technocrats, experts, teachers, but to one degree or another, it manages to contaminate the whole of the population.

What limits will the capitalist classes encounter in their enterprise of converting across the board all human activities into a unique semiotic equivalent? Up to what point is a revolutionary class struggle still conceivable in such a system of generalized contaminations? No doubt these limits are not to be found among traditional revolutionary movements. Revolution is not uniquely played out at the level of explicit political discourse, but also on a far more molecular plane, in mutations of desire, artistic and techno-scientific mutations, etc. In this dizzying course, capitalism is engaged in systematic control of everyone on this planet. Today, it is at the apex of its power, having integrated China, but perhaps at the same time, it is about to reach an extreme threshhold of fragility. Its system of generalized dependence may be such that the slightest hitch in its functioning may create effects of which it won't be the master.

Translated by Charles Wolfe and Sande Cohen

1. Subjection understood in its cybernetic sense.
2. Marx defined surplus-value in these terms: "I call *absolute surplus-value* the surplus-value produced by the simple extension of the work day, and *relative surplus-value* the surplus-value which proceeds from the reduction of necessary time and of the corresponding change in the relative magnitude of both aspects which make up the work day." (Karl Marx, *Oeuvres*, Pléiade, vol 1. (Paris: Gallimard, p. 852).
The rate of surplus-value is represented in the following formula:

$$\frac{\text{relative}}{\text{surplus value}} = \frac{\text{surplus-value}}{\text{variable cap.}} = \frac{\text{surplus-value}}{\text{work-power value}} = \frac{\text{surplus-work}}{\text{necessary work}}$$

Marx adds: "The first two formulas express as a relation of value what the third formula expresses as a relation of time spaces in which these values are produced."

3. "True wealth being the full productive power of every individual, the standard measure won't be expressed in labor-time, but in available time. To adopt labor-time as the measure of wealth is to found the latter on poverty; it implies that leisure only exists in and by opposition to over-time work; it amounts to reducing all of time to the sole temporality of labor in which the worker is degraded to the sole role of an instrument." (Marx, *Pléiade*, v. 2, p. 308)

4. In a different register of ideas, one realizes that the present triumph of behaviorism in the U.S. doesn't result from the "progress of science," but from a more rigorous systematization of methods of social control.

5. The "mercantilist revolution" would seem to be the referent I am thinking of, in particular, the great book of Thomas Mun, *A Discourse of Trade from England into the East Indies* (1609, London, 1621), which, for Marx, represented "the conscious break of mercantilism with the system from which it came." Mun's book would become the "Gospel of mercantilism."

6. According to Marx, it is the relative and progressive diminishing of variable capital in relation to constant capital (because of machinery and concentration of factories) which introduced disequilibrium in the organic composition of the total capital of a given society. "The immediate consequence is that the rate of surplus-value expresses itself in a decreasing profit rate, where exploitation remains unchanged or even increases." (Marx, *Pléiade*, v. 2, p. 1002)

7. A multinational, after negotiating with State power, will introduce a super-modern factory in an under-developed region. Then, later, due to political motives or some "social instability," or on account of complex merchandising, it will decide to close the factory. It is impossible, in these cases, to assess the growth in fixed capital.

   In another area, say in steel production, an ultra-modern branch of industry will be toned down or dismantled because of market problems or alleged technological choices, which only express fundamental options concerning the totality of economic and social development.

8. As a number of anthropologists have shown for archaic societies, apparent exchange is always relative to actual relations of force. Exchange is always instrumentalized by power. Cf. E. R. Leach, *Critique of Anthropology.*

9. Marx, *Pléiade*, v. 1, p. 1122; v. 2, p. 1002.

10. This general movement of deterritorialization nonetheless allows archaic strata more or less territorialized to remain or, more frequently, gives them another breath by transforming their functions. In this sense, the actual "rebound" in the value of gold constitutes a surprising example. It seems to work concurrently in two opposing directions: on the one hand, as a semiotic black hole, economic stasis and inhibition; and on the other, as a diagrammatic operator of power: (1) for those who *proved capable* of inserting their semiotic intervention in "good places" and at "the right moments"; (2) for those capable of injecting abstract credit of power, at the "right time" within key economic sectors. On the dia-

grammatic function, semiotic black holes, etc., cf. *L'inconscient machinique* (Paris: Editions Recherches, 1979).

11. Beyond gold, fiduciary money, credit money, stocks and propriety titles, etc., Capital today manifests itself through semiotic operations and manipulations of power of all kinds involving information and the media.

12. Such is the role, parallel to the administration, police, justice, IRS, stock-exchange, the military, etc., of schools, social services, unions, sports, media, etc.

13. Marx, *Pléiade*, v. 1, p. 1002.

14. One finds a relative reterritorialization at this level: multinationals which are not at all reducible to the economic sub-grouping of the U.S. and are objectively cosmopolitan, are nonetheless headed in majority by U.S. citizens.

15. The dialectical mechanism of Marx at times led him to envision a quasi-spontaneous and involuntary generation of this type of transformation: "While the system of bourgeois economy develops bit by bit, its negation does as well as the ultimate extension of this system. Here we have in mind the process of instant production. If we consider bourgeois society as a whole, we see that the final result of social production is society itself, in other words, man himself in his social relations." (Marx, *Pléiade*, v. 2, p. 311)

16. Such a proposition can only be heard if one conceives desire not as some indifferentiated energetic drive, but resulting from a highly elaborated assemblage of deterritorialized machinics.

25

THE UNCONSCIOUS IS TURNED
TOWARD THE FUTURE

Q: As a psychoanalyst, a writer, but also a militant, you occupy a special position in the political scene. Most intellectuals disappointed by Marxism are concerned exclusively with human rights and the defense of a number of humanist ideals, but you maintain an offensive attitude toward Western social structures, that of a revolutionary intellectual. How do you manage to sustain this dual activity?

FG: I believe I am neither an intellectual nor a revolutionary. I'm just pursuing something I started long ago, perhaps with a certain imperviousness to hazards of the present situation. And sometimes, in the eyes of influential people, I even feel like a "half-wit," someone kind of backward. It's true that I have a rather particular vision of things, which perhaps comes from the fact that I am very short-sighted. I have a tendency to stick a bit too closely to a text as well as to an event. That is perhaps why I got interested in analysis at a very young age and why I forged parallel visions for myself, a naïve vision, and to compensate for it, politically and philosophically, an "armed" vision. The passage from this molecular vision, sticking closely to texts and events, to a more theoretical dimension is never easy for me to make. But I remain convinced that molecular transformations are the true fabric of long-term historical transformations.

Q: People often object to your penchant for abstraction, shock formulas. For once could you be more concrete about what you mean by molecular transformations?

FG: Let's take an example: the technology of the pill. Here's something that deeply transformed relations to the sexual body, to conjugality and the family. It's only a little gesture, an evening ritual, a monthly purchase at the pharmacy, but it radically alters the socius. Another example: the relationship to justice. The creation of a very "politically committed" association of magistrates like the "Union of Magistrates" refers to an invisible transformation of the relationship to the thing judged, to the judicial institution, to legal texts, etc. Whether these transformations are positive or negative, this isn't the place to debate that. The same holds true in a multitude of domains that have to do with neighborhood, information, or even movement, speed, the kind of translations Paul Virilio talks about. All these mutations, which I have termed molecular, are what I wanted to bring to bear upon a different conception of the unconscious and also of history.

Q: This conception only widens the gulf that separates daily life from traditional conceptions concerning the transformation of society. It is an incentive to redefine the role of organizations, groups, in short, the political struggle. Don't parties, trade unions, leftist groups have anything left to say in your opinion?

FG: Let me state it very clearly: I do not believe in either the death of politics or in social implosion, dear to our friend Baudrillard. On the other hand, two notions seem to have collapsed: that of ideology and that of group.

Reference to ideology masks the connections between different "machines" at work in the social process. It might have to do with machines of a scientific nature, an aesthetic, institutional nature, but also technical machines, logical machines that intertwine their effects in order to trigger off an event, something historically important, as well as a microscopic, almost imperceptible decision-making process. Reference to ideologies does not account for such events. For example, the eruption of what one could call "the Khomeini effect." One could ask: who are the Chi'ites? Should we interpret this movement in terms of religious fanaticism? One invokes paranoia; but where does this paranoia originate? In Freud? In Bleuler? In ethology? Carter's advisors are tearing their hair out trying to grasp the possible causes of such a phenomenon, which never have the systemic or structural character of ideologies. It is always due to the interaction of very heterogeneous factors stemming from different logics, or from a multivalent logic, that results in the coexistence of systems—I prefer to say machines—plugged into the real. Unlike Althusser, I do not rigidly oppose ideological discourse to scientific discourse. I would approach scientific or aesthetic discursivity in the same way.

Another notion in crisis is that of the group. There are social aggregates that have no specificity of group action whatsoever, and, conversely, there are isolated individuals who shape the socius "from within," so to speak; writers like Beckett, like Proust, have effected direct transformations on the social unconscious. It does not specifically involve effects of communication occurring within a group; the group is only the medium through which a multiplicity of components circulate.

At one time I came up with the idea of the "subject-group." I contrasted these with "subjected groups" in an attempt to define modes of intervention which I described as micro-political. I've changed my mind: there are no subject-groups, but arrangements of enunciation, of subjectivization, pragmatic arrangements which do not coincide with circumscribed groups. These arrangements can involve individuals, but also ways of seeing the world, emotional systems, conceptual machines, memory devices, economic, social components, elements of all kinds.

Q: In your last book, *L'Inconscient machinique* [*The Machinic Unconscious*],[1] there is a long passage on "schizoanalysis." Is this a new technique of treatment, a sort of superpsychoanalysis that therapists seduced by your proposal should attempt to use by drawing up "maps of the unconscious"? Or is it just a pretext to refine the criticism of psychoanalysis and enrich your conception of the unconscious?

FG: Your question brings us back to the debate between technology and ideology. In my opinion this opposition does not hold up. Yet this question is very present in current, internal debates at the Réseau Alternatif à la Psychiatrie.[2] Should one reject everything that exists in the technical domain and merely wage war on the political front, in such a way as to bring together political struggle and the transformation of psychiatry? Should one, on the contrary, try to salvage existing techniques and put them to best use? I answer: neither. Ideological battles cannot be dissociated from technologies (for example, technologies of information or of group manipulation). Moreover, when one tries to be a strict technician, and believes to be merely applying the principles of psychoanalysis, or family therapy, or psycho-pharmacology, one is not freed from micro-political fields for all that. Under these conditions, it is impossible to circumscribe a legitimate technical object. The schizo-analytical aphorisms I set forth in my book have no other goal than to suggest intellectual tools, a conceptual machine, that can be transformed according to each person's liking. It is not a super-psychoanalysis, or a univocal reading of the political.

Q: By turning to animal ethology, particularly the study of birds, aren't you outlining a sort of human ethology, an individual surrounded by "visagéité" (*faceness*), obsessed by "refrains," in short, an "alienated" individual who no longer has anything human about him?

FG: Rather than the unfortunate term "alienation," which no longer means much of anything, I prefer turning to the notion of "subjection" which I contrast with that of "subjugation": subjection deals with people, power relations, and subjugation with machinic relations and power relations. It is at an extrapersonal level that relations of subjugation are established. What happens to an individual in his machinic environment is always below or beyond his person. Beside affective, perceptive, intellectual and discursive components, there exists ethological components which psychologists and anthropologists have not taken sufficiently into account. Research in human ethology demonstrates the existence of non-verbal systems of communication and specific territorializations. In particular, I have in mind "greeting behaviors," automatic, subliminal smiles, which can only be detected in slow motion film and which one finds again in all cultural areas. The way these features of visagéité work cannot be explained by analyses such as those by Spitz, concerning interhuman relations at the infant stage (identification with the mother, etc.) . It happens at a level of expression which cannot be mechanically explained by an intra-familial system. It does not imply the existence of a univocal determinist causality. It is interesting to study how individuals and groups juggle with these pre-coded features of visagéité, with these expressive refrains, a bit like a pianist arrives at mastering reflexes which, in the beginning, seemed completely mechanical. The work of actors—those Georges Aperghis directs in the field of musical theater, for example—heads in this direction. Distinctions between the innate, the acquired, learning, the imprint, are being called into question by this current research. There is a continuum between these domains which, in my opinion, could be illuminated by the concept of arrangement I mentioned earlier. How can one otherwise understand that systems of genetic encoding manage to "pick up" new information, new behaviors, new morphological systems? The formation of the biosphere, and of what I have called the *mechanosphere,* does not result from chance, but from modes of concatenation by blocks of semiotic sequences and chains of highly differentiated encodings.

Q: The work of Proust gives you opportunity to demonstrate the methods evoked above. How can *Remembrance of Things Past* constitute a type of "scientific work," as you assert?

FG: I have always been exasperated, as many people have, by psychoanalytical readings of literary works. "Beneath" the purely literary work one seeks to discover the real man, his inhibitions, his anxieties, his affective problems, familial problems, etc. Here again, this raises the question of methodology. If one believes the unconscious is something buried in the past, crystallized in the form of signifying chains, certain keys should be enough to find the complexions or "mathemes" that compose it. But if one starts from the transsemiotic unconscious, which is not solely structured by signifiers, and no longer turned toward the past but toward the future, an unconscious that bears the capacity to "engineer" new objects, new realities, then everything changes. To make a comparison, if you want to study computer science, it's better to go into research departments or workshops where new computers with the greatest technological capabilities are being built rather than limit yourself to standard models that were built fifteen years ago. Well, this is the same thing. If you want to analyze your unconscious, rather than going to Freud and Lacan, refer to the richest authors—Proust, Beckett, Joyce, Faulkner, Kafka or Artaud—because scarcely anything better has been done since. Interpret Freud, Jung and the others through Proust and not vice versa. The unconscious has to be built, invented. Proust is one of the greatest analysts who ever existed, because he was able to detect modes of communication, major routes between music, painting, social relations, life in the salons, physical sensations, etc. He worked the unconscious as transsemiotic matter.

Q: In this analysis of Proust's work, you set forth the idea that music and in particular "Vinteuil's little phrase" constitutes not only "the national hymn of Swann's love," but structures the whole of the novel, the shape of the sentences, the outline of the plot, etc.

FG: Yes, a certain system of refrain structures (I prefer to say "machinates") both Vinteuil's little phrase—the novel never stops presenting it and then withdrawing it—and the story of Vinteuil and his daughter; and beyond, the whole strategy of the novel (the fact, for example, that a character who has drifted off is replicated or disappears). A certain kind of music is linked to the "Baron de Charlus" construction; another to the branch of the "young girls" and to a different conception of homosexuality which merges into a vector of becoming woman ("enriched" and multidimensional homosexuality). When I say that the unconscious is made of multiple components, turned toward the future, etc., one might well wonder what holds all these components together. For the time being, I reply: "abstract machines" carried by this sort of refrain, a notion close to René Thom's "logos," but different in that these machines do not lend themselves to a mathematical or structuralist reduction. Nor do they come down to an undifferentiated whole, to a muddle of interactions. An abstract machine can be adjacent to a technological mutation; it can result from extraordinary marriages such as that of Khomeini-Kissinger: an ayatollah in his monastery dreams of killing the Shah; a brilliant manipulator dreams of salvaging the fortune of this same Shah: the result is fabulous…. But one could very well have imagined other, much quieter marriages such as that of Sadat-Carter… and thus, other refrains, another international music.

Translated by Jeanine Herman

1. Félix Guattari, *L'Inconscient machinique*. (Paris: Recherches, 1979).
2. The Alternative Psychiatric Network is an international collective that gathers together psychiatrists, nurses, and psychiatric patients for a radical transformation of the approach to mental illness.

26

THE REFRAIN OF BEING AND MEANING: ANALYSIS OF A DREAM ABOUT A.D.

T hat dream "non-sense" might be meaningful relates back to the oldest forms of subjectivation. Breaks in syntax, semantic proliferation, pragmatic inductions: all dream realms play a role of bifurcation in relation to meanings and norms prevalent during a state of wakefulness. The subject of this paper is to show that, in order to reach consciousness, it is not necessary to oppose the basic logic of latent contents to that of repression. It is possible to use a model in which the unconscious is open to the future and able to integrate any heterogeneous, semiotic components which may interfere. Then, meaningful distortions no longer arise from an interpretation of underlying contents. Instead, they become part of a machinic set-up entirely on the text's surface. Rather than be mutilated by symbolic castration, recurring incomplete goals act instead as autonomous purveyors of subjectivation. The rupture, the breach of meaning, is nothing else than the manifestation of subjectivation in its earliest stage. It is the necessary and adequate fractalization which enables something to appear where the access before was blocked. It is the deterritorializing opening. To illustrate this problematic, I have chosen one of my own dreams containing numerous over-determinations, presented as a hologram, which have been recurrent themes throughout all major turning-points in my life.[1]

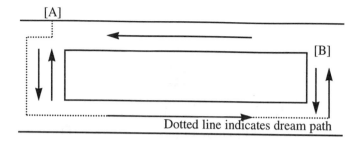

Dotted line indicates dream path

DREAM TEXT

In the company of Yasha David and his wife, I come out of house [A], which is next to a large, rectangular-shaped town square, which seems to belong to a large, provincial town, rather than to a big city. The streets running along the two longer sides of the town square are one-way in opposite directions, whereas those along the shorter sides are two-way. All together, this constitutes the circuit along which I travel for about three quarters of the dream.

We are on the verge of separating and I tell myself that I do not remember exactly where I parked my car. I suggest, first of all, looking around the town square. Yasha believes he remembers where the car is. He and his wife help me look for it. We arrive at point [B], located at the right of the town square. Then, I have an urge to congratulate Yasha on the success of our joint venture. However, I refrain from saying what I was about to say, since I realize that I would have called him Gilles [Deleuze]. I speak of the risks we shared; we were at the edge of an abyss. "Let me start over," it was as if we were hanging onto the wall of an abyss. But, eventually, we made it out all right. Feeling an outburst of affection, I want to kiss them both. Again, I refrain from acting on my first impulse since I remember hearing that Yasha is very jealous over his wife. So, I settle for hugging them both.

ASSOCIATIVE REMARKS AND NARRATIVE DEVELOPMENTS

Yasha David: A Czechoslovakian intellectual and refugee living in France, with whom I worked for over a year on several large exhibits commemorating the centennial of Kafka's birth. Those in charge at the Pompidou Center made it so difficult that, on several occasions, we thought we would have to abandon the project.

Yasha David's wife: I do not know her very well, since we have crossed paths only two or three times. In transcribing this dream, I realized that the woman in my dream was not her but the wife of another friend, Helena Gallard (who, in reality, writes her first name "Alena"). Alena is also Czechoslovakian and also worked on the Kafka exhibit, though only in the preparatory stages. I have confused Yasha David's wife and Alena several times in the past. Alena, her husband Jean Gallard and I have met several times in the past in Mexico City, Paris and Amsterdam. I like this couple very much, perhaps even bordering on fascination. However, I have a feeling that there are problems in the relationship of which I know nothing.

THE RECTANGULAR-SHAPED TOWN SQUARE

I am reminded first of all of the main town square in the eastern province of an old Mexican city, whose name I know well but cannot remember when writing the dream. I finally find it by cross-checking, Michoacan. The name of the city must be Pascuaro. I stayed overnight in a hotel next to the town square. I was very much impressed by its provincial charm and the fact that it seemed destined to remain the same throughout the centuries. I remember thinking, "This is where I would like to end my life." In the background of this Mexican memory is the echo of another very old one, of a large, shadowy public square in the town of Louviers in Normandy. I lived with my maternal grandmother on Rooster Street ("rue au coq") which runs into the town square. Several days after writing down this dream, I realized with surprise—I was overwhelmed by the new evidence—that the square in my dream had to be the main square of Mer. Mer is a small village on the Loire river, close to where I currently spend half of the week. Nevertheless, my dream is not about the Mer of today, but that of over forty years ago during what was called "the exodus," when millions of French people prepared to flee the 1940 German invasion. I do not know how, but my parents had managed to rent a small house right at point [A] of the town square as I depicted it from my dream. We anticipated staying through the war, ready to move south of the Loire, if need be. I was literally thrilled with this possibility (I must say that I lived through this entire period of upheaval as if it were an extraordinary adventure). However, at dawn the very next day, we had to leave immediately since we heard that all bridges on the Loire in the Germans' path were to be blown up.

THE DIRECTION OF TRAFFIC AROUND THE TOWN SQUARE

The existence of a vectorial element superimposed over the figural dream representation refers to two formative components: (1) a dream, going back about a year, that I named "the wooden floor dance dream," in which my second son, a very young child, moved away from me in an emotionally charged atmosphere. We were at a ball; I ended up exiting through the door on the right side of the large quadrilateral-shaped room. Then, after returning through the door on the left, I proceeded to weave my way back through the dancers from the left to the right side. (2) a graph, also quadrilateral, depicting a new definition of the Unconscious by transforming four basic entities: the Flows, the Machinic Phylum, the Existential Territories, the Intangible Universe. But one question evoked by this graph (which, by the way, had already inspired the formal composition of the "wooden floor dance dream") remained unanswered. It was about the symmetry, which was too conspicuous for my taste, of inter-entity transformations along the absissae and the ordinates of my diagram. In the dream exposed here, an area— the upper part of the trajectory—can be perceived as, if not impassable, then at least as requiring a detour and consequently a break in symmetry. The hesitations, doubts, inhibitions, forgetfulness and slips of the tongue which make up the texture of this dream all seem to gravitate towards this very area which, only recently, I had described as "vacuolic."[2]

THE FORGOTTEN CAR

I forgot two aspects of my car: its place within the dream context and its name. While writing the dream, the initials BMW appeared under my pen instead of Renault. This substitution of a car that I owned twenty years ago for one that I currently own also refers back to another dream. At this point, we can already consider that we are dealing with a dream intersection rather than a meaningful, self-contained entity. This type of dream activity is much more frequent than is commonly believed.[3] In this other dream, I had also forgotten my car, the BMW I owned before. However, the setting was in the troubled years during which I owned it, more precisely, those around 1968. I was walking down Gay-Lussac Street—a name that I often block-out—looking for my car. Eventually, I went on my way by bicycle. On the other side of Boulevard Saint Michel,[4] I discovered I was in a Socialist Party meeting; the French ecologists were being expelled by numerous guards led by Lionel Jospin in person.[5] Considering that the current issues arise from the act of forgetting the Renault:

—A hole is created in space by the missing car; this spatial "gap" of a familiar object, which in some way is a part of my ego, enters together with the opening of the door to the house [A]. This parenthesis of an element of the ego does not affect the dream car's basic character, meaning that it remains a Renault;

—I feel that going from the word "Renault," written out, to "BMW," an acronym, has a certain quality of meaning;

—I experience some hesitation regarding the sequence of events between forgetting the car's location and the near slip of Yasha David's name. This hesitation echoes my confusion when Yasha David states that he might remember where I left the car;

—Finally, I cannot refrain from mentioning the mechanical association, however stupid it may be, which consists of prolonging the question of that which is forgotten, in the form of a: where is the car...? type of analysis. It is true that recently I reread the Freud-Fliess correspondence and I wondered about the strange, disguised, homosexual relationship on which Freud built the text of his self-analysis.

THE SLIP OF THE TONGUE IN THE DREAM

Gilles Deleuze's name came to mind instead of Yasha David's in this duplicated deeper consciousness that I created in my dream. This substitution will function as a matrix of enunciation which will generate dialogical polyphonic progressions, as defined by Mikhail Bakhtin,[6] using essentially feminine characters—Adelaide, Arlette Donati, Alena Gallard, Micheline Kao, my mother, my grandmother, etc.—harmonic constellations in the heterogenous texts that we will examine later.

THE ABYSS

There are three associative orientations:

—a speleological reference which I cannot seem to identify;

—a text by Samuel Beckett, which I believe is entitled "Le Dépeupleur," where an entire population survives by hanging on to a circular wall;

—a test that I invented as a youth and pompously baptized "The sociological-existential integration test," in which the initial rules are progressively cancelled as the game is being played.

INHIBITION WHEN CONFRONTED WITH JEALOUSY

I was robbed recently, and a good twenty years of my notes were stolen. A friend offered to help reconstruct my "memories" by interviewing both my friends and me on my past. When she said that she would interview Arlette Donati, with whom I lived for seven years during this period in the 60s, I thought it likely that she would describe some of my jealous behavior towards her—that I prefer to forget. Here, however, the classical logic of Freudian denial comes into play: "I am not jealous, since it is Yasha David who is jealous."

POLYPHONIC ANALYSIS OF
MANIFEST LINES OF SUBJECTIVATION

Here, one must identify lines of parallel and intercrossed meaning in the same manner as Bakhtin's dialogism. Only later will we seek to qualify the meaning synapses which, from a deterritorializing and fractalizing rupture, will act as a catalyst for the function of setting up a Constellation Reference Universe. Initially, we will distinguish the manifest phylum of discursive meaning, as they appear in the written text of the dream, and the latent phylum, as they develop during the oral clarification in an "associative" perspective.

There are five principal manifest phylum:

I) around the town, the town square, and the closed circuit of streets which encircle it;

II) the forgotten car;

III) Yasha David and the slip of the tongue in the dream which he incurs regarding Gilles Deleuze;

IV) an abyss;

V) the inhibition when faced with jealousy.

The third manifest phylum, the only one which puts forth proper names, is distinct from the others due to its function as a synaptic operator. Also worthy of note is that these components are heterogenous.

The first one appears as a visual iconic representation which we will classify under Existential territory (Et).

The second one evokes an absent vehicle; a potentiality which may or may not exist, which we will classify under Discursive phylum. The third one is a psychopathological mental process of daily life which we will classify under Synapses.

The fourth one is a significant text which becomes an iconic statement during the associative developments. In this respect, it is the opposite of Existential territory; it is a chaotic black hole. The fifth one is a "Coarté effect" (using Rorschach's definition), that we will put with the non-discursive Reference Universes.

ANALYSIS OF LATENT LINES OF SUBJECTIVATION

Development of the first component. The dream place reference was immediately identified from an iconic point of view, however, it took me several days to find the proper name of the town in question. It was the town of Mer. The other references—Pascuaro in Mexico, Louvier in Normandy—remain in the background of the first one, despite the fact that, initially, they are mentioned before Mer. (It is as if I had to break through successive levels of resistance.) One should avoid leaping too quickly to the conclusion that the phonetic structure "mère" (mother in French) arises from the lexeme "Mer." Mer is a proper name to which I more readily associate my father, who made the decision, at the time of the exodus, for us to find lodgings in this town and exactly at the town square. For me, the fact that the last "e" and the accent of the word "mère" are missing from Mer is significant. It is the "mère," or mother, less a few things; the mother freed of responsibilities and restrictions. It is the "père," or father, who is much freer of movement and also much more distant.

The town square of Louviers (which is roughly adjacent to a park where I believe my mother took me in a baby carriage), however, represents solely a maternal background.

After examining the works of the dream's central synapse, we will then return to the third dimension of the constellation—the Mexican town square of Pascuaro with its connotation of sweet death. All that we can retain for now is that the door of the house at [A] leads to a composite father/mother existential territory.

Development of the second component. What actually happened following the cultural exhibit at the Georges Pompidou Center in which Gilles Deleuze participated, was that I offered to drive Yasha David home. We walked together to the parking lot underneath the Pompidou Center. I realized that I had forgotten where I left the car. We went in circles for a long time among the different levels, before I remembered to my embarrassment that I came on foot. That was what really happened; however, I have dreamed very often of forgetting my car.

The same is true here; I cannot approach the turnoff on rue Gay-Lussac,[7] the ecologists, the Socialist party, etc., without first working through the synapse; in the meantime, it is important to note that the car theme, for me, is that of a desiring machine. My life changed dramatically after I got my driver's license—very late, since I was already 35. An indirect consequence is that I became more independent, which eventually led, among other things, to a divorce. It was my father, who on his deathbed, insisted quite adamantly that I obtain my license. He felt isolated, too dependent on my mother. He wanted me to come and see him more often. I also remember that he had given me a fifty franc bill so that I would register for the driver's test. That made a big impression on me because he was completely unaware of the fact that fifty francs was no longer worth very much.

ANALYSIS OF THE SYNAPTIC COMPONENT

The de-territorializing and fractalizing dream agent is an abstract tool which appears thanks to two elements:

—the act of forgetting (the car);

—the slip of the tongue (concerning Yasha David's name).

These two elements can be expressed within one single structure written in three parts:

	Renault	Mer	Yasha David
I am looking for my _____	in _____	with _____	
	BMW	Gay-Lussac	Gilles Deleuze
	(forgotten)	Street	(slip of tongue)

It must be noted that the first articulation is already organized in a complex manner. I dream that I have forgotten my car, but, at the same time, I forget the type of car, substituting it with another—the BMW.

Twenty years ago, during the events of 1968, I owned a BMW. I have memories of driving through very violent demonstrations at the wheel of this car. I lived with Arlette Donati at the time and my collaboration with Gilles Deleuze started shortly thereafter. Thus, a Renault, from the Yasha David period in the present, exists with a more prestigious BMW, from the 1968, Arlette Donati,[8] Gilles Deleuze period in the past. Yet, the way the past period represses the present one is not according to simple dynamic opposition. It contains a dialectic dimension which produces machinic gains which will operate in other ways of subjectivation. This is essentially a de-territorializing movement appearing in the passage from the whole word Renault to the acronym BMW. Afterwards, we will see that this "acronym-ization" will spread over to the neighboring proper names, thus, allowing the first, abstract, machine core to develop. At the time of this dream, I was having a very problematic relationship with an Italian woman named Adelaide, whom I called A.D.

Thus, the following transformation can be diagrammed:

1984	Renault	A.D.	Yasha David
1968	BMW	Arlette Donati	Gilles Deleuze

It is as if the acronymization of 1968 moved up to 1984 transforming Arlette Donati into A.D. (Adelaide).

HARMONIC CONSTELLATION ANALYSIS OF TEXT LEVELS

Polyphonic lines developed according to their own spaces of meaning as a function of their respective machinic propositions—which are themselves set in extrinsic, rhizomatic coordinates. So, the town square developed into the town of Mer, Louviers, Pascuaro, and then into the father/mother, etc. Currently, the point is to determine core de-territorialized texts expressed in the dream as well as in reality, since from the point of view of producing subjectivity—which is the one I adopt here—there is no longer any reason to keep the latent unconscious contents separate from consciously expressed texts. These "assigning" or "interpreting" agents, as defined by C. S. Peirce, are non-discursive inasmuch as they make up de-territorialized universes, which give rise to the organization of heterogenous means of semiotization.

An example of this type of heterogenous component, which generates discontinuous structure fragments, is the transformation of Renault into the acronym BMW, or the name Arlette Donati slipping into A.D. In addition, in the last exam-

FÉLIX GUATTARI

ple, the de-territorialization of the abbreviation is correlative to a phonological re-territorialization since this is the level on which A.D. operates within the name Adelaide.

It is important to note also that these sources of partial texts cannot, as such, be designated through syntagmatic links and paradigmatic axes. Here, they are merely linked to proper names, summoned by three women whom I loved successively: Micheline Kao, Arlette Donati and A.D. It is as if code names or inchoative verbs acted as agents of this very same non-significant rupture, opening the door to the beginning of a stated existential function. Instead of being prisoner to a significant quadrature, the synaptic semiotic link here is in a position to generate a fractal proliferation which will explore the resolution of a problematic in limbo; that of the relationship with birth and death inasmuch as it can generate inhibition.

An initial partial harmonic core revolves around dream components I and IV (i.e., that of the father/mother territory and of the abyss) attracting him to the components of a spoken field, in relation to their intrinsic coordinates. One must remember that the predominant form of expression of component I is essentially visual. After leaving [A], I enter the superimposed background world of mother (*mère*) Louviers—Pascuaro. This iconic component is, however, duplicated and even disturbed by a certain phonological syncretism which becomes evident at two points:

—the transformation of Mer to *mère;*[9]

—the transformation of Michoacan to Micheline Kao who, in a way, was my first wife, even though we were not officially married. These superimposed background worlds make up a sort of glass palace at the bottom of which I perceive an abyss-zone at point [B], through the doubts, the missing items; the caesure relating to the act of forgetting the car.

The Existential territory of Mer remains closed like a bicycle circuit. Nevertheless, it is cracked: an abyss lives tangentially in it. I can only apprehend this abyss from the exterior, metaphorically or metonymically, through proper names which are stuck onto it associatively.

It is the second harmonic core which will enable me to define it better. It results from the application of the synapse constituted by component III as the second machinic component and the fifth emotive component. The Renault-BMW passage causes me to transit a regressive/mortiferous world towards a type of initiation course. I proceed down Gay-Lussac Street, first on foot, then by bicycle. It is obvious that this street evokes "homosexuality," yet the memories of the violent demonstrations of 1968 are stronger. I arrived too late the morning of May 10th, after the battle, to look for injured friends. Anyway, I felt uncomfortable during the street fighting; I was inhibited in terms of physical confrontation with the police. Thus, here we can find a two-fold matrix of the coarté effect: inhibition when faced with combat and when faced with homosexuality.

Yet, this inhibition has an evolution; since the background worlds here cease to be stacked one on the other as in a mirror. Instead, they create a processual chain at the meeting with the Ecologists, the dispute with Jospin and, in endless continuity, the memory of my ethnological friends: Cartry, Clastres, Adler etc., and of the first psychotic patient I had in therapy—who I took to visit them on a motorcycle, exactly the opposite side of Gay-Lussac Street (Monsier le Prince Street), etc. And, I must add Lucien Sebag[10] and another dream which took place opposite the university classroom at Mutalité. In this dream, the theme of death and music was intermingled. In essence, it was an entire world of diverse life activities made up of creative machinic links.

It is the semiotic diversification with the grapheme game and the phoneme around A.D., as in a crossword puzzle, that allows me to articulate and differentiate the imaginary blockage which is provoked by the territorialized component of Mer.

Nevertheless, a residual reterritorialization appears with the jealousy coarté effect. Throughout these various eras with Arlette Donati and A.D., though I was an avid believer in sexual liberation, I still became jealous whenever any of my partners took advantage of this liberation. This core of inhibition, which, with Arlette Donati, was present for a long time—causing me to look for her several times in my BMW, reappears in the ambivalence about Yasha and Gilles. Though, here, it is a neutral core, since accepted social behavior does not allow the problematic of jealousy in this situation.

A final analysis of the dream: beyond the fixing of native lands, the problematic of a desirous machine can start processual existential lines in motion. However, something continues to go wrong: a forgotten item, an inhibition, a lack of consistency, etc. Under these conditions, it is better not to be too abrupt and certainly not to forget the self-analysis of the slip of the tongue and of the forgotten item within the dream. This is the only way to conjure up a death fear, characterized both as essential and superficial, by the gesture of a dying father handing me a fifty franc bill.

Translated by Jill Johnson

1. A paper delivered at the Cerisy Colloquium: "Temps et devenir à partir de l'oeuvre de Prigogine," June 1983.
2. *Psychanalyse et transversalité* (Paris: Ed. Maspero, 1972).
3. Ancient societies, notably the Australian aborigines, are used to considering oneiric performances as not only diachronic progressions, but also as dreams experienced collectively, playing a fundamental role in establishing relations of filiation, planning rituals and setting all other types of traditions. Cf. Barbara Glowczewski. Paper on the dreams of the Walpiri in "Chimère," No. 1, Spring 1987.
4. A place where, even longer ago, I met daily with Lucien Sebag, Pierre Clastres and a whole group of students.
5. Secretary General of the Socialist Party at the time.
6. Mikhail Bakhtine, *The Dialogic Imagination*. (University of Texas Press, 1981).

7. The rue Gay-Lussac, in the Latin District, was at the heart of the May '68 rebellion. [Ed.]

8. Arlette Donati, a psychiatrist at the La Borde clinic, was Guattari's companion at the time.

9. The assimilation of "Mer" (sea) and *"mère"* (mother) is a standard psychoanalytic pun. [Ed.]

10. Pierre Clastres and Lucien Sebag, both anthropologists and close friends of Félix Guattari, died prematurely (Sebag committed suicide and Clastres died in a car accident.) [Ed.]

27

SYSTEMS, STRUCTURES AND
CAPITALIST PROCESSES
FÉLIX GUATTARI AND ERIC ALLIEZ

The question of capitalism may be considered from multiple angles, but economics and "the social" de facto constitute a necessary starting point.

From the first angle, capitalism may be defined as the general function of semiotization of a system of production, of circulation and distribution. Capitalism, the method of Capital, will then be considered as a procedure allowing merchandise, goods, activities and services to be valorized through indexing systems governed by a particular syntax apt to overcode and control. Such a "formalist" definition is possible, for despite the fact that it is inseparable from the technical and socio-economic arrangements that it strives to direct, this semiotic system nonetheless possesses an intrinsic coherence. In this regard, the capitalistic modes of writing could be compared to mathematical structures whose axiomatic consistency is not affected by the applications that can be performed in extra-mathematical fields. I suggest that this first level be called *semiotic machine of capitalism or semiotic of capitalistic valorization.*

From the second angle, capitalism will rather appear as the generator of a particular type of social relations: segregational laws, customs, and practices here move to the first rank. The processes of economic writing may vary; what is primary is the conservation of a certain type of social order founded on the division of roles between those who monopolize power and those who are submitted to it, and this applies just as much in the areas of work and economic life as in those of life-style, knowledge, and culture. All of these divisions cross over with divisions of sexes, classes, ages, and races, and end up making up, in their final form, the concrete segments of the socius. This second level, for which I suggest the name of *system of segmentarity of capitalism or capitalistic segmentarity,* also seems to preserve its own system of "axiomatic" coherence, whichever its transformations or upheavals imposed by history may be.

Capitalism is coded, but not in the manner of a "tablet of the law." The social order that it governs evolves as much as its economic syntaxes do. In this realm, as in many others, the influences are not unilateral, and we are never faced with a one-way causality. There is no question here, then, of opposing this semiotic machine and that system of segmentarity. These two components always go together, and their distinction will only be pertinent insofar as it will allow one to shed light on their own interactions with a third fundamental level, which is that of production. Let us specify right away that the latter must be not identified with what Marxists call "relations of production," or "infrastructure economic relations." Some of that is true, but it is quite different for technical machines and desiring machines. The notion of productive component (or processual component) will include both material machinic forces, human labor, social relations and investments of desire, inasmuch as all develop potentially evolving and creative relations. (These productive relations will also be termed diagrammatic, as opposed to the representative and/or programmatic relations of the first two levels.)

Is it legitimate to keep speaking of capitalism as a general entity? Aren't the formal definitions that are proposed a priori condemned to obliterate its diversification in time and in space? Since Marx, a double-tiered question has been asked: that of the place of capitalism in history and the place of history in capitalism. The sole element of historical continuity which appears to be able to characterize the various vicissitudes of modern capitalism indeed seems to be this *processual character* of the technico-scientific transformations it rests on. One can "find" capitalism in all places and times as soon as one considers it from the point of view of the exploitation of the proletarian classes, or of the mobilization of means of economic semiotization which are favorable to the rise of big markets such as fiduciary currency, bills of exchange, shares, bonds, credit currency, etc. But the capitalisms of the last three centuries only really "took off" from the moment that science, industrial and commercial technology and the socius irreversibly linked their common fate together. And everything leads one to believe that in the absence of such a machinic nexus in constant mutation, the societies within which the contemporary capitalistic formulas proliferated would probably have been unable to overcome the traumas of the great crises and world wars, and would certainly have met the same end as some great civilizations: a sudden, "unexplainable" death, or an interminable agony.

A calculator, Capital has also become a prediction machine, the computer of the socius, the homing head[1] of innovative techniques. Its raw material, its basic nutrition is made up of human labor and machinic labor, or, to be more specific, of the power of the dominant groups over human labor and of the power of the machines set up by this human labor. In other terms, what Capital capitalizes is not just social power—for on that account, there would be no cause for differentiating it historically from the prior systems of exploitation—but above all, *machinic power.* Let's say that with regard to the powers-that-be and potencies in general, it is at once a *mode of evaluation* and a *technical means of control.* All of its "mystery" lies in the fact that it is thus able to connect, within the same general system of equivalency, entities which at first sight seem radically heterogeneous: material and economic *goods,* individual and collective human *activities,* and technical, industrial and scientific *processes.* And the key of this mystery lies in the fact that it does not merely standardize, compare, order, and computerize these various areas, but that, in each operation, it extracts one and the same element, which might be called *machinic exploitation value* or *machinic surplus-value of the code.* It is through machinic valorization that capitalism infiltrates itself, not only within the material machines of economic production (crafts, manufacturing, industry…), but also within the immaterial machinisms at work at the heart of the most varied human activities (productive-unproductive, public-private, real-imaginary...). Hence a "latent" market of machinic values and values of desire is necessarily added to, and overdetermines, any "manifest" economic market of exchange-values.[2] It is from this double-market system that the essentially inegalitarian and manipulative character of any operation of exchange in a capitalist context stems, insofar as its function is always ultimately:

1) to connect heterogeneous domains and asymmetrical potencies and powers;

2) to control the social arrangements and the arrangements of desire, which are organized in such a way as to program what the modes of sensibility, tastes, and choices of each individual should be.

Fernand Braudel showed that this fundamentally inegalitarian character of the capitalist markets was much more visible, much less "dressed-up" in the era of world-economies centered around cities such as Venice, Antwerp, Genoa, or Amsterdam, than in the era of the contemporary world market. The capitalist proto-markets deployed themselves in concentric zones from metropolises which held all of the essential economic keys and recovered the greater part of surplus-values, while in their periphery, they tended towards a kind of "zero degree," due to the lethargy of the exchanges and the low level of the prices prevalent there.[3] Even today it is obvious that the exploitation of the Third World is not at all a matter of egalitarian exchanges, but rather of a kind of pillage "compensated" by the exportation of glass-ware, Coca Cola and luxury gadgets destined to a handful of autochthonous privileged ones. This does not prevent the "new economists" of the Chicago School, the "neo-liberals," from preaching the redeeming virtues of the capitalist market, in all places and in all situations.

Were one to listen to them, only the capitalist market would be able to guarantee an optimal arbitration between individual preferences with the least cost and constraint.[4] According to the proponents of this kind of theory, the inequality of exchanges ultimately would only stem from "imperfections" in the structures of the *cost of information* in society.[5] A little more effort with costs and everything will be all right. However, it is obvious that, whether it is well or poorly informed, the Third World does not "exchange" its labor and its wealth for cases of Coca Cola or even barrels of petrol. It is set upon and bled to death by the intrusion of the dominant economies. And the same holds, in other proportions however, in the Third and Fourth Worlds within the well-off countries.

This pseudo-egalitarian make-up of "exchanges" on the world market is not only done so as to mask the procedures of social subjection.[6] It complements the techniques meant to integrate the collective subjectivity in view of obtaining optimal libidinal consent from it, and even an active submission to the relations of exploitation and segregation. Contrary to what the theorists of "public choice" claim, the growth of information—particularly of the mass media information directed by the system—can only accentuate the inegalitarian effects of these techniques of integration. The project which aimed to "complete the theory of production and of the exchange of goods or merchant service with an equivalent theory somehow compatible with the functioning of *political markets*"[7] might have come from the best of intentions, but it was definitely incomplete, and it went wrong; economic, political, and institutional markets are one thing, machinic and libidinal markets are another.

And it is essentially on the side of the latter that one will be able to grasp the essential workings of social valorization and machinic creativity, in short, the essential workings of history. To achieve that goal, theories of the "political market," far from striving to become equivalent, "compatible" with those of the economic market, would be better advised to promote all at once a vision of the political, market economics, machinic values and values of desire which would be radically heterogeneous and antagonistic to that of the present system.

With regard to machinic value and values of desire, the pertinence of the distinction between goods and activities seems to dwindle. In a certain type of arrangement, human activities, which are duly controlled and piloted by capitalism, are transformed into machinic goods, while the evolution of other arrangements makes some productive goods lose their economic relevance, thereby having their "machinic virulence" devalued. In the first case, a power of activity (power assets) is transformed into a highly valorizable *machinic potency*; in the second case, a machinic potency (potency assets) swings over to the side of *formal powers*. Henceforth, a definition of Capital which would really take into account the factors of production and their evolutionary dynamic would invoke the association of economic modes of evaluation which had been divergent or contradictory until then: statistical evaluation of supply and demand by market *prices*; "objective" evaluation of *quantities of labor* incorporated by manufactured goods; "subjective" evaluation, of the marginalist type, of anticipated profits in economic transactions; accounting evaluation, integrating financial and fiscal components, and amortization data.

These formulas of evaluation, which economists general-ly present as excluding one another,[8] have in fact never ceased to be in contact—either by competing, or by complementing each other—in real economic history.[9] Thus there is no reason to qualify each one of them in a univocal manner. Their differ-ent forms of existence (commercial, industrial, financial, monopolistic, statist or bureaucratic valorization) in reality result from bringing one of their fundamental components to the fore, "selected" from one set of basic components, which has been reduced here to three terms—the *processes* of machinic production; the *structures* of social segmentarity; the dominant economic semiotic *systems*.

Starting with this minimal model—a necessary model, but barely sufficient, for one is never faced with simple components, but with clusters of components, which themselves are struc-tured according to their own systems of priorities—let us exam-ine at present the kind of generative chemistry of the arrange-ments of economic valorization resulting from the combination of priorities between these basic components. In the following table of capitalistic arrangements of valorization, 1) structures of social segmentarity will only be considered from the angle of the economic problematic of the state—the consequences of a cen-tralized management of an important part of economic fluxes (discernable within the national accounting) on the stratification of segmentary relations; 2) systems of economic semiotization will only be considered from the angle of the problematic of the *market* (in the broad sense evoked above, of markets of goods, of men, of ideas, of phantasies…); 3) productive processes will not be specified otherwise.

The object of this table, I must emphasize, is by no means to present a general typology of the historical forms of capital-ism, but only to show that capitalism is not identified with one formula alone (for example that of market economy). One

SIX FORMULAS OF CAPITALISTIC AGENCEMENTS OF VALORIZATION
(THE PRIORITIES BETWEEN COMPONENTS ARE INDICATED BY ARROWS)

Order of Priorities	Examples
a) State > Production > Market	Asiatic mode of production[10] War economy of Nazi type
b) Market > Production > State	Commercial proto-capitalism World-Economies centered on a network of cities[11]
c) Market > State > Production	Liberal capitalism
d) Production > State > Market	Monopolistic colonial economy
e) Production > Market > State	World-Wide Integrated Capitalism
f) State > Market > Production	State capitalism (of the USSR type)

could complexify and refine it by introducing additional components, or by differentiating the components belonging to each cluster, whose partitions are not airtight (there is "machinic production" within the semiotic machinery of the market and within the state; there is "state power" at the heart of the most liberal economic syntaxes; besides they never stop playing a determining role in productive spheres). It is only suggested here in order to bring out—out of some correlations inherent to the second system of connection internal to each formula—certain affinities between systems apparently quite far from one another, but which go in the same direction (or the opposite direction) of history.

More generally: 1) the capacity for the arrangements to assume major historical upheavals (or, to paraphrase Ilya

Prigogine's favorite formula, their capacity for piloting "processes far from historical equilibriums") will depend on the primacy of productive components; 2) their degree of resistance to change will depend on the primacy of the components of social segmentarities (axioms of clanic, ethnic, religious, urbanistic, caste or class stratification...); 3) their power of integration, their capacity to "colonize" not only economic life, but social life, libidinal life, in other words, their capacity to transform the socius, to subject it to the machinic phylum, will depend on the more or less innovative character of their semiotics of valorization (the fact that they would or would not be capable of adapting themselves, of enriching themselves through new procedures; their degree of "diagrammaticity"). The fact that the "direction of history" is related here to the evolutionary phylum of production does not necessarily have as a consequence, let it be noted, a finalization of history on transcendent objects. The existence of a "machinic direction" of history in no way prevents the latter from "going off in every direction." The *machinic phylum* inhabits and orients the *historical rhizome* of capitalism, but without ever mastering its fate, which continues to be played out equally with social segmentarity and the evolution of economic modes of valorization.

Let us take up these various formulas of priorities again:

1) MARKET PRIORITIES

—priority (b), for instance that of commercial proto-capitalism from the 13th to the 17th century, relegates the question of the state to the third place. (Questions of state came so far behind commercial interests, for the merchants of the United Dutch Provinces in the 17th century, that no one was really scandalized by the fact that these merchants were providing their Portuguese or French enemies with weapons.[12] It brings together a specific problem with the enlargement and the consolidation of capitalism to the whole of society; these start off with a kind of Baroque efflorescence of all productive, cultural and institutional spheres.

—priority (c), for instance that of the *"savage" liberalism of 19th century capitalism,* relegates the question of production to the third place. It brings together a specific historical problem with the constitution of territorialized states. Paradoxically, liberalism was always more preoccupied with the constitution of a state apparatus than with a generalized increase in production. The existence of a large market is not enough for it. A central regulation—as flexible as it might be—is also absolutely necessary to it. The "remote control" of production from a proliferating market complements the interventions and arbitrations of territorialized states, without which the system would run up against its own limits. It would prove especially incapable of producing basic equipments (public equipments, collective equipments, military equipments, etc.).

2) STATE PRIORITIES:

—priority (a), for instance that of the *Asiatic mode of production,* or the *war economy of Nazi type* (forced labor, relatively secondary role of the monetary economy, incarnation of the omnipotence of the state in the Fuhrer or the Pharaoh, etc.), relegates the question of the market to the third place. It involves specific historical problems: (1) with the management of the accumulation of capital. Surplus-value must accumulate in priority out of state power and its military machine; the growth of the economic and social powers of the various aristocratic strata must be limited, because it would ultimately threaten the caste in power; it would lead to the constitution of social classes. In the case of the "Asiatic" empires, this regulation can be effected by halting production,[13] by massive sacrificial consummation, sumptuary construction, luxury consumption, etc. In the case of the Nazi regimes, by internal exterminations and war. (2) with outside machinic intrusions, especially innovations in military techniques that the state cannot adopt in due time, due to their conservatism, to their reluctance of letting any creative initiative develop. (Certain Asiatic empires were liquidated in just a few years by nomadic war machines bearing military innovations.)

—priority (f), for instance that of *Soviet State capitalisms* (plans of the Stalinist type, etc.), whose affinities with the Asiatic mode of production have often been emphasized—the Chinese model, at least that of the Maoist period, with its methods of massive subjection of collective labor-power, maybe more closely related to formula (a) than to formula (f)—but relegates the question of production to the third place. It brings a specific historical problem to bear with the question of the instruments of economic semiotization, especially with the establishment of markets, involving not only economic values, but also values of creation, innovation, and desires. In this type of system, the deregulation of market systems, together with a hyper-stratification of social segmentarity, is correlative to an authoritarian management which can only subsist insofar as its sphere of influence is not overly exposed to outside influences, to the competition of other branches of the productive machinic phylum. Thus the Gulag is ultimately only tenable inasmuch as the Soviet economy continues to partially freeze innovative arrangements in advanced technological, scientific and cultural domains. This problematic is prolonged henceforth by that of demands connected to a democratization of the social-semiotic management apparatus of the system. (Example: the "self-management" struggles of the Polish workers).

3) PRODUCTION PRIORITIES:

—priority (d), for instance that of *classical imperialist exploitation,* constitutes a form of accumulation which is adjacent to the great capitalist entities, without any notable machinic basis,[14] and disregarding the effects of disorganization on the colonized socius. The commercial monopoly of the periphery tends to favor tendencies to monopoly capitalism within metropolises, and to reinforce state powers. This brings together a specific historical question with the reconstitution of the devastated socius of the colonies, including the creation of the state in the most artificial forms.

—priority (c), for instance of *World-Wide Integrated Capitalism,* establishes itself "above" and "below" capitalist and pre-capitalist segmentary relations (that is, at a level which is at once world-wide and molecular), through semiotic means of evaluation and valorization of Capital which are entirely novel in their increased capacity to integrate machinically the whole of human activities and faculties. The specific historical question which is brought in here concerns the potential limits of this integrative potency. It is not obvious, indeed, that World-Wide Integrated Capitalism can indefinitely manage to innovate and retrieve techniques and subjectivities. It is once again appropriate to emphasize that World-Wide Integrated Capitalism is not a self-sufficient entity. Even though today it pretends to be "the highest stage of capitalism" (to take up an expression that Lenin applied to imperialism), after all, it is only one capitalistic formula among others. Besides, it adapts to the survival of large zones of archaic economy, it lives in symbiosis with liberal and colonial economies of the classical type, it coexists with economies of the Stalinist type.... "Progressive" in the domain of technico-scientific mutations, it has become thoroughly conservative in the social domain (not for ideological reasons, but for functional reasons). Hence one may rightfully ask if one is not presented here with one of its unsurmountable contradictions. The capacities of adaptation and reconversion of the economic arrangements of enunciation of World-Wide Integrated Capitalism may perhaps arrive at their limit with the renewal of the capacity of resistance of all of the social layers which refuse its "one-dimensionalizing" finalities. To be sure, the internal contradictions of World-Wide

Integrated Capitalism are not such that it must ineluctably succumb to them. But its illness might nonetheless be deadly: it results from the accumulation of all the lateral crises that it engenders. The potency of the productive process of World-Wide Integrated Capitalism seems inexorable, and its social effects, unavoidable; but it upsets so many things, bruises so many other modes of life and of social valorization, that it does not seem absurd to count on the development of new collective answers—new arrangements of enunciation, of evaluation and action, stemming from the most diverse horizons—finally being able to demote it. (The appearance of new popular war machines of the Nicaragua type, the self-management struggles of great magnitude in Eastern Europe, the struggles for self-valorization of work of the Italian style, the multitude of vectors of molecular revolution in all the spheres of society).

I believe that it is only through this hypothesis that the objectives of a revolutionary transformation of society can be redefined.

Translated by Charles Wolfe

1. Oskar Lange compares the capitalist market to a "proto-computer"; cit. in Fernand Braudel.
2. Cf. the distinction Braudel makes between "trade," essentially inequalitarian exchange, and "market," self-regulating market of prices.
3. Braudel considers that each world-economy was necessarily centered on a single world-city. But perhaps he is too systematic on this point. One can entertain the opposite hypothesis, that urban and capitalistic processes did not develop according to a mono-centric model, but according to the essentially multi-polar machinic rhizome of "archipelagos of villages."
4. Cf. Henri Lepage, *Demain le capitalisme* (Paris: Livre de Poche), p. 419.
5. Vera Lutz, *Central Planning for the Market Economy* (London: Longmans, 1969).
6. Quantity of subjection of human activity, focused on the technico-semiotic machines of the system. Subjection is understood here in a cybernetic sense.
7. James Buchanan, cit. in Henri Lepage, p. 38. Cf. the ravages made in Pinochet's Chile by Milton Friedman's "Chicago boys." (Jacqueline de Linares, "Le Matin de Paris," Sept. 11, 1980.)
8. On these modes of evaluation of Capital, cf. Alain Cotta, *Théorie générale du capital, de la crois-*

260

sance et des fluctuations (Paris, 1967) and the entry "Capital" in the *Encyclopedia Universalis*.

9. Examples of complementarity: the fact that the proto-capitalism of the 15th and 16th centuries, even though it was predominantly merchant and financial, became industrial in some circumstances (cf. the revival of Antwerp by industrialization, evoked by Fernand Braudel, op. cit., vol. 3, p. 127); the fact that market economies, whatever their apparent "liberalism" may be, have always contained a dose of State intervention, or that "centralized" planification (for instance, the Stalinist Plans) has always preserved a minimum of the market economy, whether within its sphere of influence, or in its relation to the world market.

10. Example: China in the 2nd and 3rd centuries B.C. Cf. Karl-August Wittfogel, *Oriental Despotism: A Comparative Study of Total Power* (New Haven, CT: Yale University Press, 1957).

11. Examples: Venice, Antwerp, Genoa, Amsterdam, between the 13th and 17th centuries.

12. Cf. Fernand Braudel, vol. 3, pp. 172-173.

13. Etienne Balazs, *La Bureaucratie céleste* (Paris: Gallimard, 1968).

14. And which doubtless even slows the development of productive machinisms within metropolises: cf. F. Sternberg, *Kapitalismus und Sozialismus vor dem Weltgericht* (1951): "The alliance between European imperialism and colonial feudalism [...] slowed industrial development, and in general, the progressive development of the economy in colonial empires, in an extraordinary manner." Cit. by Maximilien Rubel in K. Marx, *Oeuvres* (Paris: Gallimard-Pléiade, 1965), vol. 1, p. 1708.

28

FOUR TRUTHS FOR PSYCHIATRY

Obviously, the stagnation in which psychiatry and psychological movements have been mired for a number of years is not independent of contemporary economic and social convolutions. The protest and counter-culture movements of the 60s must have appeared, for those most intensely involved, to be the first fruits of profound transformations that would gradually win over the entire social fabric. But nothing like this has happened, although history may still have some surprises in store for us. In the meantime, it must be admitted that the repeated crises of the last few years vitally concern these movements. One can even wonder about whether they are one of their essential "objectives." Whatever were the hopes, the utopias, the innovative experiments of that period, only a hazy memory remains; touching to some, hateful and vengeful to others, and indifferent to most.

This does not mean, however, that the alternative undertakings and movements have been definitively swept out of the way or have lost all legitimacy. New generations have picked up the baton, with perhaps fewer dreams, more realism, less mythic and theoretic scaffolding.... For my part, I remain convinced that the problems of that period, far from having been "surpassed," still influence the future of our societies. A choice must be made for a reorientation of human ends involving all kinds of reappropriations of individual and collective territories, to stemming the race towards a collective murderous and suicidal madness, whose indices and symptoms are amply visible in current events.

It is in this context that we should reevaluate the attempts to transform psychiatry in the past decades. Let us summarize the most salient: the first version of the movement for institutional therapy, under the impetus of people like Daumezon, Le Guillant, Bonnafé, etc., led to a humanization of the old psychiatric hospitals, with the beginnings of community healthcare in psychiatry, day clinics, protected workshops, home visits, etc. The second version of institutional psychotherapy, redefined by François Tosquelles, Jean Oury and Gt Psy, used psychoanalytical concepts and practices, different movements of alternatives to psychiatry, etc. Each of these carried with it a part of the truth, but none of them was in a position to confront the upheavals that were simultaneously occurring throughout society. Beyond their particular contributions—which I would be the last to underestimate—the question of a radical conversion of psychiatry, what in other registers could be called a change in paradigm, has always been avoided.

I am not, of course, in a position to set up an exhaustive cartography, but I would like to present some facts that constitute the necessary conditions for any progressive "boost" to this rather neglected domain. It appears to me that there are four levels of intervention, to which are indissolubly associated four truths, relating to:

1) the transformation of existing "heavy" facilities;

2) the strengthening of alternative experiments;

3) the mobilization of a wide range of social partnerships around these themes;

4) the development of new methods of analyzing unconscious subjectivity, on individual and collective levels.

We must stay clear of the dogmatic blindness and corporatist bickerings that have for so long hampered our reflections and practices. In this area, as in many others, one truth does not drive away another: there is no universal recipe, no single remedy can be applied in a single fashion. The first criterion is the possibility of involving social operators willing to be responsible at every level.

I will now try to show with a few examples how recent attempts to change psychiatry involved at least one of the "four truths," and how they fell short for not having engaged them all concurrently—which would have required the existence of collective arrangements capable of translating them into action.

In the years following World War II, what has been called the "first psychiatric revolution" led to noticeable improvements in the material and moral conditions of a number of French psychiatric hospitals. This would not have been possible without the conjunction of the following factors: (1) A strong current of progressive psychiatrists. (2) A powerful majority of psychiatric nurses who fought to change the conditions of mental asylum-institutions, for example with the creation of special training programs promoting active methods. (3) A nucleus of functionaries at the Ministry of Health who were working in the same directions.

Thus the particular conditions for intervening effectively on the first level of "heavy" facilities were in fact met. But none of the other three levels were engaged (that of alternatives, that of social mobilization, that of the analysis of subjectivity) even though they were often debated among the community hospitals which resulted in effect from this movement.

Community experiences in England, which developed in the wake of Maxwell Jones, then Ronald Laing, David Cooper and the Philadelphia Association, had a certain social intelligence and an undeniable social analytic sensibility in their favor. But they received no support from either the state or from what is traditionally called the left, so they were not able to gather strength to evolve.

If we now turn to the experience of La Borde, a clinic with about one hundred beds (over which Jean Oury has been the principal coordinator for some thirty years, and to which I remain principally attached) one finds a quite extraordinary institutional machinery, working as a "collective analyzer," which I consider tremendously interesting. Exterior support was no less wanting in this case, although in different modalities than those of the preceding examples. Let us just say that this clinic, although recognized by the social security system, has always been systematically marginalized from an economic point of view and, paradoxically, rather than improving since the arrival of the socialist governemt, its situation has only gotten worse. While some people treat it like an historical monument, it remains more vital than ever. It has been sustained by never flagging popular support, as the participation of more than a hundred French and international trainees and visiting practitioners attest to each year. And yet it remains isolated.

Still, this experiment could only have achieved its goal through a proliferating network of alternative initiatives. One question it implicitly raises concerns the role of hospitalization. Obviously it is urgent to put an end to all methods of incarceration. But this does not mean that it should be abandoned in every respect. For a number of "mental dissidents," reinsertion into what are called the normal structures of society is out of the question. In this regard, it is time to dispel the myth that returning patients to the family, or maintaining them there by force, or through guilt, is the solution. Other modalities of individual and collective life can be invented, and it is there that an immense space for research and experimentation opens up.

I could enumerate other examples that put the disharmony of the four levels of intervention into relief. But I will content myself with one illustration, involving Psychiatria Democratica and the work of Franco Basaglia, whose memory I here commemorate. This movement was the first to intensely explore the potentialities offered by field-work when it is associated with a mobilization of the left, public awareness and systematic pressure on public authorities. Unfortunately, and for a long time this was a point of contention between my friend Franco

Basaglia and myself, it was the analytical dimension that was toned down, sometimes even vehemently refused.

Why, you may ask, this insistence, like a leitmotif, on the fourth analytic dimension? Should it really be considered as one of the principle touchstones of our problem? Without expatiating at great length, I'd say that with it comes a healing of the leprosy of our psychiatric institutions and, beyond this, of the welfare system, with the hopeless serialization of individuals that it induces not only on its "users," but also on its therapeutic, technical and administrative "practitioners." Fostering large-scale institutional analyses would require permanent work on the subjectivity produced through all kinds of connections to aid, education, etc.

A certain type of subjectivity, which I would call capitalistic, is overtaking the whole planet: an equalized subjectivity, with standardized fantasies and massive consumption of infantalizing reassurances. It causes every kind of passivity, degeneration of democratic values, collective racist impulses.... Today it is massively secreted by the media, community centers and alleged cultural institutions. It not only involves conscious ideological formations, but also collective unconscious emotions. Psychiatry and the various psychiatric and psychological domains have a special responsibility in relation to it, whether they underwrite its current forms, or try to turn it into non-alienating directions. Alternatives to psychiatry and psychoanalysis are important on that account. They will have no real impact unless they manage to ally themselves with other movements bent on changing subjectivity in various ways, i.e., through ecological, ethnic, feminist, antiracist and, more generally, through alternative practices that open up positive perspectives for the widening mass of the "marginal" and the unprotected.

But this implies at the same time that parties, groups, communities, collectives and individuals willing to work in that direction are capable of self-transforming, and stop tracing their organizations and their unconscious representations on repressive models. To do so, they would have to act not only as political and social instruments in relation to themselves and to the outside, but as collective analytical arrangements of these unconsious processes. Everything can be invented.

This is pretty much what we have been trying to do in the Alternative Network to Psychiatry. Since its creation in 1975 it has periodically organized international debates between the most diverse, most heterogeneous components of the psychiatric and psychological professions and alternative movements. Many other comparable efforts exist. I am thinking particularly of the encounters in mental ecology, organized by the Topia Group of Bologna, led by Franco Berardi. What is more than ever at stake is the right to singularity, to freedom of individual and collective creation away from technocratic conformism, postmodernist arrogance and the levelling of subjectivity in the wake of new technologies.

These are some of the elements I hope to bring into the debate. Now, in conclusion, permit me to make these comments.

It was certainly of the utmost importance to challenge the old legislation, and any backward step towards reinstating former asylum structures would be totally reactionary and absurd. If specific hospital rest-facilities must be re-established—and I think this is absolutely necessary—they should be conceived as sites for evolving research and experimentation. Reimplanting them within general hospitals would obviously be counter-indicated.

Only new forms of social mobilization will help mentalities to evolve and dissipate the menace of "anti-crazy" racism. In the final analysis initiative and decisions in this area do not belong to traditional political formations, tied up as they generally are in their bureaucratic choke-collar, but to the reinvention of a new type of social and alternative movement.

Translated by Chet Wiener

29

INSTITUTIONAL SCHIZO–ANALYSIS

It is during the discussions we had within the Psychoanalytic Workshop (Gt Psy), spurned by Tosquelles' injunction to move on with "both feet," one Marxist and the other Freudian, that I began to reflect on what another analytical path could be, which I called "institutional analysis" at the time, an expression I didn't really succeed in imposing within this milieu, but which proliferated outside of it. It was about bringing forth a field which was not merely that of institutional therapy, institutional pedagogy or the fight for social emancipation, but which implied an analytical method capable of cutting through all these fields (hence the theme of "transversality").

I reached the conclusion that the Gt Psy debates, on "institutional transfer," for example, were not specific in relation to mental illness, and could also concern relations of the individual to the collectivity, the environment, aesthetic productions, etc.

My intention was not to diminish individual singularities and the prepersonal side of the analysis, in the world of psychosis for instance. Nothing was further from my mind than proposing a psycho-sociological model which could claim to be a global alternative to existing methods analyzing the unconscious. Beginning with this period my thinking revolved around procedures that I now call *metamodelization*. That is, say, something which does not establish itself as an overcoding of existing models, but as a procedure of "automodelization" which takes over all or parts of the existing models in order to construct its own cartographies, its own references and therefore its own analytical approach and methodology. Then, ultimately, I tried to elaborate a method of analysis of unconscious formations that would rely neither on the individuation of subjectivity, nor on its embodiment in groups and institutions. What Tosquelles was doing at Saint Alban and at La Borde for me was already the beginning of a decentering which made it possible to remove analysis from the personological and family–based framework to account for *assemblages of enunciation* of another scale (either of a larger social scale, or an infra-individual scale).

This is where the ulterior problematic stemmed from: *Capitalism and Schizophrenia*, in collaboration with Gilles Deleuze, which revolved around the way pre-personal subjectivity works—below the totalities of the person and the individual—and the supra-personal, which deals with group phenomena, social dimensions and assemblages of enunciation involving "machinic components," such as computer components. What seemed urgent to me, finally, was to reclaim what was most important in Freud and Marx, that subjective formations don't, could not and should not coincide with an individual "profile." Subjectivity establishes itself, at a minimum, in a complex relation to the other, mother, father, family, caste relations, class struggles, in short all levels of social interaction. These are the things that Lacan focused on with his recentering of the unconscious onto language, which unfortunately didn't prevent him from falling back onto universals, structural "mathemes" which reintroduced this subjective individuation he had thrown out of the door of analytical practice by way of the window of theoretical fantasies.

From the moment one considers that subjectivity cannot be assimilated to a black box set in the cerebral circumvolutions, but that it is being produced at all levels of the "pre-personal" and the social, the analysis of the unconscious must account for "machinic circuits" and assemblages of subjectivation, which cannot be in any way reduced to interpersonal relations based on an oedipal axiomatic.

I do not claim, I have never claimed to be engaging in an analysis of a scientific sort. I have even come to think that a cartography of subjectivity, to have any analytical value, that is to say to be processual, by definition must distance itself from any scientific ideal. It seems to be that the phenomena of class struggle, as they can be read from the history of the working class (and therefore not only through the analysis of Marxist theorists) are necessarily inscribed within a genealogy of *subjective orientations.* All together, therefore, they constitute objective power struggles and enterprises producing subjectivity. One cannot understand the history of the working class movement if one refuses to see that during certain periods, the institutions of the working class movement engendered new types of subjectivity and, to push things a little further, I'll even venture to say produced different "human races." In 1871 a certain type of Communard became so "mutant" that the Versailles bourgeoisie had no other solution but to exterminate it. They were perceived as a diabolical threat. The Paris Commune was exterminated the way the Protestants were exterminated during the Saint Barthelemy massacre. History also furnishes us with examples of *subjectivity wars,* which one cannot fully understand without the concept of the mutations we mentioned above. For example, Lenin explicitly envisaged the invention of a new mode of militant subjectivity that would differ from the social-democratic subjectivity integrated into capitalism.

The large scale capitalist production of subjectivity by the collective apparatus today is of a very different nature than that of "pre-capitalist" societies, based on a direct subordination or indirect symbolic infeodation, within relatively well defined territories, or that of proto-capitalist societies, based on a sub-jective assignment of class or caste, within a general deterrito-rialization of fluxes (demographic, work related, exchanges, cultural…). Today it is not only economic and social territories that are deterritorialized, but also the modes of subjectivation which tend to result from a completely artificial production. Included are the subjective territorialities of the ego, the super ego, the family, the primary group, etc., which are fashioned by the productive machine. All this creates a paradoxical cock-tail of *hyper-segregation* and *generalized communication.*

In this context, how does one put together again a dis-alienated, de-serialized subjectivity, which I call "processual," because it creates its own existence in a process of singular-ization, engendering itself as an *existential territory* the more it set itself up as an analytical cartography? This is the question I have been working on for years. Nothing seems more urgent in view of the popularity of and return to orthodoxies, post-modernisms and neo-conservatisms.

Q: Could we come back to an idea that is seductive but not always easy to understand: that of the machine? After all, it is a crucial concept, this idea of the machine. As I understand it, it is linked to what you have developed concerning subjectivi-ty, or micro-political assemblages, as you also called it. What is your present position on this theory of machines which you define as *desiring machines*?

FG: They are not only desiring. And one should take note that I am not the only one to have broadened the use of the term machine: biologists, mathematicians, they do it as well. It is not enough to think of the machine only in terms of tech-nology: before being technological, the machine is diagram-matic, to borrow semiotician Charles Sanders Peirce's expres-sion. It is made up of diagrams, plans and equations, etc.

Besides and articulated with technological, chemical and biological machines, one must accept the existence of machines which I call semiotic or diagrammatic, theoretical machines, and abstract machines, including political, economic machines, etc. Think of the "Apollo" program launched by Kennedy: without the political machine behind the project, the engine would never have been built. Without the will and somewhat mad desire, not only Kennedy's, but also of the generations that have dreamed of going to the moon, the machine would never have lifted off. All this to say that this type of technological machine brings into play semiotic, economic, political and institutional machines (the Army and Air Force did not want to have NASA run the project...). If one really wants to describe how historical mutations occur, I think it is necessary to forge an extended concept of the machine that would account for what it is in all its aspects. There are its visible synchronic dimensions, but also its virtual diachronic dimensions: a machine is always the final outcome of a series of previous machines and perpetuates the evolutionary phylum of future machines: it is a material and semiotic assemblage which not only has the virtue of traversing time and space, but also very diverse levels of existence concerning the brain, biology, feelings, collective investments.... In other words, machines essentially are transversalist.

Q: I would like to get back to this concept of the machine. Where do you stand today in relation to your writing on this idea of desire as a construct?

FG: Our conception of desire was the opposite of an ode to spontaneity, of a praise of disorderly liberation. It was precisely to underscore the artificial "constructivist" nature of desire that we defined it as "machinic," which is to say in conjunction with the most actual machinic phylum, the most "urgent." We were far from Reich, far from the orgone drives.

As I see it, desire is a *process of singularization*, a point of proliferation and creation of the possible within an established system. This process may go through stases of marginality, "minor becomings" bringing out cores of singularity. In time sequences when everyone is bored, an event occurs which, for no obvious reason, changes the outlook. An unexpected process brings out different universes of reference; one sees things differently; not only does subjectivity change, but also all the space of the possible, all the life projects. Desire is always like that: somebody falls in love in a universe that seemed closed and which all of a sudden reveals other possibilities. Love and sexuality are only semiotizations of these mutations of desire. Desire is the fact that in a closed world, a process arises that secretes other systems of reference, which authorize, although nothing is ever guaranteed, the opening of new degrees of freedom.

Q: In my view you made an important proposition, talking about desire in *The Molecular Revolution*, when you said that it is integrated, or part of and situated in the infrastructure.

FG: To say of desire that it is part of the infrastructure is the same as saying that subjectivity produces reality. Desire is not an ideological superstructure. The old base structures, the old territories of reference, ecological, anthropological with their intrinsic systems of modelization have been deterritorialized by the economy and capitalist subjectivity. It is no longer, in terms of a deterritorialized curriculum, a local "initiation," as was the case in archaic societies, that one becomes somebody or something. Only academics still believe that. Today most people do not know anymore who or what they are.

Henceforth individuated subjectivity has become the target of a type of industrial production. Let us take an historical example. Two countries emerged completely destroyed after World War II: Germany and Japan. They were not only physically crushed, as Bremen under the bombs; they were socially and psychologically devastated and on top of it permanently occupied. This resulted in two economic "miracles." And, paradoxically, these countries had no material advantages—no raw materials, no capital reserves. But they recreated a prodigious "capital of subjectivity" (capital of knowledge, of collective intelligence and of will to survive). In fact they invented new modes of subjectivity from this very devastation. The Japanese, in particular, reclaimed elements of their archaic subjectivity and transfered them in the most "advanced" forms of social and material production. This illustrates quite well how the production of subjectivity came to occupy the infrastructural position. But this is only one way of saying it, because they are no more "infra" than "supra," which are after all very lame concepts. I only define them that way out of provocation. What is important is that this is a complex way of producing subjectivity that made it possible to launch a multitude of creative processes—of which some are actually hyper-alienating. Such examples show us that it is not only on a biological, libidinal, economic or geopolitical base that collective subjectivity is established. It can also be found at the root of these assemblages. Most governments today are confronted with problems of subjectivity. Nation–related questions are poisoning the capitalist system, in the East and West. This is called the Palestinian, Basque, Black, Polish, Jewish, and Afghani problem…. Theoretically, governments have all the means necessary to find rational solutions to these problems. But this would mean neutralizing the resistance of a collective subjectivity, converting it into a "subjectivity of equivalence" where each individual, each function, each thought would be standardized as in a game of Lego blocks. And there are areas where this does not work, because subjectivity is not just produced by the capitalist machine, but by you and me, in your institution, family, sometimes alone; it can be written in a desire, novel, trip etc. This is a big problem.

Q: It also changes work.

FG: Yes, it changes everything. As soon as you introduce this desire for singularization as an essential component of our contemporary crisis, one can no longer view things in the same way as the present "tenants" of the economy want you to see it. In the name of the crisis, we are being ordered to put our educational, urban and social problems aside. We will first deal with the economic crisis! The question of desire is always for later.

Q: Is schizo-analysis a method? How do you situate it in what you said so far?

FG: For me it is important to take a number of analytical dimensions into account in their relation to singularities, to the processes of singularization. If one does not introduce them into social practices, be they political or labor conflicts, everyday struggles, ecological or other, then you have guaranteed failure and demoralization. One must constitute networks and rhizomes to get out of the systems of modelization in which we are stuck.

I repeat: schizo-analysis is not an alternative modelization. It is the search for a meta-modelization. It attempts to understand how we got to this point. "What's your model like?" It does not work? Well, I don't know, but let's work together! We will try to graft other models. Perhaps it will be better or it will be worse. We'll see. There is no way we'll import a standard model. And the truth criterion, in all this, is precisely when a meta-modelization turns into an auto-modelization, a self-management of the model, if you like.

This would imply a theoretical approach, quite complex actually, to account for the transfers of subjectivization from one field to another and transformations of systems of meanings between various semiotic components. What influence, for instance, can an economic problem have on an obsessional syndrome? It is not easy. Generalities on partial objects and the signifier are not enough. One must be wary here of master key concepts, beginning with the concept of sexuality. Infantile sexuality, adolescent sexuality and adult sexuality partake of totally different worlds, for which no general category of libido can account for, and between which there is no direct causal relationship.

Q: What are the pragmatic results of a schizo-analyst technician?

FG: There could never be a schizo-analyst technician; this would be a contradiction in terms. If schizo-analysis must exist, it is because it already exists everywhere; and not just among schizophrenics, but in the schizes, the lines of escape, the processual ruptures which are facilitated by a cartographic auto-orientation. Its goal? One could say that it doesn't have any, because it is not so much the end that matters but the "middle," the process as it processualizes itself. This calls for a blind trust in the movement of deterritorialization at work. When you are working on a project, for example, an institutional project, a film, or a novel you can internalize an existing model (the Stendhal novel, or the Marcel Lherbier film style). What you have then is a consumer object which can be located in terms of means and end. With schizo-analysis, it's rather the other way around. Objectality is detotalized. One leaves pre-organized programs. One attempts to deploy fields of the possible carried by an assemblage of enunciation. You begin a novel without knowing where it will take you; maybe it won't be a novel at all. But it will be an analytical process; an analytical cartography without a guaranteed outcome. For me, this idea of process is fundamental. It assumes that one has discarded the idea that one must absolutely master an object or a subject—and that the analytical research is given a dimension of finitude, singularity, existential delimitation, precariousness in relation to time and values. Such an ethical and micro-political decentering implies a complete reversal in relation to the actual educational system. This does not mean that the ends yield to the means. Because the formula falls apart: there are neither ends nor means; only processes; nothing but processes; processes auto–constructing life, auto–constructing the world, with mutant, unforeseen, unheard-of affects. If everything is written beforehand, rather die on the spot. No point in waiting for the end of the film, everybody knows it already.

Q: The strange thing is that paradoxically it looks like idealism, whereas this changes the perspectives, and what you are saying with this is something very materialistic, even if it's not obvious for our own mentalities.

FG: What is idealistic—in the positive sense of the term— is to think that one can have an impact on the course of things through an idealistic involvement. Destiny is not inscribed in an infrastructure. Capitalist societies secrete a society, a subjectivity which is in no way natural, in no way necessary. One could very well do something else. What I refuse is the idea of an inevitable and necessary program. One seems to think that history is programmed like a computer. This is what I mean by making the "unconscious work." It is not just simply discovering it, but first and foremost bringing it to produce its own lines of singularity, its own cartography, in fact its own existence. In short, there are no recipes.

Translated by Bernard Schütze

BIBLIOGRAPHY

"Molecular Revolutions" is the (yet unpublished) transcript of Guattari's address to the Schizo–Culture Conference organized by Semiotext(e) in November, 1975 at Columbia University in New York. Translated by David L. Sweet.

About two thousand people attended the various workshops, lectures, discussions on psychiatry, madness, political repression, Portugal, etc. Lecturers included Ti-Grace Atkinson, William Burroughs, John Cage, Gilles Deleuze, Richard Foreman, Michel Foucault, Félix Guattari, Joel Kovel, R. D. Laing and Jean-François Lyotard. The atmosphere was very heated, and Michel Foucault, who was publicly accused by various *agents provocateurs* of being paid by the CIA, got very upset. This was "the last counter–culture conference of the '60s," he said privately (and somewhat derisively) to Sylvère Lotringer, who directed the Conference. It was, in fact, the first encounter in the United States between post-'68 French theorists, the New York art world, and the American "radical" academic constituency, and a number of clashes ensued.

Guattari's improvised evening address was cut short by hecklers, presumably followers of Ti-Grace Atkinson, who spoke right after him on the podium.

"Desire is Power, Power is Desire" is Guattari's (yet unpublished) response to the Schizo–Culture Conference, in November 1975. Translated by David L. Sweet.

"Letter to the Tribunal" is a response to the French government censorship of a special Gay Issue of *Recherches*, no. 12, "Trois milliards de pervers: Grande Encyclopédie des Homosexualités" (Three Billion Perverts: Great Encyclopedia of Homosexualities), published in March, 1973. The issue was confiscated and all the copies destroyed. Félix Guattari, director of the magazine, was fined for publishing "a detailed exposition of depravity and sexual deviations... the libidinous exhibition of a minority of perverts." Translated by Jarred Becker.

"To Have Done With the Massacre of the Body," an unsigned essay published in the censored *Recherches* issue on homosexualities (none of the pieces were signed), may be attributed to Guattari. Translated by Jarred Becker.

"I Have Even Met Happy Drag Queens" was first published in *Libération*, April 3, 1975. Reprinted in *La Révolution moléculaire* (Paris: Ed. Recherches, 1977). First translated by Rachel McComas in the "Polysexuality" issue of *Semiotext(e)*, Vol. IV, No. 1, 1981, François Peraldi, ed.

"Becoming–Woman" is a fragment of an interview with Christian Descamps first published in *La Quinzaine Littéraire*, August 1975. Reprinted in *La Révolution moléculaire*. First translated by Rachel McComas and Stamos Metzidakis in the "Polysexuality" issue of *Semiotext(e)*, Vol. IV, No. 1, 1981, François Peraldi, ed.

"A Liberation of Desire," an interview conducted (and translated) by George Stambolian, was first published in *Homosexuality and French Literature*, G. Stambolian and Elaine Marks, eds. (Ithaca: Cornell University Press, 1979).

"The Adolescent Revolution," an interview conducted by Christian Poslianec, was originally published in *Sexpol*, 1979: "Des madame–Dolto partout." Reprinted in Guattari's *Les Années d'Hiver, 1980–85*. (Paris: Barrault, 1986). Translated by Chet Wiener.

"Popular Free Radio" was first published both in *La Nouvelle Critique* and *Rouge*, in June, 1979. First translated by David L. Sweet and published in the "Radiotext(e)" issue of *Semiotext(e)*, #16, 1992, Neil Strauss and Dave Mandl, eds.

"Why Italy?" was published in the "Italy: Autonomia" issue of *Semiotext(e)*, Vol. III, No. 3, 1980, Christian Marrazzi and Sylvère Lotringer, eds. This interview took place several months before leaders of the Italian Autonomist movement were arrested on April 7, 1979. Translated by John Johnston. Not published in French.

"Utopia Today" is Guattari's response to a survey by *La Quinzaine Littéraire*, no. 53, 1983. Translated by Jeanine Herman.

"The New Alliance," an interview conducted by Sylvère Lotringer, was first published in *Impulse* [Toronto] 10, no. 2, Winter 1982. Translated by Arthur Evans and John Johnston.

"Machinic Junkies," an interview conducted by Jean–Francis Held, was first published in *Les Nouvelles*, April 12–18, 1984. Reprinted in Guattari's *Les Années d'Hiver, 1980–85*. Translated by Chet Wiener.

"Entering the Post–Media Era." Unpublished manuscript. Translated by Chet Wiener.

"Regimes, Pathways, Subjects" was first published in *Chimères* 4, Winter 1987 as "De la production de subjectivité." Translated by Brian Massumi in *Zone* 6, "Incorporations," 1992, Jonathan Crary and Sanford Kwinter, eds.

"Did You See the War?", an interview with "Canal Déchaîné" held in January 1991. First published in *Chimères*, Summer 1994. Translated by Andrea Loselle.

"Cinema of Desire," a paper delivered in Bologna, Italy at a conference on Eroticism and Cinema in December, 1973. Reprinted in *La Révolution moléculaire*. First translated as "Cinematic Desiring Machines" in *Critical Theory* 3 (7), August 3–9, 1988. Translated by David L. Sweet.

"The Poor Man's Couch" was first published in *Communications* 23, 1975 as "Le divan du pauvre." Translated by Gianna Quach.

"Cinema Fou" [La ballade sauvage], interview with Delfeuil du Ton published in *Libération*, July 17, 1975. [On Terence Malick's *Badlands*.] Reprinted in *La Révolution moléculaire*. Translated by David L. Sweet.

"Not So Mad" [Fou à Délier], first published in *Cinématographie* 18, April 1976. Interview with Jean–Noël Keller. Reprinted in *La Révolution moléculaire*. Translated by Gianna Quach.

"Like the Echo of a Collective Melancholia," first translated by Mark Polizzotti in "The German Issue" of *Semiotext(e)*, Vol. IV, No. 2, 1982, Sylvère Lotringer, ed.

"Freudo–Marxism" was originally written in 1977 for *Le Nouvel Observateur*, which never published it. First translated by Janis Forman in "Anti–Oedipus," *Semiotext(e)*, Vol. II, No. 3, 1977, Sylvère Lotringer, ed.

"Beyond the Psychoanalytical Unconscious," lecture written in 1977, delivered in Mexico City, October, 1981. Published in *Réseaux–Systèmes–Agencements* 7, 1983. [*Les Années d'Hiver*]. Translated by Chet Wiener.

"Capital as the Integral of Power Formation" [Le Capital comme intégrale des formations de pouvoir], was published in the 10/18 UGE version of *La Révolution moléculaire*. Translated by Charles Wolfe and Sande Cohen.

"The Unconscious is Turned Toward the Future," an (unpublished) interview by Numa Murard and Luc Rozensweig for *Recherches*, 1980. Translated by Jeanine Herman. [Ed.'s title]

"The Refrain of Being and Meaning: Analysis of a Dream About A. D." in *New Observations* 74, Feb/March 1980. Translated by Jill Johnson.

"Systems, Structures and Capitalistic Processes," by Félix Guattari and Eric Alliez, 1983. First published in *Change International*

Deux, 1984. Reprinted in *Les Années d'Hiver, 1980–1985.*
Translated by Charles Wolfe.

"Four Truths for Psychiatry," from a conference on Psychiatry and
Institutions sponsored by the Italian Socialist Party, Rome, 1985.
First published in *Les Années d'Hiver, 1980–1985.* Translated by
Chet Wiener.

"Institutional Schizo–Analysis," unpublished manuscript, 1985.
Translated by Bernard Schültze.

▲ SEMIOTEXT(E) NATIVE AGENTS SERIES ▲
CHRIS KRAUS, EDITOR

CRACKING THE MOVEMENT: SQUATTING BEYOND THE MEDIA
Foundation for the Advancement of Illegal Knowledge

THE LIZARD CLUB, Steve Abbott

WHORE CARNIVAL, Shannon Bell, ed.

CRIMES OF CULTURE, Richard Kostelanetz

CAPITAL AND COMMUNITY, Jacques Camatte

THE ROOT IS MAN, Dwight Macdonald

PIRATE UTOPIAS: MOORISH CORSAIRS & EUROPEAN RENEGADOES
Peter Lamborn Wilson

▲ AUTONOMEDIA BOOK SERIES ▲

SOUNDING OFF! MUSIC AS SUBVERSION/ RESISTANCE/REVOLUTION
Ron Sakolsky & Fred Wei-Han Ho, eds.

UNBEARABLES, The Unbearables

THE DAUGHTER, Roberta Allen

FILE UNDER POPULAR, Chris Cutler

MAGPIE REVERIES, James Koehnline

ON ANARCHY & SCHIZOANALYSIS, Rolando Perez

GOD & PLASTIC SURGERY: MARX, NIETZSCHE, FREUD & THE OBVIOUS
Jeremy Barris

MARX BEYOND MARX: LESSONS ON THE GRÜNDRISSE, Antonio Negri

RETHINKING MARXISM, Steve Resnick & Rick Wolff, eds.

THE TOUCH, Michael Brownstein

GULLIVER, Michael Ryan

MODEL CHILDREN: INSIDE THE REPUBLIC OF RED SCARVES, Paul Thorez

SCANDAL: ESSAYS IN ISLAMIC HERESY, Peter Lamborn Wilson

THE NEW ENCLOSURES, Midnight Notes Collective

THE ARCANE OF REPRODUCTION: HOUSEWORK,
PROSTITUTION, LABOR & CAPITAL, Leopoldina Fortunati

CLIPPED COINS, ABUSED WORDS, CIVIL GOVERNMENT:
JOHN LOCKE'S PHILOSOPHY OF MONEY, C. George Caffentzis

TROTSKYISM AND MAOISM: THEORY & PRACTICE IN FRANCE & THE U.S.
A. Belden Fields

FILM & POLITICS IN THE THIRD WORLD, John Downing, ed.

COLUMBUS & OTHER CANNIBALS:
WÉTIKO DISEASE & THE WHITE MAN, Jack Forbes

ENRAGÉS & SITUATIONISTS IN THE OCCUPATION
MOVEMENT, MAY '68, René Viénet

CASSETTE MYTHOS: NEW MUSIC UNDERGROUND, Robin James, ed.

XEROX PIRATES: "HIGH" TECH & THE NEW COLLAGE UNDERGROUND
Autonomedia Collective, eds.

THE NARRATIVE BODY, Eldon Garnet

POPULAR REALITY, Irreverend David Crowbar, ed.

ZEROWORK: THE ANTI-WORK ANTHOLOGY, Bob Black & Tad Kepley, eds.

MIDNIGHT OIL: WORK, ENERGY, WAR, 1973–1992
Midnight Notes Collective

A DAY IN THE LIFE: TALES FROM THE LOWER EAST SIDE
Alan Moore & Josh Gosniak, eds.

GONE TO CROATAN: ORIGINS OF NORTH AMERICAN DROPOUT CULTURE
James Koehnline & Ron Sakolsky, eds.

ABOUT FACE: RACE IN POSTMODERN AMERICA
Timothy Maliqalim Simone

HORSEXE: ESSAY ON TRANSSEXUALITY, Catherine Millot

DEMONO (THE BOXED GAME), P.M.

FORMAT AND ANXIETY: COLLECTED ESSAYS ON MEDIA, Paul Goodman

BLOOD & VOLTS: EDISON, TESLA & THE ELECTRIC CHAIR, Th. Metzger

DAMNED UNIVERSE OF CHARLES FORT, Louis Kaplan, ed.

BY ANY MEANS NECESSARY: OUTLAW MANIFESTOS
& EPHEMERA 1965–70, Peter Stansill & David Zane Mairowitz, eds.

OFFICIAL KGB HANDBOOK, USSR Committee for State Security

WILD CHILDREN, David Mandl & Peter Lamborn Wilson., eds.

▲ AUTONOMEDIA DISTRIBUTION ▲

FELIX: REVIEW OF TELEVISION & VIDEO CULTURE
Kathy High, ed.

LUSITANIA: A JOURNAL OF REFLECTION & OCEANOGRAPHY
Martim Avillez, ed.

DRUNKEN BOAT: ANARCHIST REVIEW OF LITERATURE & ARTS
Max Blechman, ed.

RACE TRAITOR: A JOURNAL OF THE NEW ABOLITIONISM
John Garvey & Noel Ignatiev, eds.

XXX FRUIT, Anne-christine d'Adesky, et al., eds.

COURAGE TO STAND ALONE: CONVERSATIONS WITH U.G.
KRISHNAMURTI, Ellen Chrystal & Henk Shoenville, eds. Plover Press

RADIO SERMONETTES: Moorish Orthodox Radio Crusade Collective
Libertarian Book Club

AIMLESS WANDERING: CHUANG TZU'S CHAOS LINGUISTICS
Hakim Bey Xexoxial Editions

ALL COTTON BRIEFS: EXPANDED EDITION
M. Kasper Benzene Books

O TRIBE THAT LOVES BOYS: POETRY OF ABU NUWAS
Translated & introduced by Hakim Bey Entimos Press & The Abu Nuwas Society